MACRO-ECONOMIC POLICY

Also by J. O. N. Perkins
International Policy for the World Economy

Other books for students

The Growth of the International Economy, 1820–1960:
An Introductory Text by
A. G. KENWOOD AND A. L. LOUGHEED
University of Queensland

Australian Economic Development in the Twentieth Century
edited by
COLIN FORSTER
Australian National University

The Economics of Socialism
J. WILCZYNSKI,
Royal Military College, Duntroon

Acceptable Inequalities
IAN BOWEN
University of Western Australia

The Politics of New States
edited by
R. D. SCOTT
Queen's University, Belfast, formerly University of Sydney

MACRO-ECONOMIC POLICY
A Comparative Study

AUSTRALIA CANADA NEW ZEALAND SOUTH AFRICA

by

J. O. N. PERKINS
editor
Professor of Economics, University of Melbourne

M. D. ENGLISH
University of Alberta
formerly Lecturer in Economics, University of Melbourne

J. P. NIEUWENHUYSEN
Senior Lecturer in Economics, University of Melbourne

J. W. ROWE
Professor of Economics, Massey University, New Zealand

UNIVERSITY OF TORONTO PRESS

First published in 1973 in Canada and
the United States by University of Toronto Press
Toronto and Buffalo

ISBN 0-8020-1968-4
ISBN (microfiche) 0-8020-0311-7

Printed in Great Britain

Preface

The idea for this book occurred to us when three of the authors – one hailing originally from South Africa, one coming from Canada – found themselves occupying neighbouring rooms in the University of Melbourne. It seemed to us that Australia, Canada and South Africa could probably learn something from each others' experience in macro-economic policy, and we therefore felt it worth while to consider and compare some of the macro-economic problems and policies of this group of countries, together with New Zealand, the other country whose economy seemed to have most in common with the other three. The absence of any such study seemed likely to be partly the result of the wide geographical separation of the countries concerned, and of the associated lack of frequent opportunities for economists from these four countries to work together. In the course of a visit to Melbourne of the New Zealand economist who agreed to become our co-author, we planned, and co-ordinated (so far as it seemed useful to do so), the outline and general approach of the work embodied in this book.

If such a book had been written entirely by authors living and working in their own country, this sort of co-operation would have been much more difficult. On the other hand, to offset the complementary disadvantage that two of the authors wrote most of their respective chapters while they were away from the country in which they were specializing, we were fortunate that both of them were able to put the final touches to their work in the countries about which they were writing. In addition, both of them had previously had many years first-hand experience of those countries' economies. All of us had some knowledge of more than one of the countries discussed in this book, and two of us had worked for considerable periods in more than one of them.

This background is given in order to emphasize that we would wish the book to be regarded as a whole, and not merely as a group of unrelated studies of the various countries. Indeed, readers who are especially interested in appraising and improving macro-economic policy in one of the countries discussed may find that the experience of the other three countries is at least as relevant for this purpose –

whether as an example to follow or one to avoid – as that of the country with which they are principally concerned.

The relative neglect in the literature of the problems and policies of this group of countries also seemed especially strange in view of their relevance for many other types of economy. All of the rich, highly developed, countries share with our group of countries a common set of problems that includes 'Keynesian' unemployment and more recently 'stagflation'; whilst the less developed countries share with our group the problems associated with a high degree of dependence on primary exports, and, indeed, on external transactions generally, as well as some of those resulting from having capital markets that are generally somewhat less highly developed than those of the USA or Western Europe. In some respects, then, the group of countries discussed in this book is intermediate between the more developed and the less developed types of economy, and the experience of the group therefore seems to be relevant to an unusually wide range of other countries.

Each of the authors has benefited from the comments of one or more of his co-authors, as well as from discussions with a number of other economists.

The typing of the final manuscript was very capably handled by Mrs J. Vike and Mrs M. Verduci of the secretarial staff of the Department of Economics of the University of Melbourne.

Melbourne, Australia   J. O. N. PERKINS
February 1972

Chapter 2

AUSTRALIA*

J. O. N. PERKINS and J. P. NIEUWENHUYSEN

The Australian economy shares with Canada, South Africa and New Zealand a high degree of dependence upon capital inflow and primary exports, a high degree of industrialization and a generally high standard of living. Like the others the Australian economy is greatly influenced by changes in the rate of growth of world trade and in the readiness of investors in other countries to send capital to Australia; and it naturally shares this set of problems with the less developed countries of the world. On the other hand, the high degree of industrialization and absence of disguised unemployment mean that 'Keynesian'-type full employment policies, and other types of measures to affect the level of demand and the degree of inflation are generally as applicable in Australia as in any of the 'developed' countries of the world; so that Australia's experiences in the fields of monetary and budgetary policy are in most respects of interest and relevance to, say, Britain and the USA – as is the experience of these countries to Australia.

It is true that in earlier decades the relative immaturity of the capital market in Australia made comparisons of her experience and policies with those of, say, Britain or the USA much less useful, so that the types of central banking control used in Australia had at that time had much more in common with those applied in many less developed countries. Moreover, it remains true that the degree of reliance on direct controls over bank liquidity in Australia even in the early 1960s makes her experience in these matters more directly comparable with that of countries relying more on such measures than do Britain or the USA, for example. But the growing use of market measures of monetary control in Australia now makes her experience of monetary policy (as well as budgetary policy) of much greater relevance than it used to be for countries such as Britain and the USA with well-developed capital markets, as well as to less developed countries that are in the process of developing a range of different measures of central banking control.

*The section on Wages Policy on pp. 46–9 is written by J. P. Nieuwenhuysen; the remainder is by J. O. N. Perkins.

17

This analysis of the main features of macro-economic policy in Australia will first outline the main problems of internal and external balance that arose during the period 1960–71, and the use made of the various weapons of macro-economic policy in meeting these problems. There will then be some discussion of the role of Australia's system of determining award wages, coupled with the absence of prices and incomes policies as normally understood, followed by a brief discussion of the lack of any form of indicative economic planning. A concluding section will suggest some of the principal conclusions to be drawn for future policy, principally with the aim of emphasizing those lessons that are likely to be useful not only for Australia but also for the economies of the many other countries, both highly developed and less developed, that resemble Australia in a number of the relevant respects.

During the period 1959/60 to 1970/1 the Australian economy achieved a real rate of growth of nearly 6 per cent per annum. Over the second half of the decade the rate of growth was appreciably higher than in earlier years, despite the fact that rural output was considerably curtailed in several of these years by severe drought.

This rate of economic growth was sustained to some extent by a rate of immigration of about 1 per cent per annum – which was probably greater than that of any country of comparable living standards. In addition, the natural rate of increase of the population was also approaching 1 per cent, and the work force was growing even faster than the 2 per cent growth rate of population, partly because of a heavy concentration of the population into the age groups being added each year to the work force, and partly because of a sustained rise in the proportion of married women entering the work force. Towards the end of the decade the work force was in fact rising at around 3 per cent per annum.

The other main factor helping to maintain this rate of growth was the relatively high rate of savings, coupled with a capital inflow, the value of which was equivalent to about a tenth of annual real investment. A large part of the relatively high level of investment was of course required to provide equipment and various services for the rapidly growing population; but a considerable part of it helped to make possible the rise in productivity, which was of the order of $2\frac{1}{2}$ per cent per annum.

THE MANAGEMENT OF THE AUSTRALIAN ECONOMY 1960–71

The degree of success achieved in managing the Australian economy during the 1960s varied from conspicuous failure – by present-day standards – up to about 1962/3 to remarkable success in the later years of the decade. In the early 1960s there were serious problems, when an external deficit and domestic inflation in 1960 led to excessively anti-inflationary domestic policies beginning late in 1960, and a consequent recession in 1961/2. These years were in marked contrast with the remarkable absence of either serious inflation or unemployment, or of external difficulties, in the last three years of the decade. Between these two extremes were periods of both fair success in managing the economy (in and around 1964), and of a minor lapse from full employment growth (in 1966/7). A fairly mild form of 'stagflation' occurred in 1970/1.

One may view these variations of experience as partly resulting from world-wide fluctuations in the rate of economic growth and trade, which were inevitably reflected in the Australian economy. For 1960, 1964 and 1968/9 were periods of rapid growth in world trade and incomes, whereas in 1961/2 and 1966/7 world trade and output were expanding much less rapidly. Moreover, towards the end of the decade world trade exhibited a rapid expansion not paralleled in earlier years of the decade; and the greater success of the Australian economy in reconciling high growth rates with external balance may well be attributed in part to this. But, in addition, there was the special feature of the remarkable burst of mineral discoveries in Australia during the 1960s, which were beginning to affect the level of exports noticeably by the end of the decade, and which had acted as a strong magnet for capital inflow throughout the second half of the 1960s. By its consequently strong upward effect on the country's receipts of foreign exchange and their generally favourabe effect on business activity and expectations, the mineral boom undoubtedly greatly facilitated the task of maintaining a high growth rate without balance of payments difficulties. But such conditions could well have led to serious inflation if policies had been insufficiently restraining. The authorities must therefore certainly be given due credit for their role in maintaining internal and external balance, even though their task was greatly facilitated by circumstances largely beyond their control. In short, the course of the 1960s in Australia may be described as a (discontinuous) progress from a situation where serious problems of internal and external balance – due in part to uncontrollable outside factors – were handled with less than adequacy to one in which outside factors were so favourable that mismanagement of the economy would have been somewhat difficult, but one in which the authorities showed that they had learned much from their mistakes of earlier years.

It is true also that the apparatus for managing the economy was a good deal more adequate in the later years than it had been in earlier periods. For the central bank had by the end of the 1960s a much more complete range of weapons available to it (which it was able and willing to use) than had been true in earlier periods. The rapid development of financial institutions, especially of an officially backed short-term money market and the growth of the bond market, during the period also facilitated the operation of monetary measures; whilst a greater readiness to vary tax rates and rates of government expenditure over the period, and especially a greater readiness to use interest rates, also played an important role in providing the authorities with more adequate means to manage the economy. These helpful developments were partly a natural consequence of the increasing sophistication of financial institutions, and of the wider spread among the public generally of understanding of the economic system and of economic policy; but they also owed something to the efforts of the authorities to develop a suitable range of weapons to affect the level of demand.

The two main (actual or potential) deficiencies were (as we shall see in later sections) the absence of any official prices and incomes policy, and the general reluctance to make use of the exchange rate (and the absence of other measures aimed directly at affecting the balance of payments, once import controls had been abandoned in 1960). It is true that the Arbitration Commission gradually evolved a system of wage decisions that exhibited a considerable degree of enlightenment, and that the relevance of its decisions for wages generally, and so for a large proportion of incomes, played an important role in an area where other countries have tried (often with conspicuously little success) to affect the general level of prices and incomes. It is also true that the decision not to devalue with sterling in 1967 was an important example of a sort of negative use of exchange-rate policy on an isolated occasion. It nevertheless remains true that Australia would be fortunate indeed to maintain throughout the 1970s the successful management of the economy achieved in 1967–9 without a more conscious and thoroughgoing prices and incomes policy and a more flexible attitude to the use of the exchange rate. Both these deficiencies were evident in 1971, when unemployment rose to a high level (by recent Australian standards) whilst inflation was accelerating, and when the government's failure to allow an adequate appreciation led to an excessive accumulation of international reserves.

EXTERNAL BALANCE

Let us now consider how far Australia has been successful in achieving 'external balance' – the avoidance of serious balance of payments deficits on a scale leading to dangerously low reserves, and, on the other hand, the avoidance of surpluses on a scale that would cause an unnecessarily large piling up of international reserves.

As a background to an outline of Australia's experience in this matter during the 1960s it is worth mentioning the periods of severe balance of payments difficulties during the 1950s, especially that of 1951/2 (which led to the imposition of import controls that were not finally removed until 1960) and that of 1955/6. The prolonged difficulties of the 1950s were gradually alleviated by an improvement in exports in the later 1950s together with some retardation of domestic growth, which curbed the expansion of imports. Consequently, the Australian government felt able to remove import controls in 1960. But the emergence of a situation of full or over-full employment in 1960 led to a very rapid expansion of imports, which raised doubts about whether the Australian economy would be able to sustain the level of imports resulting from the absence of import controls (at least at the prevailing exchange rate), though part of the rise could be attributed to temporary rather than lasting factors, including the once-for-all replenishing of the stocks of imported goods that had not been freely available for so long, and perhaps also to a stock-piling of imports in the fear that the freedom from import controls could not last.

The consequent reduction of Australia's international reserves was somewhat alleviated by borrowing from the International Monetary Fund; but taking together both international reserves and readily available IMF drawing rights, this indicator of Australia's international liquidity had been reduced by the end of 1960 to a level that was, in relation to the country's imports, or total current debits, not very far in excess of the levels to which the reserves had fallen in the years of severe balance of payments troubles in the mid-1950s. The reserves were re-built during the recession of 1961/2 – especially in relation to the depressed level of imports during that period – and then rose progressively, with a minor interruption in 1964/5, up to 1966. From that level, which was felt to be fairly comfortable, despite the fact that its relationship to the level of imports was not very much higher than in the crisis year 1960, there were small falls in the years 1965/6 and 1966/7, which reduced this measure of

Table 2.1. *Australia: International liquidity*

($A million)

	1959/60	1960/1	1961/2	1962/3	1963/4	1964/5	1965/6	1966/7	1967/8	1968/9	1969/70	1970/1
Changes in reserves and other international monetary movements	+15	−81	+177	+150	+447	−297	+57	−124	+79	+148	+37	+602
Reserves and Special Drawing Rights at end of year	926	963	1,049	1,200	1,650	1,355	1,414	1,264	1,345	1,514	1,636	2,316

Source: Commonwealth Bureau of Census and Statistics, *Balance of Payments.*

international liquidity to much the same sort of relationship to imports that used to cause anxiety in the 1950s; some rise in the reserves in 1968/9 and 1969/70, thanks mainly to a very rapid rise in mineral exports and capital inflow, and the initial creation of Special Drawing Rights with the International Monetary Fund, did not alter this broad picture, but a very big rise occurred in 1970/1, as Table 2.1 shows.

It is true that one cannot regard the relationship between reserves (including readily available liquidity from the IMF) and imports as being by any means a complete measure of reserve adequacy. In particular, the adequacy of a country's reserves depends also to a large extent on its balance of payments prospects; and the feeling in Australia in the later 1960s was that these were excellent, in view of the rapid build-up of exports from minerals that was occurring, and which was likely to go very much further in the 1970s; and also in view of the very high and sustained rate of capital inflow – which was in large measure related to the prospects of the Australian mineral industry. But at the same time there were certain adverse factors, especially the growing difficulties of Australia's rural exports, with world wool prices falling at the end of the 1960s and a world wheat surplus also tending to worsen the prospects of one of Australia's other leading rural exports.

But, taking the 1960s as a whole, one may say that after the balance of payments crisis in 1960 the balance of payments became progressively less of a restraint on policy decisions. It is true that initially the improvement was largely a result of the 1961/2 recession, which cannot be considered as having been an appropriate means of strengthening the country's balance of payments, in view of the loss of potential output that it involved. But thereafter the general level of the country's reserves was generally neither excessive nor so low as to cause serious anxiety (though, as we have seen, this was largely because of the greatly improved prospects for mineral exports and capital inflow). There was a period about 1964 when one could argue that the reserves were beginning to rise unduly high, but the resumption of a high level of domestic activity in 1964/5 and the consequent expansion of imports reduced the reserves in the following year to a level where they could not be regarded as excessive. During 1970/1, however, the reserves rose to an excessively high level.

But such an examination of the results tells us little about how far macro-economic policy was responsible for the generally satisfactory outcome (at least from about 1962/3 onwards) on the side of external balance. It has to be admitted that a great deal of the success was due to a very high level of capital inflow during the middle and later 1960s, which could not reasonably have been foreseen and which was related to only a minor extent to the government's macro-economic policies. One can certainly argue that the political stability of Australia and the generally very favourable official attitude to capital inflow (coupled with less attractive conditions for capital in many other other countries, especially ones that might have been attractive alternative sources of minerals) were important influences on capital inflow and the balance of payments; and the generally high level of domestic activity (with the exception of 1966/7) without any serious inflation or appreciable risk of devaluation, presumably helped to attract capital inflow. Nevertheless, it is reasonable to argue that Australia was fortunate that capital inflow rose, under the influence of the major mineral developments, to such a high level in the later 1960s, and that if it had not done so, the government's policies might well have scored less highly on the criterion of external balance.

There were, indeed, few cases after 1960/1 when the government could reasonably be said to be taking decisions of macro-economic policy that were consciously and intentionally directed towards affecting the state of the balance of payments – except, of course, in the negative sense that as external considerations were not a serious restraint on policy in this period, macro-economic policy generally was able to be more expansionary than would otherwise have been possible. One exception to this generalization is the failure to use an appreciable reduction of interest rates as a potentially worthwhile stimulant to the level of demand when the economy was operating below full employment potential in 1966/7. This seems to have been largely because the authorities wanted to avoid the adverse effect on capital inflow that they feared would result from a reduction in interest rates in Australia, especially in view of the fact that interest rates in the rest of the world were already tending to rise in relation to those in Australia. It is true that the ready availability of bank credit in Australia (and, indeed, of credit generally), presumably tended to make many companies with parent companies overseas borrow rather more within Australia, and consequently to bring in rather less capital, than would otherwise have occurred, especially in view of limitations on capital outflow imposed during the second half of the 1960s by Britain and the USA: and a further reduction of interest rates in Australia would certainly have accentuated this tendency. But the stimulus to activity within Australia that would have resulted from a reduction of interest rates would have probably done even more to stimulate capital inflow, by improving the profit prospects of overseas capital in Australia. In any case, if the authorities were really inhibited from taking this expansionary action by fears of the effect of lower interest rates upon capital inflow, the consequent loss of potential output in Australia must be counted a very considerable cost of the policy. One might reasonably doubt whether such capital inflow as may have been attracted by the policy of refraining from reducing interest rates was really worth having at the cost of the output forgone. At the very least, if fears about capital inflow really did lead to policies that had the effect of maintaining less than full employment, the episode would suggest that the Australian economy had been allowed to become unwarrantably dependent on capital inflow for maintaining a satisfactory external balance. The appropriate remedy for such a situation would be to ensure the maintenance of full employment, and then to devalue if the balance of payments deteriorated uncomfortably. But this alternative also was presumably one that the Australian government would have been inhibited from adopting by probably exaggerated fears of its adverse effect on capital inflow (to judge by its expressed views on the matter at the time of the decision not to devalue with Britain late in 1967). There was, however, in theory at least, the further alternative of varying the policy mix of budgetary and monetary measures in such a way as to maintain both full employment and external balance, if one felt that a more expansionary budget, rather than lower interest rates, could have been used to restore full employment without the adverse effects on capital inflow that might have resulted from lower interest rates. It may well be that this was the course the Australian authorities had in mind, whether or not they consciously spelt it out in this manner: for in fact the restoration of full employment in 1968/9 owed little to monetary policy (at least in the shape of lower interest rates) and most to the expansionary effects of the budget of 1967 (especially the rapid rise in defence spending). But it did not, apparently, prove possible to take expansionary budgetary action on a sufficient scale and at the right time to avoid considerable losses of potential output in 1966/7; and this suggests that it was of questionable wisdom to have refrained from using to the full the more flexible weapon of monetary policy to restore full employment in 1966/7.

Furthermore, the informal control over local borrowing by overseas firms in Australia, exercised by the Reserve Bank from 1966 onwards, was partly directed at preventing the sharp reduction in capital inflow (as a result of the stimulus to increase the local borrowing by these firms) that might have resulted when interest rates in Australia lagged well behind those in the rest of the world. It may be doubted how far an informal control such as this could offset this incentive for greater local borrowing if the interest-rate differential became large; but if the availability of this control did something to reduce the inhibition the authorities apparently felt against keeping interest rates in Australia down in 1966/7, it may have been worth while on this account, in any event.

It seems that a consideration of the effect of monetary measures on capital inflow was one factor that influenced the government in deciding to raise interest rates in the first half of 1970. It is true that some policy to restrain demand was probably in any event required at the time for internal reasons, and that the alternative of a less expansionary budget was probably ruled out for political reasons associated with the general election late in 1969, and the subsequent reluctance that the government would presumably have felt to reverse this budgetary policy early in 1970 so soon after being returned to power. But the other important consideration was that interest rates in Australia began to lag behind the increases occurring in many other countries in the early part of 1970, and there was apparently some fear that this situation might adversely affect capital inflow. In any event, whatever the precise mixture of motives in bringing about the tightening of monetary policy in the first half of 1970, it certainly appeared to have the effect of increasing net capital inflow in the months immediately following the increase in officially controlled interest rates.

Capital inflow reached very high levels in 1970/1. In addition to the continued attraction of the good long-term prospects for Australian minerals (even despite some weakening of Japanese demand for them during 1971), the general strength of the Australian balance of payments was itself a factor encouraging capital inflow in a situation where general adjustments of exchange rates seemed likely, and where the exchange rate of the us dollar was under suspicion. In particular, American companies operating in Australia seem to have deferred the remittance of dividends earned in Australia, in expectation of the devaluation of the us dollar that in fact occurred late in 1971. There was also reason to believe that the official Australian 'guide-lines', limiting the borrowing in Australia by overseas-owned companies, were leading such companies to bring more capital into Australia than they would otherwise have done. Furthermore, an increasing number of Australian firms were discovering the advantages of borrowing overseas, partly to shield themselves from the seasonal stringency of cash that occurs with the concentration of certain tax payments into the March quarter (which had been particularly tight in 1970 as a result of anti-inflationary monetary measures).

Exchange-rate policy in the 1960s

No use was made of variations in the exchange rate as a means of reconciling internal and external balance during the 1960s (nor indeed, during the 1950s). The only practical consideration of whether to vary the exchange rate occurred in November 1967, as a result of the devaluation of sterling. In contrast to what happened when sterling was devalued in 1949 (when Australia had devalued with sterling), in 1967 Australia retained the prevailing parity against the United States dollar (and therefore, of course, against all other currencies that did not devalue).

On a number of occasions when the Australian balance of payments was in difficulties during the 1950s there was some discussion, at least among academic observers, of whether it would be preferable to devalue, rather than to retain import controls. Even after import controls had been abandoned in 1960, the balance of payments crisis of late 1960 might reasonably have suggested that an appropriate policy would have been devaluation, for this would certainly have made it possible to secure a stronger balance of payments without the period of severe recession that followed in 1961/2, which was (by accident rather than design) in fact the means employed to eliminate the external deficit.

But the gradual strengthening of the Australian balance of payments during the 1960s, even after the recovery to full employment, made any serious discussion of devaluation seem inappropriate on balance of payments grounds. For the rapid rise in capital inflow and in mineral exports made it possible to finance a very rapid rise in both visible imports and invisible debits without this bringing about any serious strain on the reserves.

At the time of the devaluation of sterling in November 1967 there therefore seemed to be no good case on balance of payments grounds for a devaluation of the Australian dollar. The government appears also to have been influenced by a wish to contribute towards ensuring that the devaluation of sterling was as successful as possible in improving Britain's balance of payments, which was, of course, more likely if relatively few other countries devalued at the same time. But the dominant considerations in the decision were probably ones of prestige, including a feeling that capital inflow would be encouraged if Australia could show the rest of the world that its currency was strong enough to be able to avoid devaluing with sterling, and thus to emphasize the extent to which the Australian dollar was now (in some sense or other) independent of sterling. In the short run, at least, this calculation seems to have been correct; for many overseas investors may have had their confidence in the Australian dollar strengthened by the decision not to devalue, and a number of investors, in Continental Europe especially, may well have had their attention drawn to the prospective profitability and security of investing in Australia by this decision of the Australian government not to devalue with sterling. At a time of relative strength in the balance of payments of a country heavily dependent on long-term capital inflow, perhaps it can therefore be argued that the international publicity given to the strength of its balance of payments by a decision not to devalue in such circumstances may have a strongly favourable effect on capital inflow – though this is not a consideration that has (so far as the writer is aware) ever been introduced into theoretical discussions of the criteria for judging the desirability of devaluing. But it remains true that a decision not to devalue must tend to weaken the current account, and will certainly be likely also to have adverse effects on capital inflow into a country whose balance of payments is at all weak at the time (as was that of New Zealand in 1967). One should therefore exercise great caution about generalizing from Australia's experience in late 1967 – the relevant features of which might well never be repeated. For the essential consideration was that the greatly improved outlook for the Australian economy arising out of the remarkable mineral developments during the 1960s had not up to that time been fully appreciated by potential investors in many countries, so that – once they became aware of the position – there were good grounds for believing that overseas investors had scope for profitability increasing the scale of their investment in Australia; and the Australian government was therefore probably right in its judgment at the time that the decision not to devalue would do a good deal to draw the attention of international investors to these prospects. But in any situation where the prospects for profitably and secure investment in Australia were already fully appreciated by investors in other countries one could not reasonably expect a decision not to devalue to have any comparable favourable effect on capital inflow. It would therefore be dangerous to use this experience as a precedent in any future period when exchange-rate policy is being determined – or for any other country whose circumstances did not have these special features that presumably did something to increase the flow of capital to Australia in 1967/8.

Between 1967 and 1969 it proved possible to keep the Australian balance of payments in a comfortable state virtually as a by-product of keeping the economy reasonably close to full employment. In other words, with budgetary and monetary measures operating on the level of domestic demand with the prime aim of maintaining internal balance, it happened that external balance turned out to be neither unduly weak nor unnecessarily strong. But it has to be recognized that such an outcome is by no means automatic. It is virtually certain that there will be periods when the balance of payments will become unduly strong or weak if the level of domestic demand is kept (so far as possible) near the point where full employment prevails. It will then be necessary to use the exchange rate, as well as operating on internal forms of expenditure, if internal and external balance are to be successfully reconciled – assuming that such alternatives as import controls, flat-rate tariffs on imports, and a successful and flexible prices and incomes policy are ruled out as either undesirable or impracticable.

Import controls had acted as this second arm of macro-economic policy in Australia during the 1950s. The recession of the early 1960s was in part the price paid for trying to reconcile internal and external balance without such a second arm of policy; and the 1966/7 lapse from full employment also (fortuitously) played the same role to a more moderate extent. But it would require an excess of optimism to expect that such a second weapon of macro-economic policy could be dispensed with indefinitely, even though, by a happy accident, in 1967–9 external balance emerged as an almost incidental by-product of the maintenance of internal balance.

There is another aspect of the decision not to devalue in November 1967 which is of importance if one accepts the argument that a better allocation of resources in the Australian economy would result if the Australian dollar were devalued, and if tariffs on imports and a number of special forms of assistance to primary producers were simultaneously reduced. For it would have been politically easier to devalue in November 1967 than it is likely to be in any other foreseeable circumstances; and the consequent improvement in the allocation of resources that would probably have resulted from the combination of devaluation with a reduction in tariffs and subsidies would itself have increased the country's economic growth in the long run. It would, incidentally, also eventually presumably have thereby increased capital inflow – the effect on which seems to have bulked large in the government's considerations at the time. It is beyond the scope of the present study to discuss policies relating to the allocation of resources as such; but an inefficient allocation of resources, such as almost certainly resulted from Australia's over-valued exchange rate supported by high tariffs, clearly affects the rate of growth and therefore has an important bearing upon macro-economic policies. If, therefore, one seeks to draw general conclusions from Australia's decisions about the exchange rate in 1967, they should be cautious ones from a long-run point of view. One could reasonably be satisfied with the decision not to devalue in 1967 only if one could count on the Australian government being ready in appropriate future circumstances to devalue (whether to overcome an existing external deficit, or to forestall the occurrence of a deficit that would otherwise result from a general reduction in tariffs, and in certain subsidies and other forms of assistance to primary industries). If, on the other hand, one has not that degree of confidence in the future flexibility of official policies in this matter one could argue that a golden opportunity was lost in 1967 to achieve a better allocation of resources and a higher rate of growth, by devaluing and simultaneously reforming tariff policy and other measures that impeded an appropriate allocation of the country's resources.

Exchange-rate policy in 1971
A very large rise occurred in Australia's international reserves during the course of 1970 and 1971, so that in the aftermath of the United States measures of August 1971, when the future of most exchange rates was under discussion, there was a strong case to be made for an appreciation of the Australian dollar – certainly as against the US dollar, and probably also against the average of other currencies.

It is true that a still stronger case could be made for reducing or eliminating tariffs, and for then adjusting the exchange rate in whatever way was necessary to keep the reserves at a reasonable level. But the prospect of a speedy and whole-hearted movement in the direction of lower tariffs seemed non-existent, so that with the reserves accumulating to an unnecessarily high level, an appreciation seemed a wise course. It is true that the rise in the reserves resulted largely from a rapid increase in capital inflow, which could well have fallen away sharply, whilst the uncertain prospects for many primary exports (with the prospect of a slowing down in the rate of growth of the Japanese economy, and of Britain entering the EEC) led many observers to counsel caution about the balance of payments outlook. But such views were really arguments for pursuing a sufficiently flexible exchange-rate policy to make any necessary future adjustments of the parity as conditions changed, rather than against appreciating in the conditions prevailing in 1971.

The case for some degree of appreciation in 1971 was reinforced by the existence of a substantial measure of internal inflation (at least by Australian standards) which an appreciation (or a tariff cut) would have helped to alleviate. It is true that there was also some tendency for demand to lapse below full employment growth rates, and that an appreciation would have increased this tendency; but such effects could always have been offset by a sufficiently expansionary budgetary and monetary policy.

The most powerful opposition to any appreciation (even in relation to the US dollar, which was itself worth less than it had been earlier in 1971, in terms of most major currencies) came predominantly from the powerful rural sector, which was in considerable difficulties, largely because of low wool prices, and also from mining companies, whose profits would have been reduced – especially as many of their export contracts, for iron ore and coal especially, had been fixed in terms of US dollars. Many manufacturing industries would also have opposed an appreciation, as making it harder for their products to compete with imports.

The government therefore decided, for the period August–December 1971, to keep the Australian dollar pegged to sterling, which amounted to a considerable depreciation in relation to the Japanese yen, and a small appreciation relative to the United States dollar. This intermediate course had the argument of practical convenience to recommend it – the Australian currency having been normally fixed in terms of sterling; but there was no presumption that whatever fluctuations might occur in the exchange rate for sterling in terms of other currencies would happen also to be the fluctuations most appropriate to the Australian currency. Indeed, with the three major currencies of prime interest to Australia having fluctuated in relation to one another, and being likely to alter their relative parities further, the only logical course had become that of fixing the rate on none of them (except in the trivial sense that the daily quotation had to be in terms of some currency), but, on the contrary, to pursue a flexible exchange-rate policy. This could have been done either by making frequent small alterations or by allowing a fluctuating rate on the Canadian model.

In this situation of balance of payments strength and high reserves, coupled with an uncomfortably rapid rate of increase in the domestic price level, it is strange that the government did not take advantage of the exchange-rate adjustments made by many countries late in 1971 to bring about an effective appreciation of the Australian dollar. It is true that it did not succumb to the pressure of rural and mineral exporting interests for the Australian dollar to be depreciated all the way with the US dollar; and the Liberal party leaders of the governing coalition would have apparently preferred to remain at the former parity against sterling. But the final decision, made in response to Country party insistence that some effective devaluation should occur in order to assist the depressed rural sector, was in effect to depreciate against the average of other countries – to an extent officially estimated as about $1\frac{3}{4}$ per cent (though the basis of this estimate was not made clear). But this was done by the curious, indeed ingenious, but none the less reprehensible, device of perverting to a quite inappropriate purpose the wider spread around the notified par value that the Group of Ten major countries had agreed upon with IMF approval about a week earlier. The wider band – of $2\frac{1}{4}$ per cent on either side of par – was intended to enable countries with a temporarily strong balance of payments to appreciate towards the top of this band, and to enable countries with a weak balance of payments to depreciate towards the bottom end of it, without having to change their official par values. But the Australian government used the wider band to establish an effective market rate at the lower end of the band, despite its high level of reserves and strong balance of payments.[1] This was apparently done in order to be able to inform the rest of the world that the official parity of the Australian dollar against gold had not been changed when the US dollar devalued, whilst at the same time the Country party could rightly claim that it had secured an effective devaluation of the Australian dollar against other currencies generally.

The real reason for this decision was therefore purely a matter of domestic politics, though a more efficient way of assisting the rural sector would have been to adopt the exchange rate that was

[1] The decision to fix the actual market rate for the Australian dollar at the lower end of the permitted margin about the fixed official parity left room for a substantial market appreciation (by up to $4\frac{1}{2}$ per cent) if the balance of payments remained strong, without any need to change the official parity. The government thus had scope to use this margin to reduce the reserves to a more reasonable level (if the balance of payments generally remained strong). But at the time of writing it seems virtually certain that domestic political considerations would make it difficult to make this sensible use of this greater permitted range of flexibility.

Contents

Chapter 1

INTRODUCTION

J. O. N. PERKINS

Australia, Canada, New Zealand and South Africa share with each other far more economic characteristics than does any of them with most of the other countries of the world. Their economies contrast with almost all the other countries that enjoy high living standards in being greatly dependent on the export of primary products (especially if 'primary' is defined to include minerals and base metals); though it is true that manufactured exports have been of growing importance for all the four countries in recent years, and for Canada manufactures are now about as important as primary products in total exports. This emphasis on primary exports is associated with the high ratio of economically useful natural resources to population in each of these countries. The four countries contrast with the less developed countries of the world in their much higher living standards, and also (with the exception of South Africa) in the relative absence of disguised unemployment, and of a subsistence sector. On the other hand, they have in common with the less developed countries of the world the major role played by primary products in their exports, although for many less developed countries primary products make up an even greater proportion of total exports. Finally, they share with underdeveloped countries the characteristic of generally running a current account deficit in their balance of payments, though for the four rich primary-exporting countries this deficit is financed largely by private capital inflow, whereas various types of official grants and loans are the means of financing the current account deficit of most of the less developed countries.

The characteristics that the four countries share, and which distinguish them in one way or another from other economies of the world, have implications for many areas of their economic policies. The importance of the balance of payments, and especially that of fluctuations in their exports and in their long-term private capital inflow, presents special problems for them. This is not, of course, to deny that comparable problems may arise for other countries also.

But for other rich countries there is generally no comparable degree of dependence on a net inflow of private long-term capital; and for the other industralized countries the fluctuations of capital inflows that do occur tend to be to a larger extent of short-term capital (as well as being often offset by inter-central bank lines of credit, whereas there is little or no possibility of this form of financing for any of the four countries except Canada). Moreover, other rich countries that have a considerable gross inflow of private capital have usually at least as large a gross long-term capital outflow.

The four rich primary-exporting countries also share with one another the general characteristic of a high rate of growth of population, partly as a consequence of relatively high net immigration rates. Their work forces are thus increasing more rapidly than those of other countries with high living standards. This characteristic is also associated with their large net inflows of private capital; for the high ratio of natural resources to population makes these countries attractive for the two relatively scarce factors of production, labour and capital. The high rate of population growth itself tends also to encourage capital inflow, for the rapidly growing population generally has a high level of education and skill, and is fairly fully employed, and with high living standards. In these respects they contrast with most poorer countries with populations growing at comparable rates, for which a fast population growth is not likely to be an especially strong attraction to capital inflow.

These characteristics make the experiences of each of the four countries in the various fields of economic policy of special relevance to the remaining countries in the group. It is therefore strange that little or no attempt seems to have been made to compare the experience of these countries in the principal fields of economic policy, with a view to assessing what each of them could learn from the others. Whereas the experiences of the USA and Britain in the main fields of economic policy receive a good deal of public discussion in the four countries, relatively little public discussion of policy in them has taken explicit account of the experience of the rest of the four.

Part of the explanation for this neglect presumably lies in the geographical separation of these four economies, and the relative inadequacies of lines of communication among them. For example, publications discussing economic policy in the USA and Britain are much more readily available in the four countries than are those discussing policies in other rich primary-exporting countries. Even between two such close neighbours as Australia and New Zealand, the exchange of ideas on economic issues – at any rate, through the public press – is very much less than the press discussion in each of them of economic policies in Britain, both in their own publications and in the wide range of American and British publications available in each country. The relative geographical proximity of these two countries is, in short, scarcely more conducive to the interchange of published ideas and information in these areas of policy than the greater distances that separate these two countries from Canada and South Africa. Political considerations may well have also played a part in limiting the interest of Australians, Canadians, and New Zealanders in economic events and policies in South Africa (and perhaps also in limiting South African interest in the other three); but if this is so it is quite irrational. Whatever one's views about the political situation in a particular country, this is no justification for failing to take full advantage of any opportunity to learn from its economic experience.

The present study attempts to contribute towards filling this gap in the literature. The aim is to assess the principal lessons that can be drawn from the experiences of each of these countries in the main areas of macro-economic policy, that is, the maintenance of full employment without inflation ('internal balance') and the maintenance and restoration of an adequately (but not excessively) strong balance of payments situation ('external balance'). The period under review has been the years 1960 to 1970 or 1971, but the contributors have been free to extend their reviews into earlier years if this helps them to make the points that seem most relevant and important for the four countries concerned. The approaches of the four authors have been co-ordinated. They have nevertheless remained free to develop their approach as seemed best to each of them in the light of his own interests, and of the nature of the problems of the economy on which he was writing, but in full awareness of the general aims of the study, which had been decided by the group before the work began.

Although the four countries have been considered primarily for the relevance that the experience of each of them should have for the other countries in the group, the study of macro-economic problems in this group of countries should also have a wider interest. For it is relevant in many ways to the discussion of macro-economic problems in the developed economies generally, and also has some bearing on a number of aspects of policy in less developed countries.

In the first place the four countries are comparable to the economies of Western Europe, North America and Japan in being concerned with the types of short-term macro-economic policies that are essentially similar to the policies operated in all the developed countries. In particular, where appreciable unemployment arises in any of them, it is likely to be generally 'Keynesian' – in the sense that it can be overcome by raising the level of effective demand: though it is, of course, true that almost all these countries have also pockets of regional unemployment to which policies of this sort are not necessarily applicable.

Within the group of developed countries (including the four discussed in detail in this book) a common body of experience in macro-economic policy is being gradually accumulated which is of clear relevance to all of them. For they are all concerned with using broadly similar budgetary and monetary policy for maintaining full employment without serious inflation and a healthy balance of payments, and they are all concerned with the problems of whether or not some form of prices and incomes policy is feasible or desirable. Moreover, they are all closely integrated parts of the market economy of the Western world, with their industries linked closely together by the operation of multi-national firms, and by the operations of financial institutions with interests that spread across their national frontiers and cover the four countries (as well as those of Europe, North America, and to an increasing extent Japan).

The experience of the rich industrialized countries of Europe, North America, and Japan is not closely relevant to policy in the less developed countries. But the group discussed in this book have enough characteristics in common with less developed countries for their experience to be clearly relevant also for many less developed countries.

It is true that the relevance of the experience of these four countries for the policies of the less developed countries is not, at least at first sight, so great as one would expect it to be for the richer, industrialized, developed countries. But in some respects the group of four countries occupies an intermediate position between the two main types of economy, and shares a number of relevant characteristics with the less developed group.

In particular, the stage of development of the capital markets and of financial institutions in the four countries has been (at least until very recently) rather less advanced than in many European and North American industrialized countries, and the rate of development of these capital markets in recent decades suggests ways in which similar markets in the less developed countries are likely to develop in the decades ahead. Certainly, the problems and opportunities for the operation of monetary and financial policy in many developing countries that are likely to be experienced in coming years have similarities to those of the four countries, with their capital markets at various stages of development, and strongly influenced by the capital markets of major financial centres in other countries (notably New York and London). In particular, the role of net long-term private capital inflow in the four countries and also in a number of less developed countries raises common problems relating to the efficacy of monetary policy for internal balance and also for balance of payments policy. These common interests have been the background to the advice that has been given by the Australian central bank (for example) in the setting up of a central bank in Malaysia and to a smaller extent in certain African countries. (This common interest with less developed countries in financial matters naturally extends far beyond the field of macro-economic policy covered in this book: it may be at least as important in matters relating to the efficient operation of the capital market for achieving an allocation of funds such as will facilitate a high rate of economic growth.)

The plan of the book is to discuss first the experience of each of the four countries separately, and then to compare their experiences in a final chapter. There is no particular reason for the order in which the countries are discussed here. They have been placed alphabetically, and the chapters on each country may be read separately or in any order. The writers would strongly urge, however, that readers in any one of these countries should not confine their attention to the discussion of the experience of their own country: for the experience of each and all of the countries is likely to afford some guidance for policy decisions in each of the others. It is to be hoped that when future policy decisions (in these and other countries) are made, and when there is discussion of the policies by official observers, this will take place against the background of the accumulated body of experience of all of these countries (as well, of course, as that of others). The major decisions about the development and use of the tools of macro-economic policy – such as the types of budgetary weapons, the form of monetary and other financial measures, the use of the exchange rate – can best be taken after giving due attention to the experience of countries whose measures have differed somewhat from those of one's own country; and whose successful use of exchange rate flexibility, direct controls over financial institutions or open-market operations (for example) may therefore suggest new ways of applying or developing such measures – or, alternatively, pitfalls to avoid in applying them.

The government of a country, and observers discussing its measures and policy instruments, are naturally generally familiar with the lessons that can be derived from the experience of their own country. But other countries also have often accumulated experience that could usefully be taken into account when important policy decisions are made in one's own country. If politicians, bankers, civil servants, journalists, academics and students in these four countries become more aware of what can be learned from the economic experience of the others, this should greatly increase the likelihood of the adoption of sound future policies in all of them.

thought to be in the best interests of the country, and then (where it was felt to be justifiable) to assist those rural industries that needed it, in whatever was believed to be the most efficient way possible. But the government attempted to justify its decision by pointing out that the balance of payments was not really as strong as it looked, as some of the recent very high capital inflow had presumably been due to temporary factors. In fact, however, even the most generous reasonable allowance for this consideration would still have left Australia's reserves and balance of payments among the strongest in the world. In such a situation the effective devaluation was thus difficult or impossible to justify internationally. The failure to appreciate was still harder to justify in the prevailing context of the need to check the rise in the domestic price level, for which purpose a substantial appreciation would have been appropriate. The downward effect of any appreciation on the flagging level of domestic activity at the time could quite easily have been offset by tax cuts or by a rise in government spending (or both). One could naturally (as for any surplus country at any time) suggest various considerations that might worsen the balance of payments in the reasonably near future, and so make an appreciation unjustifiable in retrospect. But one could also have found arguments for an opposite viewpoint. In any event, even if subsequent events led to a deterioration of the balance of payments – or, indeed to a further improvement in it – the right policy would then be to realign the exchange rate at that later date, to meet any such fundamental change in the outlook as might occur. Views about possible future changes in the outlook could be no justification for failing to adopt a realistic exchange rate at the time.

A further feature of the exchange-rate decision reached late in 1971 was that henceforth the Australian dollar was to be fixed in terms of the US dollar instead of in sterling. There can be no quarrel with this if it is to be considered purely as a matter of administrative convenience. But the danger is that this matter of the way in which the rate is quoted by the Reserve Bank (there being no foreign exchange market in Australia) may lead to a continuance of the prevailing rate against the US dollar in circumstances when this is not appropriate. Indeed, there is some reason to believe that the expectation that sterling would be likely to devalue against the US dollar before long played the major part in influencing the authorities to take this course, as fixing the rate on the US dollar would in that event make a future devaluation of the Australian dollar to that extent less likely. But this consideration should serve to emphasize the point that the method that happens to be chosen for the day-to-day exchange-rate quotation should not be allowed to determine future movements in the exchange rate for the Australian dollar. With the prospect of major currencies varying against one another from day to day more often than in the past, there is no presumption that the rate on any one of them should remain fixed for long. The administrative decision as to which of them should be the one in which the rate is fixed from day to day should not be allowed to influence the fundamental decision about the level of the exchange rate; only the state of the reserves and the overall balance of payments are relevant to this.

INTERNAL BALANCE

During the 1960s the Australian government generally achieved a high degree of success (by world standards) in maintaining internal balance, once the considerable recession (considerable, that is, by post-war standards) of 1961/2 had been left behind, as Table 2.2 shows.

A measure of the general success in avoiding serious excess demand is that the number of registered unemployed never fell to the very low level of about ¾ per cent (of total employees plus defence forces and unemployed) to which it fell in 1954/5 and 1955/6. After the recession of 1961/2 (when the percentage was about 2½-3 per cent of the work force), the average percentage unemployment for the succeeding years varied between 1·2 and 1·8 per cent. It is true that at the peak of activity in 1965 and 1970 the percentage dipped to just over 1 per cent; and at both those peaks of activity one could say that the upper limit of what most observers would regard as reasonably full capacity was reached, though perhaps it was not exceeded. At the other extreme, in 1966/7 the percentage unemployed rose to a level that was certainly higher than the government would have wished, though this occurred partly for temporary reasons associated with drought, rather than with inadequate demand of the more usual type. Approximate measures of the extent to which the economy was operating below capacity in the non-farm sector are probably a better indication than unemployment of the success in achieving internal balance. Such a measure suggests that in 1964/5 the economy was operating well up to or even above its sustainable level of capacity operation, and that for a while in 1966/7 it was operating at perhaps about 1 per cent below the average degree of capacity utilization (or about 4 per cent less than the degree of utilization experienced in the peak year of

Table 2.2. *Australia: Inflation and unemployment*

	1960/1	1961/2	1962/3	1963/4	1964/5	1965/6	1966/7	1967/8	1968/9	1969/70	1970/1	1971/2 (Estimated)
Implicit GNP deflator (Per cent rise in year)	4·5	0·9	1·0	2·4	2·4	2·8	3·2	2·7	3·7	4·8	6·2	7
Consumer price index (Per cent rise in year)	4·1	0·4	0·2	1·0	3·7	3·7	2·6	3·4	2·6	3·2	4·7	6
Registered unemployed (Per cent of non-rural employees)	2·0	3·3	2·6	1·8	1·2	1·4	1·6	1·7	1·5	1·3	1·6	1·8

Sources: Commonwealth Bureau of Census and Statistics, Department of Labour and National Service, University of Melbourne Institute of Applied Economic and Social Research.

35

1964/5). During the recession of 1961/2 it was operating at about 4 per cent below the average degree of capacity utilization, or about 6 per cent below the peak degree of capacity utilization achieved in 1959/60.[2] Even though the recession of 1961/2 therefore represented a failure by these high standards, something remarkably close to internal balance without either serious inflation or high unemployment was maintained from 1963 to 1970, though a (fairly mild) form of 'stagflation' arose in 1971.

It is true that there was another lapse from full capacity growth in 1970/1. But in the early 1970s unemployment never approached the high rates reached during the same years in Britain or North America (even if every reasonable allowance is made for differences in recording unemployment in the various countries); nor did the rate of price increase (as indicated by the available indexes) reach the corresponding maximum rates of increase that occurred in the same period in Britain or New Zealand, even though inflation in Australia in 1970/1 was certainly high by past Australian standards, being well in excess of the moderate rates of inflation experienced since the end of the Korean boom of 1950/1. Australia did, then, experience a form of 'stagflation' – that is, less than full employment growth coupled with rising prices – in the early 1970s, but the dimensions of the problem were small compared with the stagflation prevailing in the same period in Britain and North America, as unemployment in Australia was much less than in those countries.

Budgetary and monetary policy
During the 1950s the budget had been used increasingly as a means of maintaining internal and external balance. This is not to say that the timing of budgetary measures was always good, but merely that its use on Keynesian principles to affect the overall level of demand had become widely accepted. It is true that journalists, members of parliament and ministers were still sometimes to be found advocating a reduction of taxes on such irrelevant grounds (as an economist would see them) as the existence of a budget surplus; but the extent of such reasoning had by the early 1960s become much rarer than it had been even during the 1950s, and it is unlikely that such pre-Keynesian attitudes played any considerable part in the major budgetary decisions.[3] Increases in taxation,

[2] I am indebted to Mr A. N. E. Jolley for these estimates.

[3] It is true, however, that until very late in the 1960s one could find examples of official statements that measured the effect of a budget by the net cash outcome in a particular year – which is not a good indication of the overall effect of a

accompanied by (belated) increases in interest rates had been used to check the booms of 1950/1 and 1955/6, though this action had been taken only when these booms were well past their peak (as can be seen in retrospect), so that the anti-inflationary budgetary and monetary measures served largely to intensify the subsequent periods of recession. But though the timing was bad – probably because of the political difficulties involved in taking unpopular budgetary and monetary action rather than from any lack of expert advice to take more timely action – the principle had thus become established during the 1950s that the main budgetary and monetary weapons could and should be used to keep the economy as close as possible to internal and external balance. In addition, the import controls imposed during the balance of payments crisis of early 1952 had been retained, though with varying severity, throughout the 1950s, and these had thus also been a macro-economic weapon of some importance.

The 1960s began with a renewed problem of boom coupled with balance of payments crisis. But the problems of this boom differed considerably from those of 1950/1 and 1955/6. In particular, the external problem was associated with the abandonment of import controls (with very few exceptions, as from March 1960), and was thus in some measure the result of what was thought of as a move from strength, the ensuing deficit being due partly to the immediate after-effects of removing the controls, when importers replenished their stocks of imported goods that were now freely available. But a high level of domestic demand also played an important part in causing the deficit; though the extent of excess demand was never great – again in contrast to earlier booms: and it was heavily concentrated in particular areas of the economy, especially building and motor vehicles. It was thus possible to argue that severe overall measures to check demand were probably not justifiable from the viewpoint of internal balance; and one may suppose that it was mainly the rapid fall in the country's international reserves that eventually precipitated action in the second half of 1960 to curb demand.

During the course of 1960 some increases had been permitted in those interest rates under official control; in this respect, therefore, one could argue that something appeared to have been learned from

budget, as many other influences on the level of demand also affect the net cash outcome in a particular year. In the later 1960s, however, budget statements tended to differentiate between changes in tax receipts resulting from changes in tax rates and those that were the result of influences originating from outside the budget.

the failure to use the weapon of higher interest rates in 1950 and 1955 until well past the peak of the boom. It is very doubtful, however, whether the increases that were permitted kept pace with the rising expectation of inflation, or with rising interest rates in the uncontrolled parts of the capital market. Indeed, the grudging and gradual edging up of bond rates probably sufficed merely to confirm the expectation of the market that further rises were likely – and so did little or nothing to persuade the public to buy bonds.

Similarly, there were a number of tax increases in the budget of August 1960, which in retrospect were probably sufficient, though they might more appropriately have been made earlier; but one may suppose that the practice of having an annual budget in August would have made it difficult (had the government wished) to vary tax rates in say, June or July. In November 1960, however, the government decided that further measures were needed to curb demand, for it was not by any means clear that the peak had passed, whilst the country's international reserves were falling towards a dangerously low level.

In the broad context of the development of budgetary and monetary weapons in Australia, the decisions of November 1960 and the subsequent months are of some importance. In the first place, those interest rates under official control were at last raised to a level where there was a strong expectation that the next change in them would be downwards – so that the level of demand, and the level of publc subscriptions to bonds at last moved in the desired direction (for – rightly or wrongly – the official view at the time was that it was still desirable to curb spending). This made it difficult for businesses to raise capital, and in any case affected business confidence so adversely that the demand for capital slackened considerably, and placed a number of businesses in considerable difficulty before very long. The rapid increase in lending to the private sector, especially through finance companies, was based on a somewhat too optimistic appraisal of the creditworthiness of a number of borrowing firms, so that some corrective was probably necessary; but if appropriate measures had been taken sooner, neither the rapid rise in lending (and so in the level of demand based upon it) nor the subsequent violent correction of this situation need have occurred.

The increased sales tax on cars, designed to check expenditure in one sector of the economy where it had been especially buoyant, was reversed some weeks later, when the demand for cars fell off rapidly. The use of sales tax as an anti-cyclical weapon was thus evident – even though the timing of its use left much to be desired, for the increase had been too late, whilst the subsequent reduction in it did little to stimulate the demand for cars, which had by then become very sharply depressed.

The other principal measure introduced late in 1960 was the so-called '30/20' ratio for insurance companies and pensions funds. This had the effect of increasing their subscriptions to government bonds, as it gave them a very strong tax incentive to hold at least 30 per cent of their assets in the form of Commonwealth government and semi-government bonds, and at least 20 per cent of them in Commonwealth government securities. In a period of boom the extra incentive to the public to hold bonds could have been useful; but this was a much more lasting measure in its effects, and was clearly not intended to be varied anti-cyclically. Indeed, from the viewpoint of monetary policy its effects were probably thoroughly undesirable, as the consequent 'locking-in' effect upon the holdings of government bonds by these institutions meant that it was less feasible to operate monetary policy in a flexible, anti-cyclical way through the bond market. For an appropriate policy would have been to encourage these holders to increase their holdings of bonds most rapidly in booms (as an anti-inflationary device), and encourage them to increase the proportion of their portfolio made up of loans to the private sector in times of recession. But in fact the immediate effect of the measures was that during 1961/2 these institutions were building up their portfolios of government bonds to the level at which they received the tax benefit, so that the availability of funds from them to the private sector was consequently sharply diminished during the recession, when increased loans to businesses and individuals would have been most useful.

Although there was some reduction in the level of certain interest rates under government control during 1961, this was quite inadequate to offset the effects of the very sharp fall in the level of confidence during the recession and the reduction in the expected rate of inflation. The authorities seem to have feared that another boom was just round the corner, and in any case they probably felt it essential to rebuild the level of the country's international reserves and repay the drawings made from the IMF before they could safely relax their monetary and budgetary measures.

This attitude was taken to a most remarkable extreme in late 1961, when, despite there being an election in a situation of what was, by recent past standards, considerable unemployment, the government went to the country on the extraordinary platform of pointing to its own financial rectitude in not taking expansionary action. A large proportion of the electorate apparently saw how inappropriate this attitude was in the circumstances, and the government went within one seat of losing power. A few months later, in February 1962, it belatedly saw the error of its ways and took reflationary budgetary action, though it was still remarkably unwilling to effect any substantial reduction in interest rates.

The most interesting feature of the tax reductions of February 1962 was that the income-tax Pay-As-You-Earn deductions were sharply reduced, by giving taxpayers a 5 per cent rebate on their year's income tax, and effecting this reduction entirely in the last four months of the financial year. This meant that when the new financial year began in July the rebate was effectively at the lower rate of 5 per cent of each month's wages, compared with 15 per cent for each of the previous four months. Over the six months February to July, therefore, three different effective rates of deduction of income tax were payable; this represents a degree of flexibility of this weapon not applied at any other time in Australia, and not (so far as this writer is aware) paralleled in any other country. This suggests that the administrative flexibility of this weapon is considerably greater than has usually been supposed; and that if governments are willing to use it anti-cyclically in this way the scope for doing so may be considerable.

It is true that this flexibility of income tax between budgets was in the downward direction. The other occasions on which supplementary budgets had been introduced (March 1956 and November 1960) had been for measures to restrain demand; and on these occasions the increases were of indirect taxes. There has not, therefore, been a case of a *rise* in income-tax rates being announced at any time other than in an August budget.

The recovery from the 1961/2 recession was gradual, and the reflationary measures turned out to be over-cautious. It is true, however, that officially controlled interest rates were reduced appreciably in the first half of 1963; and this was the year when recovery made considerable progress towards full employment. Demand expanded so rapidly that by 1964 the problem had become one of preventing demand from rising too high. Indeed, on some counts one might argue that demand had already become excessive by late in 1964; but an enlightened use of interest-rate policy in that year, implemented in part by substantial open-market sales of bonds, helped to curb the rise in domestic demand. The balance of payments and the level of the reserves had by then improved sufficiently for there to be no serious concern about the balance of payments. The 5 per cent rebate of income tax was rescinded in the 1964 budget (that is, income-tax rates were effectively increased), and company tax was raised, as were also the sales tax on cars and certain excises. In this period, therefore, for the first time monetary and budgetary measures were applied in a period of high activity in a manner, and at a time, that could reasonably be expected to prevent serious excess demand.

By the time of the 1965 budget, however, the government was clearly concerned that demand was still in danger of being excessive, especially as it contemplated a very sharp rise in its own expenditure, mainly on defence. It therefore introduced a further sharp rise in tax rates, including a surcharge (at the rate of $2\frac{1}{2}$ per cent – for the first time at this rate): this was a further refinement of the weapon of cyclically variable income-tax rates first used (in the expansionary direction) in 1962, then used to check rising demand (by the removal of the rebate) in 1964.

In the event, these measures turned out to be too strong; the economy moved during 1966 into a state of less than full employment, to a large extent because of the effects of drought in several parts of the country, and to the consequent indirect downward effects on spending, especially in rural areas. A large part of the rise in government defence expenditure was occurring outside Australia, and the internal element in it turned out not to rise as fast as the contraction of total private demand in the economy. One can perhaps understand the government's reluctance to take forthright steps to stimulate demand; for so far as drought was responsible for the lag in demand, one could reasonably suppose that it would turn out to be temporary, and so best offset by temporary measures of drought relief in the worst affected areas (which were applied on a limited scale fairly quickly). Moreover, a very sharp rise in domestic defence spending was already, so to speak, in the pipeline. Nevertheless, the 1966/7 pause was a considerable lapse below capacity operation, though not as long or as deep a lapse as that of 1961/2. The errors of policy may reasonably be considered to have been due as much to bad luck as to bad management. In any event, the changes in the structure of the economy – with the shift towards defence spending and the shift in the focus of most rapid growth towards Western Australia – probably required the creation of some slack in other parts of the economy if the transition was to be effected swiftly. Nevertheless, the lapse from full employment continued longer than one might reasonably judge to have been essential for this purpose.

41

Indeed, it continued throughout 1967/8, even though there was some revival of growth in that year, and budgetary policy contributed to the expansion. But the government failed to provide any pronounced expansionary stimulus on the tax side (not even removing the 2½ per cent levy on personal income tax), though government spending rose in 1967/8 at an above-trend rate, though not as fast as in 1966/7. There was, moreover – as in the 1961/2 recession – very little by way of reductions in interest rates (perhaps because rates in Australia were already below those in many comparable overseas countries). Furthermore the decision not to devalue in November 1967 meant that the opportunity was lost to administer what could have been a useful stimulus to domestic activity. (The alleged 'inflationary' effect of devaluing was one argument against such a policy mentioned by the Treasurer at the time, though other considerations, which have been discussed above, were presumably decisive.) Another drought was one factor to delay recovery to full employment.

Only in 1968/9 did the economy fully recover, and both budgetary and monetary policy were used to ensure that this did not bring excess demand with it. The in-built progressivity of the tax structure was an important element in restraining demand as full employment approached in 1968/9, and also when it was achieved in 1969/70 – just as it had been a factor delaying the return of full employment in 1967/8. In addition, the 1968 budget introduced small increases in certain sales tax rates and in company taxes.

When full employment was restored in 1969/70, monetary measures were gradually tightened; and in the first half of 1970 a very severe credit squeeze was imposed, partly because of a fear that there was a danger of excess demand, partly because of a desire to prevent a downturn in capital inflow (on which the strength of the balance of payments had become somewhat dependent). (There were some signs of such a downturn at the time.) The severe tightening of monetary policy about March 1970 led to a sharp fall in dwelling construction, which had expanded to an unsustainably high rate during the period of expansion; but clearly this reversal of the sharp growth in this part of the building industry went further than the authorities wished, and towards the end of 1969/70 the banks were encouraged to lend more freely for this purpose – with an immediate upward effect on this lending. If a restraining hand on demand was needed, perhaps a less expansionary budget in 1969 and a less severely restrictive monetary policy would have been preferable. But the overall effect was the continuance of virtually full employment for a third year in succession, with only a slight rise in the extent of inflation. The 1970 budget was clearly intended to hold the economy on course, the effect on demand of reductions in personal income taxation being intended to be approximately offset by rises in indirect taxes and in company taxes, with an above-trend rise in government spending presumably intended to take up any slack that might result from a slowing down in private investment spending and in dwelling construction.

The budget of 1970 was successful in preventing either excess demand or a serious lapse from full capacity operation. But by the middle of 1971 demand was slowing down and signs of some spare capacity were appearing. But at the same time the price level had been rising much faster than for many years, largely as a result of very rapid rises in salaries and wages, but probably also to some extent because of the upward effects upon costs of the increases in indirect tax rates in the 1970 budget. Even if this emphasis on indirect taxation (rather than other budgetary measures to restrain demand) was unfortunate, it is probable that a more expansionary budget in 1970 would have made prices rise even faster. In terms of its overall effect on the level of demand, therefore, the 1970 budget was probably about right.

By contrast, the budget of 1971 was totally inappropriate to the state of the economy. Even prior to the budget it was clear that demand was not expanding fast enough to maintain the economy at full capacity operation, and that a stimulus to demand was therefore desirable on that account. But the very sharp increase in inflation (as measured by the available price indexes) gave rise to an exaggerated official concern to see that demand inflation was not added to the prevailing cost inflation. This led the government to introduce a deflationary budget, which was roundly (and almost unanimously) criticized by non-official observers. There seems to have been excessive official concern – as there had been in somewhat similar circumstances in 1961/2 – that another sharp rise in demand was just about to occur, partly because of the sharp rise in the liquid asset holdings of the public in the form of savings bank deposits. Yet this rise (which was in any event mainly a recovery from an earlier temporary reduction in the rate of growth of these deposits) was itself probably an indication of a widespread public reluctance to spend, resulting from some concern about the future, which was causing consumers to build up their savings as a precaution against falling overtime earnings and declining job opportunities. One would have thought that the rational policy conclusion from this

43

state of affairs would have been to introduce a more expansionary budget, in order to offset the decline in the growth of consumption, whilst standing ready to take offsetting measures if and when any subsequent sharp rise in consumption did in fact occur.

Indeed, the official reasons that were given for the failure to introduce a more expansionary budget were so unconvincing that it is charitable to ask whether there may have been more respectable motives for the policy that ministers felt unable to express in public. It might perhaps be argued that a mild lapse from full employment seemed likely to restrain the rise in prices and money incomes, and one could understand it if political reasons prevented ministers from publicly stating any such view. But it was very doubtful whether a mild lapse from full employment would in fact have that effect, for the consequent sharp decline in productivity as output fell probably increased the likelihood of price rises by more than the restraining effect on prices of any such mild downward pressure on demand. Moreover, the tax increases introduced in the budget themselves probably increased the likelihood of cost–push inflation, both through the effects on wage demands and through the likelihood of companies passing on in the form of higher prices the effects of the higher taxes on their costs.

One might still argue, however, that a government that was really prepared to cause a considerable rise in unemployment might have succeeded in slowing down the rise in the price level, though the experience of Britain and the USA with much higher levels of unemployment and higher rates of inflation than Australia in the early 1970s provided evidence for doubting this. But the Australian government certainly never seriously contemplated a rise in un-employment of that order; and subsequent events suggested that it had not expected demand to flag as much as it did later in 1971. Indeed, the continued increase in unemployment (to only slightly more than the level that had been tolerated in 1966/7) drew forth monetary measures at the end of 1971 that were clearly aimed at stimulating demand. At that time it was announced that there would no longer be informal controls over the level of bank lending, which had been operated by regular indications from the central bank of the rate of new bank lending that it felt to be appropriate. From now onwards, therefore, the rate of bank lending was to be con-trolled only by the direct controls over their liquidity, through Statutory Reserve Deposits – which were reduced at this time as a further stimulus to bank lending – coupled with the informally agreed minimum 'L.G.S. ratio' (the ratio of the banks Liquid assets plus Government Securities to their total deposits). There were also some minor rises at the end of 1971 in government spending, mainly to provide further relief for the depressed rural sector; and bank interest rates and long-term government bond rates were eventually reduced in February 1972. Government expenditure was raised sharply later in that month.

Although the government was wise to heed belatedly the voice of its almost unanimous critics, in seeking to undo some of the deflationary effects of the budget, it was doubtful whether monetary measures were the appropriate ones on which to place the main emphasis. Presumably an expansionary supplementary budget late in 1971 would have seemed to the government to be a too obvious, and politically inconvenient, acknowledgement of the failure of its budgetary strategy. But reliance on monetary measures ran a number of risks. First, there was no evidence that spending was being held back by any shortage of bank credit, indeed, the very large capital inflow had already made the economy unusually liquid; and, in any event, during periods of excess capacity it is a well-known principle that reliance on monetary measures of expansion is likely to prove a weak reed. Secondly, in the new and unfamiliar situation where strong expectations of inflation existed at the same time as less than full capacity operation of the economy, there was a real risk that an expansionary monetary policy (assuming it successfully increased the money supply) would have most of its effects in increasing prices, rather than output. A third risk lay in the responsiveness of net capital inflows to changes in interest rates in Australia, which threw doubt on how far monetary measures alone could reduce the effective level of interest rates in an economy as open to capital inflows and outflows as Australia. For whenever bank credit is made more readily available it can reasonably be expected that companies will borrow more within Australia (except so far as the guide-lines over local borrowing by the subsidiaries of overseas companies prevent them from doing this), and to borrow somewhat less from overseas. In this and other ways net capital inflow might therefore be expected to be lower as a result of the expansionary monetary measures (so far as they succeeded in increasing bank lending): and so far as this decline in net capital inflow occurred there would be a corresponding offsetting fall in the liquidity of the economy, and to that extent expansionary monetary measures would not be effective in stimulating domestic activity. By contrast, a more expansionary budgetary policy would have tended to increase interest rates, and thus to maintain capital inflow and consequently liquidity.

Even the use that was made of some minor expansionary budgetary measures at the end of 1971 was open to some criticism (apart from the basic point that it was too slight to have much effect and too late to avoid an appreciable sacrifice of potential output). If a budgetary stimulus was to be applied there was a good case for providing it by tax cuts, as one might expect that a given budgetary stimulus provided in this way would have done more to check cost inflation than would the same stimulus provided by government spending. Moreover, so far as government spending was the chosen measure, there was a strong case for providing it by increasing certain forms of social services payments to those in greatest need, including higher unemployment benefits, which were insufficient to provide adequate compensation for the growing numbers thrown out of work through no fault of their own. (There was – again very belatedly – a considerable increase in unemployment benefits in February 1972.)

In short, the early 1970s provided some grounds for believing that the government had not succeeded in estimating correctly the degree of budgetary stimulus required to maintain full employment; for the rise in unemployment late in 1971 seems to have exceeded what the government was expecting and planning at the time of the August budget. At the same time, it must be acknowledged that the government was faced with a new and very difficult combination of problems – rising unemployment with uncomfortably rapid inflation – for which there is no easy solution, and which most other countries had been far more unsuccessful in solving. It would, however, have been possible to cut tariffs or to appreciate the Australian dollar at any time during 1970/1 and to take tougher measures to increase the degree of competition within the Australian economy; and some form of prices and incomes policy could at least have been attempted – for example, by imposing a tax at an appropriately high rate on companies whose wage bill rose by more than a stated percentage, and perhaps by some form of prices justification tribunal – even though detailed control over prices was probably undesirable, and was thought to be constitutionally impossible; but a High Court judgement in 1971 may mean the Commonwealth has this power.

AUSTRALIAN WAGES POLICY

The Organization for Economic Co-operation and Development has defined an incomes policy as being

'that the authorities have a view about the kind of evolution of

46

incomes which is consistent with their economic objectives, and in particular with price stability; that they should seek to promote public agreement on the principles which should guide the growth of incomes; and that they should induce people voluntarily to follow this guidance.'[4]

Components of an incomes policy seem to include general and particular targets for wage and price decisions and devices to induce adherence to these. In such terms, Australia has had no incomes policy. The stress laid in the above definition on government intervention and regulation of incomes and prices seems to exclude from its purview the sort of framework of policy-making that has operated in Australia. Yet Australia possesses a centralized wage authority whose criteria include general social and economic factors, and not merely narrow considerations such as the state of particular industries. But the tendency for centralization of key wage bargains and of the fixing of key wage rates (which facilitates general adjustments) occurred despite the restrictive provisions of the Australian federal system. Australian wages policy remains an adjunct of a procedure for settling disputes,[5] and Australian governments have been reluctant to intervene in wage determination in the way that overseas governments pursuing incomes policies have done. The submissions of the Federal government to the leading wages tribunal, the Commonwealth Conciliation and Arbitration Commission, have normally been confined to advice which is unspecific about the increases of award wages that it would regard as acceptable. In general, while some cabinet ministers have occasionally exhorted the Commission to adopt a 'reasonable' wage policy, Federal governments have avoided the intervention characteristic of, for example, the British experience of incomes policy.[6] But pressure for some sort of prices and incomes policy had become stronger by early 1972 – after the rapid inflation during 1971.

The main feature of the Australian wage determination system is the status and authority of tribunals created under Commonwealth and State laws to make legally binding awards. Special importance within the system attaches to the decisions of the Commonwealth

[4] OECD, *Policies for Price Stability*, Paris, 1962, p. 23.

[5] See J. E. Isaac and G. W. Ford, *Australian Labour Economics: Readings*, Sun Books, Melbourne, 1967, p. 3.

[6] See J. P. Nieuwenhuysen and N. R. Norman, 'Wages Policy in Australia: Issues and Tests', *British Journal of Industrial Relations*, November 1971; and J. P. Nieuwenhuysen, 'Australian Wages Policy: A Review of the 1960s', *Australian Economic Review*, December 1970.

Conciliation and Arbitration Commission, particularly in its major or national wage hearings, which permeate the structure of awards and are the means of exercising a centralizing control over wages. The Commission's ability to influence wages depends largely on the indirect effects of its decisions on State awards and on wages and conditions in employment areas not regulated by awards. The Commission's awards prevail over State awards where there is a conflict between the two, and for this and other reasons decisions of the Commission in national wage cases are normally (though not without exception) followed by State authorities. Substantial uniformity of award wages has been engendered in Australia through the Commonwealth and State tribunal decisions.

There has, however, been a rapid growth in over-award payments, especially in the sixties. As Professor J. E. Isaac has pointed out,

'this problem . . . threatens to undermine the control of the Commission over the level of earnings and also forces it to grant larger award increases in order to keep up with the market and to compensate award wages for rising prices which are partly, at any rate, induced by over-award pay. Under these conditions, it might be argued that the Commission, as a central wage tribunal, does more harm than good. . . . But . . . it would be quite unrealistic to expect the present Australian machinery to be unscrambled to avoid its centralizing features.'[7]

In arguments before the Arbitration Commission, the unions have maintained that the Commission's main concern should be to seek to protect the real value of awards and to enable employees to participate in the growth of productivity in the economy. In contrast to this 'prices plus productivity' approach, the employers have argued that the Commission should increase money wages in proportion with average productivity. The employers' view of a wages policy geared to changes in productivity can allow for a possible earnings drift, so that award wages may have to increase more slowly than productivity.

The complex discussions of these different views have depended on a number of intractable issues, such as the causes and extent of earnings drift, and the difficulties raised by earnings drift for a wage policy that relies on award wages only.[8] Perhaps the dominant consideration has been the implicit assumption by the employers that award wage increases are an important cause of inflation. A few

[7] *Wages and Productivity*, Cheshire, Melbourne, 1967, p. 128.
[8] See W. M. Corden, *Australian Economic Policy Discussion*, Melbourne University Press, Melbourne, 1968, chapter 1.

studies have attempted to test the statistical relationships between wage and price variations in Australia. The results seem to imply that it is unjustified in Australia to attach great importance to the possibility of causal connections between award wages and variations in the growth of prices, independently of the state of the trade cycle, productivity, and import prices.[9] The limitations of the methods employed in these studies should preclude definite policy conclusions, and the results must be used with considerable care. But in so far as the tests stress the influence of demand on price increases, they do point to the great importance in inflationary policy of demand control through monetary and fiscal measures. This at least serves to emphasize the extent to which the monetary and fiscal authorities are responsible for controlling inflation, and the probably more limited extent to which the Arbitration Commission can of its own accord inhibit price increases, if it chooses (in contrast to its practice hitherto) to make price stability its chief aim. At any rate, the conclusions of the studies are applicable to the period on which their analyses were based. The situation in 1970/1 may well have been different.

The fact that Australia has not had even a consistent award wages policy (much less an incomes policy) is underlined by the changes in criteria which the Arbitration Commission has been prepared to employ during the 1960s. In the 1961 basic wage case it was decided that major revisions of the basic wage were to occur only every three or four years instead of annually. But, because of price stability, no cost of living adjustment was necessary in 1962 and 1963. In effect, in a margins decision in 1963 and in the 1964 basic wage determination, the Commission adjusted for prices and productivity changes. But a minority judgment in 1964 foreshadowed a return to annual basic wage earnings, which began in 1965, ending the triennial review system. The 1965 majority judgment gave priority to considerations of price stability, but since 1966 another view, which appears in principle to favour a 'prices plus productivity' approach, has prevailed. This view regards price increases as a major argument in favour of wage increases, and supports the suggestion that the prevention of inflation must not assume a dominant role in the Commission's policies. It remains to be seen whether this attitude will continue in the face of the relatively more rapid rate of inflation in the early 1970s.

[9] See J. P. Nieuwenhuysen and N. R. Norman, *British Journal of Industrial Relations*, November 1971; and J. D. Pitchford, 'An Analysis of Price Movements in Australia, 1947–1968', *Australian Economic Papers*, December 1968.

PLANNING FOR GROWTH

Co-ordination of medium-term or long-term plans for economic growth between government and industry has been conspicuous by its absence in Australia. After the errors of policy that led to the recession of 1961/2, and in the light of various apparently successful forms of planning by consent in Japan and France, there was considerable public discussion of whether such long-term co-ordination of development plans of firms, industries and governments would be desirable in Australia. The Vernon Committee of Economic Enquiry, which reported in 1965, pronounced in favour of some such system in Australia: but the then Prime Minister – prompted strongly (as was widely believed) by treasury fears that some sort of Planning Council would weaken its powers of control – rejected these proposals.

Since that time there has been considerable growth of long-term planning – in the sense of looking ahead – *within* the government machine and also *within* many individual firms and industries. Each independent planning unit proceeds virtually in ignorance of the assumptions being made by the others, though sometimes hints are dropped by official spokesmen about the overall growth rate for the economy that the government is assuming. There seems to be an exaggerated fear on the part of ministers (and perhaps of some senior officials) that any firmer or more detailed attempt to exchange views about future prospects and to report on them to the public will be regarded as firm commitments, which can and will be thrown in the faces of those who have made them, when the projections turn out (as they almost invariably will) to be at variance with the outcome.

The successful management of the economy in the second half of the 1960s, and the great improvement of the long-run outlook for Australia's economic growth and her balance of payments resulting from the mineral developments in the later 1960s, accounted for the absence of any widespread discontent with the economic situation in the later 1960s, such as might have led to renewed public demands for some sort of indicative economic planning involving both official and non-official bodies, like the National Economic Development Conference in New Zealand, or the National Economic Development Council in Britain. It is difficult to believe that the long-run plans that are continually being made in many firms, industries, government departments and public utilities – which together affect (and also depend upon) the long-term prospects for the Australian economy – have a better chance of being well though out in the absence of some form of collation of their ideas about the future. For their views of future prospects would be more soundly based if there were some semi-formal means of collating, comparing, and (where it was thought appropriate) co-ordinating them. It would be a pity to delay further consideration of this matter until some future period of serious discontent with the management of the economy, partly because if it were left till then policy-makers might again react against what they might regard as a challenge to their power and a criticism of their past actions. It would be far better to consider the matter coolly, without waiting for serious public dissatisfaction about policy to arise. Even within the public sector alone there are many areas of policy about which there is probably insufficient public discussion of whether Australia is making full and proper use of her economic good fortune – for example, about education, roads, hospitals and defence. More general and detailed public discussion of these and related issues, especially of the projected growth of the various forms of public spending over the medium-term and long-term future in relation to the growth of the economy as a whole, could provide the material for a worthwhile public debate.

CONCLUSIONS FOR FUTURE POLICY

During the period 1960–71 Australia had a considerable measure of success by international standards in reconciling the twin objectives of internal and external balance. There were, however, two periods of unnecessary failures of macro-economic policy. The first was in the early 1960s, when swifter action could and should have been taken to overcome the 1961/2 recession. The second was in 1970/1 when an appalling piece of mismanagement resulted in excessively high international reserves, an unnecessary rise in unemployment and for a time a rate of growth well below capacity, coupled with an uncomfortably rapid rate of inflation, in a situation that could have been alleviated considerably by a greater readiness to modify a budgetary policy that was insufficiently expansionary, and to appreciate, and perhaps also to attempt some form of prices and incomes policy.

Through good fortune during the period 1963–9 it happened to be possible to maintain something close to both internal and external balance by operating merely on budgetary and monetary policy (that is, without the import controls that had existed during the

1950s, and without a flexible exchange rate or substitute measures such as import deposits or import surcharges which some countries applied). But it should have been inherently obvious that without the use of a flexible exchange rate (or some substitute for it) eventually internal or external balance – or perhaps both of them – would have to be sacrified to some extent if sole reliance was placed on budgetary and monetary policy. It is true that something can be done towards reconciling internal and external balance by varying the combination of monetary and budgetary measures, and this happened to some extent during the 1960s (whether or not by intention). But the use of higher interest rates to improve the balance of payments is mainly a once-for-all measure, in the sense that it does not have a continuing effect once capital flows have adjusted to it. Moreover, other policy objectives may conflict with what might on macro-economic criteria seem to be the desirable combination of monetary and budgetary policy.

It therefore seems desirable that a considerable use should be made of exchange rate flexibility in future, especially as this would enhance the usefulness of monetary policy for affecting domestic demand, and provide an additional way of influencing internal and external balance.

But if the exchange rate is not generally left free to vary, the budget will have to be the main weapon used for maintaining internal balance. As may be seen from Table 2.3, the variations in the use of budgetary policy were not great in the period from 1962/3 to 1970/1. The estimates in that table of the changes in the effect of the budget, in relation to total non-farm product (which are the work of Professor Nevile) indicate how the deflationary effect of the budget in 1960/1, which increased the depth and intensity of the recession of 1961–3, was reversed by the very expansionary budgetary measures of 1961/2 (which were heavily concentrated into the later part of that financial year), but the wide variations of 1960/1 and 1961/2 were not continued from 1962/3 to 1971/2; and that such variations in the budget as there were in those later years did not conform at all closely with the needs of the economy; for the expansionary effect as a percentage of non-farm GNP provided in the years of high activity about 1964 and again in 1970/1 exceeded that provided in the years of lower activity centred on 1967. The table also brings out the very low degree of stimulus given by the budget of August 1971 (which was less than in any year except 1960/1), despite the fact that unemployment was higher in that year than at any time since 1961/2.

Table 2.3. *Summary of Australian fiscal policy*

(Per cent of non-farm product)

| | Effect on non-farm national product | | |
	of changes in tax rates	of changes in government expenditure	(a) + (b)
	(a)	(b)	
1959/60	0·5	2·4	2·9
1960/1	−0·7	2·3	1·6
1961/2	1·0	3·5	4·5
1962/3	1·1	2·0	3·1
1963/4	0·2	3·4	3·6
1964/5	−0·6	4·1	3·5
1965/6	−1·1	4·3	3·2
1966/7	—	3·3	3·3
1967/8	—	3·3	3·3
1968/9	−0·2	3·0	2·8
1969/70	—	3·0	3·0
1970/1	—	3·3	3·3
1971/2*	−0·75	2·75	2·0

Sources: J. W. Nevile, 'Discretionary Fiscal Policy in Australia 1955 to 1970', in J. W. Nevile and D. W. Stammer (eds.) *Inflation and Unemployment* (*Pelican Readings in Australian Economic Policy*), London and Melbourne, 1972, p. 141; and J. W. Nevile, 'The Australian Economy, August 1971' *Economic Record*, September 1971. (The figures for 1970/1 are by inference from the text.)

Note: These estimates take account of the differing multiplier effects of the principal forms of government expenditure and of different taxes, Nevile's method of estimating these is explained in J. W. Nevile, *Fiscal Policy in Australia: Theory and Practice*, Cheshire, Melbourne 1970.

*August 1971 budget only; takes no account of expansionary measures in the second half of the 1971/2 year.

It might seem from the table that policy was relatively successful in those years when the stimulus given by the budget was reasonably steady in relation to total output: but this was probably because in those years the fluctuations in demand generally happened to be only small. It also suggests that when – as in 1961 and 1971 – unemployment was rising uncomfortably high the government should have been much quicker to provide an additional stimulus through the budget.

But the use made of the budget must be considered alongside the use of monetary policy, which was from 1963/4 onwards generally fairly apt, except that it was insufficiently expansionary in 1961/2, 1966/7, and again probably also in 1971. In the periods of high activity, 1964 and 1970, however, monetary policy was used to good effect in helping to restrain demand (in marked contrast to the periods of boom between 1950 and 1960). But capital flows and the fixed exchange rate weakened the force of monetary policy for affecting domestic activity.

The future of monetary, budgetary and exchange-rate policy in Australia must therefore be considered together. If it is decided to continue to make only occasional use of alterations in the exchange rate, it will be important to use the budget much more flexibly, and this will involve making variations in its overall effect fairly soon after it has become clear that the level of demand is growing much faster or slower than the full employment trend of the economy. This will normally mean being prepared to make such changes at any time in the year, and certainly not only at the time of the annual budget in August. It will still be possible for monetary measures to be varied to some extent in a helpful direction from the point of view of internal balance, provided that this does not put interest rates in Australia substantially out of line with those in the rest of the world; but when the operation of monetary policy does tend to change the relative level of interest rates in Australia, changes in net capital flows will offset the internal effects of the monetary measures, and so impair the usefulness of monetary policy for affecting internal balance, though increasing its usefulness for affecting external balance (at least temporarily) through the capital account of the balance of payments.

If, on the other hand, it is decided to allow the exchange rate to be more flexible, it will be both possible and desirable to allow monetary policy to bear the main brunt of maintaining internal balance, reserving budgetary measures mainly for affecting the allocation of resources and the distribution of income, and normally keeping its overall effect on the economy fairly steady in relation to capacity. By the same token, if policy-makers are unable or unwilling to operate budgetary policy in a flexible manner it will be the more essential to allow the exchange rate to vary.

Finally, whatever the practical and constitutional difficulties, it seems certain that future Australian governments (like those in most other countries) will have to face up to the need to devise some form of prices and incomes policy that will make possible a high level of activity without serious inflation. Direct price and wage controls are unlikely to constitute a major part of any such policy, though it would be quite reasonable for certain crucial price and wage decisions to receive public discussion and justification before they occur; and some form of constitutional power to delay or prevent increases in a few key prices and incomes might have to be taken (if the Commonwealth government does not at present possess this power). But much could be done by adopting a more whole-hearted policy for increasing the extent of competition in the economy, both by reducing those tariffs that are highly protective and by effectively preventing a wider range of restrictive practices. Moreover, a thorough examination of the tax system (which is in any event desirable on many grounds) should be undertaken with a view to considering the effects of different taxes upon the extent of cost inflation and on wage bargaining, so that such effects can be taken into account when framing budgetary policy.

Australia was generally favoured by good fortune during the period 1960/71, though its policy-makers also deserve much of the credit for the generally successful achievement (except in 1961/2 and 1970/1) of a high level of activity and relatively low inflation. But there was considerable evidence of a lack of willingness to undertake new initiatives or formulate new policies to meet new problems. The attempts at evolving a prices and incomes policy that were made in many countries had no parallel in Australia; there appeared to be little or no official understanding of the case for exchange-rate flexibility; and political pusillanimity seemed a considerable obstacle in the way of abandoning high tariffs and other forms of assistance to particular industries, whilst the idea of indicative planning for growth evoked nothing but negative official response. To all these proposals objections may reasonably be made. But it is to be hoped that Australian governments will not try to go through the 1970s making a negative response to all these and other potentially useful innovations in macro-economic policy.

Select Bibliography

Commonwealth Treasury, Canberra, *The Australian Economy* (annual).

Reserve Bank of Australia Annual Report
Australian Economic Review, published by the Institute of Applied Economic and Social Research, University of Melbourne, quarterly, 1968 onwards.
'The Australian Economy', *Economic Record*, various issues and authors, generally twice yearly, 1956 to 1967.
H. C. Coombs, *Other People's Money* (re-printed papers and addresses of the former governor of the Reserve Bank of Australia), Australian National University Press, Canberra, 1971.
J. W. Nevile, *Fiscal Policy in Australia*, Cheshire, Melbourne, 1970.
J. W. Nevile and D. W. Stammer (eds.) *Inflation and Unemployment* (*Pelican Readings in Australian Economic Policy*), London and Melbourne, 1971.
J. O. N. Perkins, *Macro-economic Policy in Australia*, Melbourne University Press, 1971.
N. Runcie (ed.) *Australian Monetary and Fiscal Policy, Selected Readings 1*, University of London Press, 1971.

Australian Wages Policy
W. M. Corden, *Australian Economic Policy Discussion*, Melbourne University Press, 1968, chapter 1.
K. J. Hancock, 'Earnings Drift in Australia', *Journal of Industrial Relations*, July 1966, 'Wage Policy and Inflation: Australia's Experience under Compulsory Arbitration', *Australian Economic Review*, 4th Quarter 1971.
J. E. Isaac, *Wages and Productivity*, Cheshire, Melbourne, 1967.
J. E. Isaac and G. W. Ford, *Australian Labour Economies: Readings*, Sun Books, Melbourne, 1967.
J. E. Isaac and D. Yerbury, 'Recent trends in Collective Bargaining in Australia', *International Labour Review*, May 1971.
J. P. Nieuwenhuysen, 'Wages Policy in Australia: A Review of the 1960's', *Australian Economic Review*, 4th quarter 1970.
J. P. Nieuwenhuysen and N. R. Norman, 'Australian Wages Policy: Issues and Tests', *British Journal of Industrial Relations*, November 1971.
Report of the (Vernon) *Committee of Economic Enquiry*, Government Printer, Canberra, 1965, chapter 7.

Chapter 3

CANADA

M. D. ENGLISH

The Canadian economy grew at a rate of about 4·8 per cent per annum in real terms from 1958 to 1969, with the growth rate somewhat higher than this in the later years.

An important influence upon this growth rate was the rapid growth of the labour force – at a rate of 2¾ per cent per annum, which was certainly one of the fastest rates of increase among Western industrialized countries. The rapid increase in the labour force was due in part to the marked increase in the size of the population of working age, partly to a rise in the participation rate of females, and to a lesser extent to immigration (which added about ¾ per cent per annum to the population over the period). Productivity, as measured by output per person employed, rose at an average rate of 2 per cent per annum during this period.

The analysis in this chapter of the main features of macro-economic policy will first discuss Canada's principal economic objectives and those special features of the Canadian economy that have helped to determine the instruments adopted in macro-economic policy and the ways in which they have been used. This will be followed by a description and analysis in chronological order of the economic circumstances and policy measures of the period from 1959 to 1971. The concluding section reviews the most important problems encountered and the most significant points about the various policy measures, and outlines some of the issues that are likely to be important in future.

Table 3.1 presents a selection of the movements in the principal economic indicators over this period, as a statistical background to illustrate the conditions prevailing in the Canadian economy during these years.

THE OBJECTIVES

Canada shares with most other modern states the broad economic objectives of full employment, a high rate of economic growth, reasonable stability of prices, a sound external position, and an

Table 3.1. *The Canadian Economy, 1958–71, selected indicators*

	Unemployment rate (per cent)	Rise in implicit price index of gross national expenditure (per cent)	Increase in GNE at 1961 prices (per cent)	Current account balance ($C m.)*	Official reserves at end of year ($US m.)
1958	7·0	1·4	2·2	−1,137	2,038
1959	6·0	2·2	4·1	−1,487	2,029
1960	7·0	1·2	2·9	−1,233	1,989
1961	7·1	0·6	2·9	−928	2,292
1962	5·9	1·4	6·9	−830	2,561
1963	5·5	1·9	5·3	−521	2,613
1964	4·7	2·4	6·9	−424	2,890
1965	3·9	3·5	6·6	−1,130	3,037
1966	3·6	4·6	7·0	−1,162	2,702
1967	4·1	3·4	3·3	−499	2,717
1968	4·8	3·6	4·9	−107	3,046
1969	4·7	4·6	5·1	−952	3,106
1970	5·9	4·1	3·3	+1,060	4,679
1971	6·4	3·4	5·4	+262	5,570

* Includes gold production available for export.

Sources: Statistics Canada, Bank of Canada.

equitable distribution of income. In addition, circumstances in Canada have brought into prominence the subsidiary objectives of balanced regional development and the maintenance of a sufficient degree of Canadian ownership and control of industry and commerce. If these goals are to have more than rhetorical importance, however, they must also be assigned weighted priorities when the inevitable conflicts arise among the objectives. In practice it is generally difficult, even by hindsight, to state at all exactly what combination of objectives policy-makers were pursuing in a given period and how closely the aims they appeared to have in mind approximated to the community's real preferences. Despite these problems, it is misleading to make inter-country comparisons of economic policy without recognition of the differing ends to which policy appears to have been directed in the various countries; and certainly the emphasis (and perhaps also the complexity) of the Canadian objectives, compared with those of the other countries, has been an important factor in accounting for many of the differences that can be observed in the use of stablization policy in the various countries.

One indication of the relative weight attached to the various goals in Canada is that the level of unemployment that is considered to be consistent with the attainment of full employment there is significantly higher than in either Australia or New Zealand – the most commonly quoted goals in Canada being the range of 3 per cent to $3\frac{1}{2}$ per cent of the labour force unemployed. It is especially significant for macro-economic policy that the national unemployment rate is an average of widely divergent regional rates. The Royal Commission on Taxation estimated that a national level of $3\frac{1}{2}$ per cent unemployment would imply that regional unemployment would range from 2·2 per cent in the prairie provinces to 6 per cent in the Atlantic Provinces. In addition, the problem of providing adequate employment opportunities for unskilled workers is especially acute, particularly among certain age groups. As structural unemployment of these types is influenced only marginally by increases in aggregate demand, considerable attention has been directed towards manpower policies of relocation and job rehabilitation; and stabilization measures have often been chosen for their effect upon particular regions, industries, or labour groups, as well as for their effect upon the level of aggregate demand. Indeed, a justifiable criticism of policy is that at certain times during the 1960s the government gave insufficient weight to the aggregative aspects of stabilization because it was devoting a disproportionate amount of attention to overcoming these 'structural rigidities'.

More weight has been attached to the objective of price stability in Canada than in either Australia or New Zealand, by comparison with that of full employment (as normally understood in each country). In the immediate post-war period the maintenance of an adequate level of employment had been of primary concern, and policy measures were almost exclusively directed towards expansion; but by the latter part of the 1950s price stability was being given increased weight, on the grounds that it was in some sense a critical factor in the long-run achievement of both a sound external position and a satisfactory increase in output and employment. Until early in 1961 James Coyne – a strong proponent of this view about the critical role of price stability – was governor of the Bank of Canada: and in 1960, with an unemployment rate of 7 per cent and with the consumer price index having shown an increase of only 1·1 per cent in the previous year, monetary policy maintained a very restrictive stance until late in the year, whilst fiscal policy was not directed towards expansion until the 'baby budget' in December of that year. It is true that the vigorous public debate of that period, the significant change of policy in December, and the government pressure on Mr Coyne culminating in his resignation are all clear indications that such a strong preference for price stability at the expense of unemployment is unlikely to be repeated. But it nevertheless proved possible in 1969 to pursue a vigorous anti-inflationary policy with little adverse comment, despite an unemployment rate of almost 5 per cent. It was thus politically feasible to pursue price stability at the cost of unemployment to an extent that would have been impossible in either Australia or New Zealand.

The objective of a high rate of growth became more prominent during the 1960s. This was partly a reflection of the international trend towards giving greater attention to promoting economic growth and partly a result of invidious comparisons of the Canadian growth rate with those of her trading partners, as well as being in part a reaction to the period of slow growth from 1951 to 1961. It is true that deficiencies in demand management, rather than any flagging of the rate of growth, were subsequently seen to have been the major problem during this period. A much more satisfactory growth rate was in fact achieved in the latter part of the 1960s; and this made it seem less urgent to try to promote economic growth by means of legislation. Many stabilization measures during the decade were, however, chosen with at least an implicit recognition of their impact upon economic growth.

The maintenance of external balance requires the utilization of foreign exchange reserves and other sources of international liquidity to offset temporary adverse fluctuations in the inflow of capital and in the current account, as well as to give time for more fundamental changes in the balance of payments to be recognized and for the appropriate policy measures to be taken. Canada's experience is of particular interest in this area of policy because of the wide range of measures that have been utilized for the purpose of restoring external balance. These have included two periods of flexible exchange rates (although at times with official intervention in the foreign exchange market), the first of these ending in effect in a devaluation and the second involving an appreciation, each of these changes being accomplished during periods when the Canadian dollar was floating. In the period from 1958 to 1961 a state of less than full employment was permitted in response to external conditions.

The maintenance of external balance was complicated by problems arising from the composition of the Canadian balance of payments. There was normally a substantial deficit on current account covered by a large capital inflow, including large amounts of direct American investment. During the 1960s the composition of the balance of payments was at least as important a source of concern as was the overall external balance. The reason for this concern (in addition to the balance of payments difficulties that arose periodically when the flow of capital fell away) was the loss of economic sovereignty that many observers believed to result from the high level of direct investment. Whilst there was no consensus about the importance or the exact nature of this problem, many Canadians feared that this might lead to a considerable restriction of their freedom of action, and this attitude fostered a few hesitant measures in the controversial area of controlling foreign investment. Although this is not really a matter of macro-economic policy, it is of some interest here in that many of the earliest steps adopted were included in policy measures designed primarily for stabilization purposes (a matter to be discussed in a later section).

Canada is a federal state, and there has been, since Confederation at least, an implicit desire to maintain some measure of regional economic balance, thus providing an additional economic objective. This desire for regional balance has been based on such diverse considerations as obtaining an equitable distribution of national income, maintaining national unity, and guarding against a tendency for areas of slow growth to retard national development. The growing awareness of the extent of regional disparities, the crisis of national unity associated with the growth of French-Canadian nationalism, and the increased attention directed to economic growth thus all combined during the 1960s to stimulate an increased effort to promote balanced regional development.

In the early years of the decade, policy measures adopted for other reasons often contained a clause favouring certain regions. As the decade progressed this approach (which was perhaps inevitable in the early stages) gave way to a more comprehensive and co-ordinated programme. The Canadian preoccupation with regional development – with the inevitable constraints that regional imbalances place upon aggregative policy measures – is probably one of the most significant sources of the differences between the policies applied in Canada and those of the other countries discussed in this book.

INFLUENCES ON POLICY

Economies may be exposed to various disturbances that will call for the use of stabilization policy. Changes in the demand for exports are a source of disturbance to the economy. Internally, fluctuations in private investment, in expenditure on consumer durables, in provincial and municipal government taxes and expenditures, and in the degree of cost inflation may pose problems for the successful use of macro-economic policy. These disturbances may be inter-related. An especially important example of this occurs in countries where investment expenditures are largely geared to exports. In Canada, although fluctuations in external demand are the single most important source of disturbances in the economy, all of the factors mentioned above have had a significant effect at some time during the period since 1958. Canada has therefore to deal with the special difficulties due to externally induced fluctuations, at the same time as having to face a wide variety of other disturbances; and all these factors present problems for both forecasting and policy.

Exports accounted for a fifth to a quarter of Canadian Gross National Expenditure in the period under study, with the annual change in the value of exports ranging from a negligible decrease in 1958 to a 14 per cent increase in 1964. These magnitudes suggest the important primary effect that external demand changes have had on production and employment. In addition, Canada shares with many other countries the problem of dependence upon a few primary products which bulk large in her exports. Fluctuations in external demand for these products are difficult to counteract. The problem cannot be solved by increasing aggregate demand, and the low mobility of factors between these industries and other sectors frustrates a more selective approach. This problem, although retaining much of its social significance, has declined in importance from the point of view of stabilization as the proportion of less specialized manufactured goods in exports has increased. Thus a particularly rapid expansion of exports occurred during 1968, despite a very weak demand for Canadian primary products. On the other hand, the role of the large wheat sales in the expansion of activity during 1963/4 attests to the important role that primary products may still play in an export-led expansion. Canada is thus very much on the borderline between the primary producing and the manufacturing countries, and her experience is therefore likely to be especially relevant to countries that are, or expect soon to be, in a similar situation where both primary products and manufactures are important exports.

As we have seen above, the Canadian economy is affected by domestic fluctuations as well as by those arising through foreign trade. For example, the annual change (from the previous year) of business gross fixed capital investment (which was only slightly smaller than exports in proportion to Gross National Expenditure) has been of significant size, ranging from a decline of 5 per cent to an increase of 20 per cent, and has at times changed independently of exports. Canada thus falls somewhere between the small European countries on the one hand, for which foreign trade is the main source of instability, and the United States on the other, for which the internal sources of disturbance to the economy are the principal ones that macro-economic policy has to counter.

In a federal state, the tax and expenditure policies of the Provincial and municipal governments may on balance be either stabilizing or destabilizing. Important factors in determining their actual impact will be the degree of autonomy, the relative size, the sensitivity of tax revenue to changes in the level of economic activity, and the degree of co-operation with the central government of the Provincial and municipal governments. In Canada, circumstances are such that considerable concern has often been expressed over the role of the junior governments in stabilization policy. While there is some evidence to suggest that, at least until 1961, Provincial and municipal expenditures did not exert a destabilizing influence upon the economy, circumstances were changing during the 1960s and on occasion this was no longer true.

The Provincial governments have considerable autonomy on both the revenue and expenditure sides of their budgets, and until the late

1960s there had never been much co-operation or even consultation with the federal government on stabilization. At the same time, the Provincial and municipal governments became an increasingly important source of expenditure during the 1960s, and by 1964 the expenditures of these two levels of government exceeded those of the federal government. The expenditure of the provincial and municipal governments as a percentage of Gross National Product rose from 12·7 per cent in 1958 to 19·2 per cent in 1968. In the same period, the federal government expenditures as a percentage of Gross National Product fell marginally from 17·9 per cent to 16·9 per cent. While it may be quite accurate to say that the federal government's role in the economy is large enough for it to pursue a successful macro-economic policy, it is nevertheless also true that it cannot be assured of success in circumstances where the Provincial and municipal expenditures change in a cyclically perverse fashion: and the possibility of this occurring on occasion increased during the 1960s. The major source of Provincial and municipal tax revenue has traditionally been indirect taxation, which is not particularly sensitive to changes in the level of economic activity. From 1958 to 1968, however, the proportion of total revenue received from direct taxes, which tends to fluctuate with business activity more than does indirect tax revenue, rose from 11·2 per cent to 21·9 per cent. In a situation in which tax revenues were likely to be spent because of the heavy demand for the services provided by the Provincial and municipal governments, this rise in the importance of their revenue from direct taxation increased the likelihood that expenditures by these levels of government would behave in a destabilizing fashion. An additional problem arose through the tying of federal government expenditures for certain programmes to Provincial expenditures on a cost-sharing basis. In these circumstances, a section of federal government expenditures were actually determined by the Provincial authorities, thus reducing the portion of the federal budget that could be used in macro-economic policy changes. Considering these factors, it is not surprising that the role of Provincial governments in national macro-economic policy presented some serious problems during the 1960s, and that these problems are ones that are still largely to be faced during the 1970s.

The price and cost performance of the Canadian economy was a persistent problem in the latter part of the decade. Measures to improve productivity were pursued throughout the decade partly in response to the goal of price stability, but it was only in 1969 that a body designed to develop an incomes policy was introduced. As the decade ended, the price and cost performance of the economy continued to be the major economic problem, and better performance in this sphere, whether achieved through an incomes policy or some other means, is an important requirement for the 1970s.

Recognition of the pervasive influence of economic events and circumstances in the United States is an extremely important special factor which cannot be avoided in any analysis of the Canadian economy. The importance of this relationship for Canada is illustrated by the fact that 60 per cent of Canadian exports are to the United States and also by the virtually free flow of capital between the two countries. Besides the obvious direct impact that changes in the level of economic activity in the United States will have, there are other important but less tangible links. Wage and price changes in the United States are observed and have an effect on the attitude towards similar changes in Canada. Business expectations are greatly influenced, both through direct connections within companies and through more indirect means, by expectations in the United States. Indeed, even such a factor as the movement of labour between the two countries may at times have a significant effect in certain industries or professions.

No country can avoid having its economic performance partly determined by economic circumstances in her trading partners. With the especially close connection between the economies of the two countries, Canada cannot realistically hope to perform much better than the United States in certain areas of policy. In a period of slack in the United States, the maintenance of full employment in Canada can be achieved, if at all, only at the cost of a large current account deficit. The success of macro-economic policy in the United States is thus a prerequisite for a good performance of macro-economic policy in Canada. Within this framework, however, there is still considerable latitude for Canada to pursue independent macro-economic policies with a good chance of success, and at times during the 1960s there were significant differences between the performances of the two economies.

MANAGEMENT OF THE CANADIAN ECONOMY SINCE 1958

The degree of success that macro-economic policy has achieved since 1958 has been as varied as the conditions with which it has had to deal. During this period the economy moved from a position of slow growth and high unemployment to one in which price stability was the crucial issue. During the years 1958 to 1961 policy measures were a conspicuous failure, even measured against the questionable set of objectives of that period. A preoccupation with objectives such as the composition of the balance of payments even at the expense of the full-employment objective, led to excessively restrictive fiscal and monetary policies in circumstances where a better mix of macro-economic instruments would have produced a closer realization of all objectives. During the recovery years from 1962 to 1965, macro-economic policy was more carefully calculated to assist in the expansion of activity, although it was still unnecessarily restrictive after the exchange crisis in 1962. This was also the period in which new courses were charted in such matters as regional development, foreign investment, and growth. In the initial stages, these measures were largely *ad hoc* and often introduced as part of a policy measure with wider objectives. As the lessons from these experiments were learned, more comprehensive and co-ordinated approached were adopted in each of these fields. Finally, the last five years of the decade saw a fairly flexible use being made of fiscal policy, frustrated somewhat by the difficulty of forecasting correctly in the rapidly changing economic circumstances, and by the inability to control the growth of government expenditures at certain crucial times, as well as by the virtually worldwide tendency towards more rapid cost and price increases.

Throughout the period under consideration the authorities had available a wide range of policy instruments. The money markets and financial institutions were already well developed by 1958 and the Bank of Canada was thus in a position to implement any reasonable policy. The monetary authorities were somewhat restricted in their use of interest-rate changes, however, by the extreme openness of the Canadian financial markets, and by the necessity to keep interest-rate levels within the bounds dictated by external requirements. The government used changes in the exchange rate and tariffs at least partially for stabilization purposes during this period, as well as a wide variety of changes in tax rates and in the rate of government expenditure. The flexibility with which macro-economic policy was used in the later years is visible in the number of supplementary budgets presented. Any failures of Canadian macro-economic policy were thus only in a small way a technical problem resulting from the lack of suitable policy instruments or the inability to change policies quickly.

The actual reasons for the deficiencies of policy during this period were quite varied. The first and most obvious shortcoming was the inability to slow down price and cost increases once started, except by allowing an inordinate amount of unemployment. Although the establishment of the Prices and Incomes Commission in 1969 may lead to some progress in this area, the tendency for periods of strain upon capacity to generate inflation (which continued for significant periods after some excess capacity appeared) placed considerable pressure upon macro-economic policy to keep the economy in the 'narrow band' around full employment. At the same time, public prominence was given to the rate of change of prices as indicating what the stance of policy ought to be. Such an approach can have serious disadvantages because the rate of change of prices generally lags behind changes in economic activity; and this is especially true of Canada with its very decentralized processes for setting wages and prices. Emphasis upon price changes is therefore likely to lead to restrictive measures being pursued for too long, and thus to unnecessarily increasing unemployment. This particular tendency was a significant factor in the unnecessarily restrictive measures of 1959.

A second difficulty has been that there was a certain amount of bad luck in basing crucial changes in the direction of policy – those of 1959, 1965 and 1967 – upon the most significant errors in forecasting made during the period; although in general forecasts have probably been as accurate as anywhere else.

A further difficulty – already discussed above – was the regional imbalances and other structural rigidities. These often tended to obscure the need for short-term demand management and were sometimes used as an excuse for poor policy performance, although the actual solutions to these problems are, of course, necessarily long term.

Finally, the rapidly changing relationship between the provincial and federal governments gave rise, at least in the later years, to some real problems in the use of macro-economic policy, and further measures to avoid this problem need to be developed.

MACRO-ECONOMIC POLICY AND CANADIAN ECONOMIC PERFORMANCE

The period from 1958 to 1961 was one of high unemployment, slow growth, and a persistent deficit on current account of over a billion dollars. Unemployment averaged 6·8 per cent of the labour force for the period, with the regional differences in employment becoming especially pronounced. Unemployment in the Maritimes remained above 10 per cent annually for the four years.

Although the recession coincided with a similar one in the United

States, there were other important forces involved. Circumstances, both internal and external, had been especially favourable for the Canadian economy during the 1950s. During the later years of that decade, the special expansionary forces that had been at work were weakening, at the same time as international markets were becoming more competitive in the goods that Canada produced. Although the environment was thus one that presented considerable difficulties for policy-makers, the inappropriate policies actually adopted did much to prevent the achievement of a more successful economic performance.

The lack of co-operation between the Bank of Canada and the government during this period was especially damaging. The government had indicated that it accepted a high level of employment as its main policy objective. James Coyne, the governor of the Bank of Canada, had very different views on the question of priorities in the objectives and equally distinctive ideas on the appropriate policies to pursue. In particular, he felt that price stability was a prerequisite for successful long-term achievement of increases in output and employment. In addition, he was very concerned with the persistently large current account deficit, and continually stressed that the nation must learn to 'live within its means'.

To achieve these ends by the means of restricting expenditure, a very restrictive monetary policy was adopted. The government, although unhappy with this policy to the extent of partially dissociating itself from it, also pursued a contractionary policy, for a variety of reasons (which are discussed below). This approach certainly achieved price stability – which is not surprising considering the level of unemployment involved – but it was completely unsuccessful in reducing the current account deficit. Canada was on a flexible exchange rate at this time. The high interest rates associated with the restrictive policy, coupled with the close relationship of the Canadian and American financial markets, served to sustain a heavy capital inflow, which caused an appreciation of the Canadian dollar. With the higher external value of the Canadian dollar, exports were discouraged and imports encouraged, thus maintaining the current account deficit. The resultant changes in imports and exports also produced a direct depressing effect upon the level of national income. While this simple explanation of the mechanics of the problem ignores possible offsetting factors such as the use of the capital inflow for direct investment (so that it never enters the foreign exchange markets), it does provide a guide to the nature of the difficulties involved with these policies.

Economic activity had started to slacken in 1957 as the investment boom in natural resources during 1955/7 lost its strength. In December 1957 a very expansionary budget was brought down which actually changed the fiscal position of the government by approximately 3 per cent of GNP. Transfer payments and the government building programme were increased, while other measures proved quite successful in stimulating residential construction.

The budget deficit resulting from the government's fiscal measures, and from the substantial refinancing of the public debt during the year 1958, necessitated heavy borrowing requirements. The large bond issue of May and the Canadian Conversion Loan of October were both supported by the Bank of Canada, and the money supply expanded rapidly in the first three-quarters of the year. Mr Coyne made it clear, however, that he felt this could be justified only by the importance of meeting the problems associated with the government cash deficit and with the refunding of the public debt. Indeed, it should be noted that the relaxation of the previous policy of restraint was over half a year late if it was intended to stimulate the economy.

In the latter part of 1958, no doubt partly as a result of the fiscal measures of late 1957, there was an encouraging upturn in economic activity and this engendered optimistic forecasts about the level of employment and the rate of growth in 1959 and 1960. At the same time, the continuation of price increases seemed to support the view that price stability would be especially difficult to maintain in the future, possibly because changes in the structure of the economy had reduced the forces restraining price increases.

As a result of these optimistic forecasts, the Bank of Canada became convinced that restraint would be required, and returned to a more stringent policy line, withdrawing its support from the Canada Conversion Loan. The resultant rise in interest rates produced a greater gap between the American and the traditionally higher Canadian interest rates than the historically normal $\frac{1}{2}$ per cent. Many corporations, municipalities, and Provinces turned to the American capital market in response to the better terms available there, thus adding to the capital inflow. This turning to the American capital market highlighted the difficulty of pursuing a monetary policy out of line with the American one; and it also illustrated another way in which the Provinces and municipalities may act in a fashion contrary to the requirements of stabilization policy.

With the optimistic forecasts, the fear of continuing inflation, and the desire to reduce the much-criticized budget deficit, the government increased taxes and reduced non-budgetary expenditures in the April 1959 budget, offsetting to a large extent the expansionary measures of the previous year. In retrospect, this was clearly most inappropriate. Although errors in prediction must bear some of the blame, the exaggerated fear that inflation might result from 'structural rigidities', at a time when the last price increases associated with the prior boom had almost worked themselves out, must be counted as the prime reason for this mistake. Although the recurrent fear that inflation is likely to be more difficult to control than in the past is perhaps quite justifiable, the tendency to focus attention upon price increases can very well lead to this type of situation in which unemployment is created with very little gain in price stability. Confusion about the budget deficits of this period also played a significant role in the restrictive policies. The large budget deficits were criticized as being a symptom of the government's inability to reverse its policies to meet the renewed threat of inflation (and, of course, on even less relevant grounds): but it is now clear that the deficit arose from the fall in revenue associated with the recession, and that the return of the economy to full employment would have brought about a budget surplus. In any event, this is one case where criticisms of the size of the actual budget deficit did affect the path of government policy.

The financial markets were quite unsettled during 1959 and there was frequent mention of a 'credit crisis'. Symptomatic of this was the indication in August by the Canadian Bankers' Association that its members had lost the ability to meet the demand for new loans and for additional amounts on outstanding credits. Also in August, the government refused to accept any of the tenders at a treasury bill auction, on the grounds that the tenders made were at interest rates that had reached an unrealistically high level in the circumstances. This was only one of several instances during that year in which the government appeared to be dissociating itself from Bank policy.

The 1960 budget contained no major changes from the previous year, and by the latter part of the year the moderate recovery dating from 1958 had spent itself. In addition to the previous reasons for the restrictive fiscal policy, fiscal restraint was clearly felt to be also necessary in order to keep down capital inflow. But, instead of doing this, it would have been better to reduce interest rates, as the main factor involved in the capital inflow was the interest-rate differential between Canada and the United States. Although fiscal policy was clearly too restrictive during 1959 and 1960, when a strongly expansionary policy was required, it is questionable how feasible an appropriately expansionary budgetary policy would have been, given the uneasy state of the credit market and the stance of monetary policy. The 'money muddle' was finally resolved with the extremely important 'baby budget' in December 1960, in which the government finally signified its intention to adopt expansionary policies to fight unemployment, and with the resignation of Mr Coyne under government pressure early in 1961.

One component of aggregate demand that proved extremely susceptible to changes in policy during this period was residential construction. In 1958 there was an increase in the amounts available to the Central Mortgage and Housing Corporation (a crown corporation) and a reduction in the minimum downpayments and income requirements for purchasing houses financed under the National Housing Act. These measures had a stimulating effect on both the building and purchasing of houses. The opposite effect (this time undesirable and probably unplanned) occurred in 1960, when government loans for housing were reduced. The experience of this period showed clearly that changes in terms or down-payments required under the National Housing Act could have a marked effect on this component of household expenditure. The construction of dwellings has, however, a high social priority in Canada and the problem in the late 1960s was to prevent the restrictive measures from having a disproportionate impact upon that sector of the economy.

The period 1961–4 was characterized by a broadly based expansion, in an atmosphere of reasonable price and cost stability, with unemployment falling steadily from its previous high levels. Supporting the expansion were the improving conditions in the United States and the more favourable conditions in world trade generally. The devaluation of the Canadian dollar in 1962 and the maintenance of reasonable cost and price stability helped to reduce the current account deficit, although it was clearly still undesirably large. Whilst there may well be a good case for a country such as Canada to run a current account deficit, it was not possible to justify such a large deficit, nor its persistence in the face of depressed internal conditions. It is therefore not surprising that the maintenance of an orderly foreign exchange market proved to be a serious problem both during the foreign exchange crisis of 1962, and also subsequently during the periods in 1963 and 1965, when there was widespread uncertainty about the likely impact on the flow of capital to Canada of the American measures taken in those years to improve the United States balance of payments.

Both fiscal and monetary policy assumed a generally more expansionary posture in Canada during this period: and this was appropriate from the viewpoint of internal balance. Fiscal policy can be criticized, however, for the length of time during which restrictive measures were maintained after the foreign exchange crisis. There was also a tendency to ignore the possibility of managing aggregate demand and to focus policy measures upon the 'structural problems' and on other factors that were seen to impede the success of any stabilization measures. Whilst the attack on these problems was certainly justified, the government's preoccupation with them often made it fail to take the appropriate measures for managing aggregate demand.

The actual start of the recovery in early 1961, was preceded by the important 'baby budget' of December 1960. In it the government firmly stated its intention to achieve the short-term goal of greater employment through expansionary measures. In the budget of June 1961 these measures were reinforced by further tax changes and increased expenditure on defence and social security. This trend continued into early 1962, when new fiscal arrangements with the provinces provided further stimulus to aggregate demand. Later in the year, however, the foreign exchange crisis led to a reversal of the trend in policy.

Exchange-rate policy
After the 'baby budget' of December 1960, the government pursued an unannounced policy of intervening in the foreign exchange market in such a way as to depress the external value of the Canadian dollar. This ended the phase of a freely fluctuating exchange rate, which had been operating successfully since 1950. During this period, short-term capital flows had generally been equilibrating, and fluctuations in the exchange rate had been small and orderly. Especially in the light of the subsequent partial freeing of the Canadian dollar in 1970, it should be noted that it was felt necessary to return to a fixed exchange rate only after a period in which foreign confidence in the management of the Canadian economy had been severely shaken.

By December 1960, the first step had already been taken in what proved to be a protracted campaign first to reduce the external value of the Canadian dollar, and later to defend the fixed exchange rate once it had been adopted. The budget speech in April had contained a warning directed to Canadian borrowers in the United States capital markets, that repayments might have to be made at a time when exchange rates had changed in a direction unfavourable to the borrowers. This warning had been sufficient to curtail severely Canadian borrowing in the New York market. But a revival of direct investment in Canada by foreigners served to maintain the size of total capital inflow.

The moving of the Canadian dollar to a significant discount on the United States dollar was an explicitly stated goal in the budget speech of June 1961. The Canadian dollar began to drift lower, and when no indication of the prospective exchange rate was given (except that the Canadian dollar would be depreciated) speculation developed. This coincided with a serious loss of foreign confidence in the management and prospects of the Canadian economy. The speculation against the Canadian dollar continued into the early part of 1962 and exchange reserves fell precipitously. On May 9th the fixing of the exchange rate at $US 0·925 was announced. The Canadian dollar immediately moved to the lower support price, and the authorities were forced to continue massive support. On June 24th the government announced a number of emergency measures designed to remove the fears of a further devaluation and to restore foreign confidence. The vagueness of the government's objectives and its hesitancy in taking decisive action were the major factors responsible for the seriousness of the crisis, and for the length of time during which policy measures had to be concentrated upon external balance. Contributing to these errors was the occurrence of a federal election in early 1962, which naturally tended to make the government unwilling to admit to the existence of a serious crisis.

There was a considerable body of opinion in Canada, and perhaps to a lesser extent outside Canada, which regarded the persistent budget deficit as one of the prime indications of the mismanagement of the economy. While this view ignored the critical factor of the large loss in revenue resulting from the operation of the economy at less than full employment, this attitude could probably not be ignored in a crisis of confidence. Thus the emergency measures adopted were directed towards reducing the budget deficit as well as reducing the current account deficit. The actual measures included a temporary surcharge on certain classes of imports; a substantial reduction in the amount of duty-free goods that Canadians travelling abroad could bring back into Canada; a reduction in the level of government expenditures by $250 million in a full fiscal year; earmarking a portion of the government's cash balances for the purpose of financing increases in the foreign exchange reserves; and the mobilization of international financial support equivalent to

$US 1,050 million in the form of cash and stand-by credits. The Bank of Canada, for its part, indicated its intention to raise interest rates and induce a capital inflow by fixing at 6 per cent the bank rate, which had for some years been permitted to float at a fixed relationship with the market rate on treasury bills. Following this indication of its intentions, the Bank proceeded with an open-market operation which led to an absolute fall in the total assets of the chartered banks. By September, with the worst of the crisis past, security prices were again allowed to rise.

Macro-economic Policy and the structure of the economy
The pace of economic expansion had slowed down somewhat by early 1963, and despite the previous rapid increase in employment the unemployment rate had fallen only slightly, because of the exceptionally fast growth of the labour force through a higher labour force participation rate and additional immigration. In such circumstances, a further stimulus to aggregate demand was advisable, but the government concentrated upon special areas of concern, particularly types of expenditure thought likely to promote long-run economic growth. An over-emphasis upon the external position was probably the basic factor involved in this decision. It was felt that an increase in demand generally would increase imports to an undesirable extent, and also that a further reduction in the budget deficit would be effective in maintaining foreign confidence. But the successful return to an expansionary monetary policy by the Bank of Canada in the latter part of the previous year without any apparent adverse repercussions on the improving external position suggests that a general stimulus to demand would not have had serious adverse effects on the capital account. The one component of aggregate demand that was encouraged by the budget was capital spending, which had as yet played only a minor role in the recovery. These measures included investment incentives through capital cost allowances, and the setting up of the Municipal Development and Loan Fund to encourage municipalities in the building up of the infra-structure.

Throughout the early 1960s, attempts to control the economy by management of aggregate demand were somewhat half-hearted, the government being preoccupied with measures directed towards overcoming regional imbalance, as well as at other 'structural' problems, at promoting long-range growth, and at limiting foreign ownership and control. In the initial years, there was considerable doubt as to the proper approach to adopt in each of these areas and a tendency to try a wide range of alternatives. Only after a few years was the programme consolidated into a more consistent framework. This approach, although perhaps providing some useful experience, seems to indicate clearly the futility of attacking such deep-seated problems as regional disparities with a series of *ad hoc* measures: and it was gradually realized that it was best to adopt a more detailed plan. Such a plan would make it easier both to achieve better results and also to have some hope of gauging the actual benefits.

These various measures to affect the structure of the economy did, however, have macro-economic effects, which were often intended. One development was the introduction of various fiscal incentives to investment. These commenced with the introduction in the December 1960 budget of accelerated depreciation for industries being newly located in areas of chronic unemployment. This approach was continued in extended form in the following few years. In 1963 generous capital cost allowances and exemption from the corporation tax for three years were introduced in the form of incentives for manufacturing and processing companies to establish new facilities in certain specified development areas. Experience showed that this was not a successful approach, as profits tended to be low during the early years of operation, thus minimizing the incentive effect. This corporate tax exemption, with the depreciation allowance remaining available, was replaced in 1965 by a system of cash grants of up to a third of the capital cost of investment in new buildings, equipment and machinery. While this movement to a system of cash grants appears now as a steady progression towards a comprehensive programme of regional development (as eventually adopted in Regional Development Incentives Act of 1969), at the time the measures were often approached as simply a regionally differentiated macro-economic policy couched in terms of employment opportunities and economic growth.

At the same time, several development corporations were established to aid in the development of certain areas or sectors of the economy. The actual amounts spent under these programmes were substantial. The agencies included those responsible for the functions of the Agricultural and Rural Development Act, as well as the Atlantic Development Board, the Area Development Agency, and the Atlantic Development Fund – all of which came into being in the three-year period starting in 1961.

Many countries find it difficult to provide employment for the unskilled worker, especially in the oldest and youngest age groups, and this is particularly true in Canada. The institution of the Vocational Training Program in 1960 was directed towards matching skills more closely with the available jobs. The government gave manpower policy a very high priority from this time onwards, with a steadily growing budgetary allocation. An example of another approach to these 'structural' problems was the introduction in 1963 of grants to cover a proportion of wages of firms that hired workers over 45 years of age, who met certain qualifications regarding the length of time they had been out of work.

A final component of the structural unemployment problem is the extreme seasonal conditions, which makes many construction projects and other operations unattractive in the winter. In an effort to overcome the serious seasonal unemployment problem in the construction industry, various incentives for the provision of winter work were established. One of these was the $500 bonus for winter-built houses adopted in 1963. This was a particularly useful measure, as it seems to have led to technological developments that overcame many of the previous problems, and eventually it proved possible to discontinue the programme after it had brought about a considerable smoothing out of the seasonal construction pattern.

Apart from these measures to remove the structural problems that had for so long been a cause of unemployment and retarded growth, efforts were also made to encourage other influences that were considered to be significant for growth prospects. It has been especially noticeable in 1961 and 1962 that private investment, which had always been a dynamic factor in previous post-war expansions, had not played a significant role in this one. In 1963 capital cost allowances were increased, as part of the measures to stimulate investment. To encourage research and development (the low level of expenditure on which was thought partly responsible for the slow rate of economic growth), taxpayers were permitted as from 1962 to deduct 150 per cent of increased expenditures on scientific research when computing their income for tax purposes. This was designed to narrow the gap between the proportion of income spent upon research and development in the United States and that in Canada, and it was hoped that it would thereby encourage technological advances that would promote economic growth.

The issue of Canadian ownership and control of the country's industry and commerce moved into prominence during this period, and a number of the policy measures adopted proved to be extremely controversial. In particular, there was especially a tendency to include incentives towards encouraging a certain proportion of

Canadian ownership of industry as a component of measures adopted for other reasons. Thus the accelerated capital cost allowances on new investment in capital machinery introduced in 1963 applied only to manufacturing or processing firms with at least 25 per cent resident ownership. Again, the rate of withholding tax payable on dividends to non-resident shareholders was made dependent upon the relative importance of resident ownership. But considerable opposition arose with the application of a sales tax to takeovers of Canadian owned companies and on sales of stock to foreigners exceeding $50,000; and this actually led to the repeal of the tax after six days. Another particularly controversial measure was the introduction in 1964 of limits upon non-resident holdings in banks and other financial institutions. This became a special point of contention because its provisions reduced the possibilities of expansion of only one bank, the Mercantile, which was owned entirely by an American bank. The nature of these measures indicate a trend in the direction of a more active policy towards foreign investment, but also indicates the lack of any readily discernible objective, or consistent approach.

The devaluation of 1962 and the accompanying measures proved to be an important watershed in the development of Canada's balance of payments position. Combined with the continuing recovery of the Canadian economy and the large wheat sales to Russia in the latter part of 1963, the devaluation and other measures provided a climate in which foreign confidence was quickly restored, and the outflow of short-term capital reversed. At the same time, the devaluation helped to reduce the current account deficit in the two years following devaluation.

Two other occasions on which external balance was threatened were associated with the announcements by the United States of policies designed to reduce her balance of payments deficit. The announcement in July 1963 of the proposed United States interest equalization tax created considerable uncertainty in Canadian financial markets, as it was apparent that only a substantial and undesirable rise in the structure of Canadian interest rates would be sufficient to offset the effects of this policy upon the flow of funds necessary to finance the deficit on current account. The problem did not arise, however, as after consultation the United States recognized the special relationship between the two economies, and exempted Canada from the tax on new securities in return for the Canadian promise to maintain a certain 'target' level of reserves and not to increase reserves by borrowing in the United States. In the second instance, Canada also received special exemptions from the guidelines on the purchase of long-term foreign securities by American non-bank financial institutions. The guidelines on US direct investment did, however, apply to Canada: but, despite some critical apprehension, they did not produce any serious additional pressures on the Canadian securities markets.

In return for the exemption from the other US measures, Canada agreed to reduce the target level for her reserves by $100 million and the government indicated its intention to repatriate its securities held in the United States if this was required in order to keep the reserves down to this target level. Although this latter undertaking did remove some of the constraints upon monetary policies which these agreements entailed, it was quite clear that, as a result of these undertakings, monetary policy could be significantly limited as an internal policy instrument from time to time, because of the large effect on capital inflow, and so on the reserves, of any market rise in Canadian interest rates above those in the USA.

The economic expansion continued vigorously into 1964, with unemployment reaching its lowest level since 1957 and productivity increasing at a faster rate than earlier in the upturn. Business investment in plant and equipment became an important factor in the expansion, after having shown only sluggish growth earlier in the period. Significantly, a large proportion of the investment was in manufacturing, in contrast to the primarily resource-oriented surge of investment in 1955–7.

With the economy now approaching a point where some sectors of the economy were reaching capacity levels, the adoption of a budget showing little change from the previous year was quite appropriate. Meanwhile, monetary policy aimed at meeting the demand for credit without any tightening in the market. This was facilitated by the large reduction in government borrowing requirements during the year as a result of a change in its budgetary position to a surplus on the national accounts basis. The monetary and fiscal positions were such that changes could be made rapidly to meet any developments in economic conditions.

The economic expansion continued strongly into 1965, but with definite signs of strain upon capacity in certain sectors. Unemployment had fallen to 3·5 per cent of the labour force by the end of the year and there were shortages of certain skilled workers and especially severe pressures upon capacity in the construction industry. Although real growth continued at a rapid rate by comparison with the last few years, productivity gains did not proceed at the pace of the previous year. Especially important was the increase in the general price level – the first significant one in several years. The rise in the price indices for each of the major categories of expenditure was greater than for the comparable ones in the United States. Moreover, after several consecutive years of increasing surpluses on merchandise trade, a rapid increase in imports caused a decline in the surplus.

In retrospect, a policy of moderate restraint was desirable, but this did not eventuate. The major change in fiscal policy was a reduction in income tax, although the expansionary effect of this was expected to be offset to a great extent by the deflationary impact upon consumption of the commencement of collections for the Canada Pension Plan on 1 January 1966. The desirability of some expansionary measures was seen as arising from forecasts that indicated a slowing down of the North American economy in the latter part of 1965. The government did, however, try to take one restraining step in August, when it was becoming apparent that aggregate demand was going to continue to grow too rapidly. Parts of the government building programme were postponed, but this measure was not sufficiently anti-inflationary in the circumstances.

In other respects the budget continued the emphasis on specific measures. In particular, the previous tax incentives both to scientific research and to capital investment in depressed areas were changed to the more economically efficient form of outright grants.

The signing of an automotive agreement with the United States during the year proved to be the most significant occurrence affecting the balance of payments. In the early 1960s the deficit on automobiles and their components in Canada's trade with the USA had been running at about $500 million a year. An attempt had been made to reduce this deficit by a scheme giving incentives for the export of automobiles, but this had not been a great success. The automotive agreement reached in 1965 allowed finished cars and components to move free of duty between car companies and parts manufacturers with plants on both sides of the border. The agreement led to a great increase of trade in automobiles and automotive components between the two countries, but was especially beneficial to Canada. By 1969, the $500 million deficit in automobiles and parts had been changed into a small surplus, as many of the component manufacturers established factories in Canada and the automotive companies built their newest and most efficient plants there. This agreement was the most important reason why the current account deficit declined so substantially (and unexpectedly) in the last years of the decade.

During 1966 costs, prices and productivity all developed less satisfactorily in Canada than in the United States. Canada's real GNP increased by more than 6 per cent during the year, but this was largely the result of the continuing rapid rise in employment. Renewed wheat sales to the Soviet Union and China and the initial effects of the automotive pact with the United States led a resurgence of export demand, which reduced the current account deficit after it had risen in the previous year. Business investment, especially in non-residential construction, was running at a very high level during the first two quarters, and costs were rising especially fast in the construction industry.

The emphasis of policy had changed in the latter part of 1965, as it became obvious that the strong demand pressures would continue. In the March 1966 budget, a quite active approach was adopted for restraining certain components of aggregate demand. The previous year's reduction in income tax was reversed for the middle and high income groups. The most significant steps, however, were the measures adopted to reduce the level of investment by providing incentives for the postponement of investment. Depreciation allowances were reduced on certain types of investment in the period April 1966 to October 1967. In addition, the sales tax on machinery and equipment, which had been introduced in 1963, was to be phased out over a period of time, and this measure provided a further incentive for firms to delay investment.

Another measure adopted was the refundable tax on corporate cash flow. Working on the assumption that the availability of internal funds is an important determination of business investment, a tax of 5 per cent was levied on the total of corporate profits plus any depreciation exceeding a $30,000 minimum. The tax collections were to be refunded at a time 18 to 36 months later, depending upon the economic circumstances. While exhibiting the commendably flexible approach to stabilization that was becoming increasingly evident, the refundable tax did perhaps lead to some additional pressure on the capital market, which was undesirable at the time, and it might also have limited the flexibility of policy at the later date. As pointed out by several observers, a temporary investment tax would have served the same purpose, and would have acted much more directly. Following these measures, business non-residential investment did decline in the latter part of the year and this was an important factor in the slight easing of demand pressures during the following year.

Credit restraint was applied until the middle of the year, after which the Bank of Canada resisted further tightening of credit conditions, indicating that the policy was having a very uneven impact, with housing and financial institutions being unduly affected. Housing starts, especially those that were largely dependent upon private financing, had declined precipitously as the institutions providing mortgage funds found it difficult to compete for funds in a situation of historically high interest rates. A preferable alternative to the general easing of credit would have been some steps designed to alleviate the excessive effects of credit restraint on the housing industry. Such a measure was adopted by the government in April and May 1967, when it authorized loans of $300 million by the Central Mortgage and Housing Corporation to builders, but this was obviously much too late. A further step, taken in September 1967, which proved very helpful in maintaining the flow of funds into the mortgage market in succeeding periods of credit restraint, was the decision to allow loans made under the National Housing Act to have interest rates related to other long-term interest rates, rather than being subject to a ceiling.

The revenue of the Provincial and municipal governments rose rapidly during 1965 and 1966, largely owing to a rapid growth of personal income tax receipts and increases in federal government transfers. With heavy demands being placed upon the Provincial and municipal governments for the social services provided by them, expenditures grew along with revenue. The rapid rise in expenditures by these levels of government clearly made stabilization more difficult during these years and this danger is inherent in a federal system in which the Provinces have so much budgetary freedom. Some tentative efforts have been directed towards overcoming this problem by closer consultation on economic affairs between the Provincial and federal governments, but it would seem likely that some regulatory device (perhaps some control by the federal government over the timing of transfers to the Provinces) will be needed to attune changes in Provincial expenditure more closely to the requirements of aggregate demand management, especially if the trend continues for a rising share of total government expenditures to be made by the Provinces. Another problem in the area of federal-Provincial fiscal relationships was that by 1966 the federal government had accumulated a number of continuing shared-cost programmes in fields primarily under Provincial jurisdiction. During this period of rapid increases in Provincial expenditures, this resulted in an undesirable and unexpected increase in expenditures by the federal government. This problem was later alleviated by the withdrawal of the federal government from these programmes in return for appropriate tax transfers. Although these adjustments did remove some of the most likely causes of conflict, this is clearly an area to which considerable attention will have to be directed in the 1970s.

The March 1966 budget had been designed to have a significant restraining effect upon the economy, despite expected increases in transfers to the Provinces and in certain other transfers. By the latter part of the year, however, it had become clear that, with demand expanding very strongly and expenditures by the government sector rising more rapidly than expected, further steps would be necessary. As a result, the government deferred the introduction of a new scholarship plan for students and the full 'medicare' plan, and cancelled the winter house-building bonus plan. A supplementary budget in December complemented these expenditure measures with increases in the manufacturers' sales tax and the old-age security tax on personal incomes.

Demand pressures eased during 1967, reflecting a decline in business investment, particularly in inventory accumulation. Despite the easing of demand, prices and costs continued to rise at an undesirable rate. Salaries rose markedly, with those in the public sector showing especially significant increases. Government expenditures continued to advance very rapidly, and there was a budget deficit (on a national accounts basis) after several years of surpluses. The financial markets seemed to have anticipated both the continuation of inflation and the quick recovery from the slowdown in the economy, as there was a heavy demand for funds in the latter part of the year. In these circumstances, with the government having heavy borrowing requirements, to finance the budget deficit and to make especially large loans to Crown corporations, there was a strong upward pressure upon interest rates. Despite the Bank of Canada's large, expansionary, open-market operations and a considerable increase in chartered bank liquidity, interest rates rose after April to levels above the peak of 1966.

With the general level of demand in the economy showing signs of easing early in the year, especially in the investment sector, the measures of the previous year – that is, the refundable tax on corporate cash flow and the reduced rates of capital cost allowance for new capital expenditures – were terminated in April. The government also authorized the Central Mortgage and Housing Corporation to undertake loans of up to $300 million to home-builders during April and May. This proved to be quite important in stimulating housing starts and again emphasized how susceptible the house-building industry is to changes in policy. The budget, which was not presented until June, was designed to be mildly expansionary. The removal of the last 6 per cent of the sales tax on production machinery was carried out immediately instead of a year later and there were some minor sales tax and tariff reductions, designed to reduce costs and prices in certain areas.

By the last quarter of the year it was quite evident that the pause in the expansion would be short, if for no other reason than the buoyant conditions in the United States. At the same time, the cost and price performance of the economy showed little improvement and the capital markets were severely strained. Reacting to the rapidly changing conditions, the government proposed significant new measures of restraint in November, including a personal income surtax for certain income groups, and higher excise taxes on liquor and tobacco. In an effort to ease the strain on the capital markets by reducing the government's cash requirements, corporate tax payments were accelerated by two months. The impact of this last measure was tempered by the plan to begin the refund of the refundable tax on corporate tax flow in June 1968.

On the external side, a halving of the current account deficit was a particularly bright feature of 1967. This was a result of merchandise exports rising more quickly than merchandise imports, especially in automotive trade with the United States, and also of a large surplus on the travel account associated with Expo and other Centennial activities.

The major problems faced by the authorities during 1968 were the continuation of inflationary pressures and the speculative attack on the Canadian dollar during the early months of the year. Merchandise exports rose very quickly in response to a resurgence of demand in the United States, and the current account deficit actually fell again, despite the ending of the influence of the Centennial activities. With demand buoyant in most sectors, employment expanded rapidly enough to absorb most of the extremely large increase in the labour force. Both the real growth rate and productivity gains were greater than in the previous year.

In these circumstances the government wished to pursue a restrictive policy, but found that the continuing rapid rise in its expenditures seriously hampered its ability to do so. In the previous two years, the large increases in wages and salaries in the public sector and a rapid growth in transfers had been important factors in the underestimation of government expenditures. In 1968 the federal government made large expenditures under certain statutory obligations, especially those with the Provinces. Throughout the years 1966 to 1968, then, the government seriously underestimated the size of its expenditures. The flexible manner in which fiscal policy was used was thus somewhat illusory; for even though the measures adopted were successful in stimulating or dampening demand in certain sectors, or in reducing or postponing certain categories of government expenditures, the underlying rate of growth of government expenditures was sufficient to swamp these effects, in a period when a contractionary policy was desirable. But it is clear that a successful restrictive fiscal policy is more likely to be achieved if it does not have to be restrictive enough to offset large, inflation-induced, increases in government expenditures, as well as to dampen demand in other sectors. The desirability (and possible scope for) avoiding rapid growth of transfers to the Provinces during inflationary periods has already been discussed. The other especially troublesome component of government expenditure during this period was wages and salaries. It is much more difficult to see any way of handling this, without distorting wage relationships in an inequitable fashion and thus creating unnecessary industrial trouble. The experience of this period thus clearly shows how difficult it is to pursue a successful stabilization policy, if large sections of government expenditures are likely to increase rapidly during inflationary periods.

The government adopted several measures during the year in an effort to control the growth of its expenditure and to reduce demand in other sectors. The personal income surtax, which had been proposed in November 1967, did not receive the approval of Parliament in February, and in its place the government proposed a surtax on both personal and corporate income, yielding a slightly smaller amount than the original measure. This was accepted by Parliament and at the same time additional cuts in expenditure were announced, as well as a freeze on the total number employed in the civil service. In the budget presented in October, the government increased income tax; introduced a corporate tax on the investment income of insurance companies; accelerated further the payments of corporate tax to an almost pay-as-you-go basis; and changed the rules by which financial institutions determine their taxable income. The government also reiterated its intention of strongly resisting increases in its expenditures; and indicated its plan to ask the Provinces for co-operation in reducing expenditures on shared-cost programmes. Significantly, these measures – which had the expected effect of improving the government's budgetary position by an amount equivalent to 1 per cent of GNP – were intended to have their primary effect on the level of activity only after a lag of six months, as a more abrupt change was felt to be too likely to disrupt the economy. More immediate effects would have been desirable in order to temper the very fast expansion of activity that occurred. The government very reasonably concluded that more abrupt changes would be inadvisable, emphasizing the deep-seated nature of the inflationary pressures upon government sector expenditures.

A speculative attack on the Canadian dollar and the difficulties of pursuing an appropriately restrictive monetary policy at a time when the level of interest rates was already at high levels by past standards, provided the two main problems for monetary policy during the year. In the atmosphere of unsettled international financial markets, speculation developed against the Canadian dollar in the first quarter of the year. The speculation was triggered by the announcement by the United States of new measures affecting capital outflows, and hinged upon the usual doubts about the viability of Canada's balance of payments position, in the event of any serious impediments to the flow of capital from the United States. In March Canada was exempted from the measures in return for the undertaking not to be used as a 'pass-through' for funds from the United States going to other countries. As there was no other reason for speculation, with the current account deficit being the lowest since 1952, exchange reserves were quickly replenished after this; and Canada was able to begin to rebuild her position with the International Monetary Fund and to repay a drawing from the Federal Reserve System under the reciprocal credit facility.

Total chartered bank assets grew by 14 per cent during the year – a rate that the Bank of Canada felt was undesirably rapid, but unavoidable in the very tight financial markets, if interest rates were not to rise to levels even more likely to disrupt the capital market. The Bank of Canada did restrict credit more actively during the exchange crisis, but eased conditions somewhat after it was over.

The continued rapid growth in prices and costs was again the most significant feature in 1969. Inflation affected almost every industrialized country during 1969, however, and the rate of increase of prices in Canada was below the average for members of the OECD – for the first time in four years. This gave only slight comfort, however, as despite the definite slowing down of the rate of expansion after the first quarter, prices increased at a slightly faster rate than in the previous year and at a much faster rate than they had in past periods with a similar level of utilization of resources.

Pronouncements by policy-makers during the year emphasized the role of 'inflationary psychology' in weakening the effectiveness of policies of restraint. Evidence of this attitude was found in the distinct reluctance of investors to commit their funds for long periods of time. While the presence of well-entrenched expectations of continued price rises may well have played a part in the persistence of the price increases, there were other more tangible contributory factors: the particularly rapid expansion of demand in the latter part of 1968 and in the early part of 1969, leading to pressures upon resources in certain sectors; the high rate of increase of prices in the United States; and the tendency of price and cost adjustments to lag well behind peaks of activity.

At the time of the budget presented in June the main concern was naturally with inflation. But there were no major changes in the general level of taxes and expenditures, as the measures taken in October 1968 had been primarily designed to produce a restraining influence during the fiscal year 1969/70. In this they were quite successful, as the change in the fiscal position of the government amounted to almost 1 per cent of GNP for fiscal year 1969/70, although (as discussed previously) this change was too late to have had its effect at the most appropriate time. In an effort to increase competition and attack 'inflationary psychology', which included the widespread expectation that cost increases could be passed on through price increases, the remaining tariff reductions of the Kennedy Round were implemented immediately, some $2\frac{1}{2}$ years ahead of the timetable for their phased introduction. This clearly indicated, as had a number of other instances in the previous few years, the desirability from the point of view of stabilization of having certain significant economic measures that could be postponed or initiated earlier if required. While capital investment projects are often cited as the only significant possibility in this area, tariff changes, introduction of new social welfare programmes, and adjustments of the tax structure for purposes other than stabilization, are all often planned far enough ahead and can certainly be made sufficiently flexible in the timing of their introduction to be used for this purpose.

A particularly interesting reason given for the choice of the tariff reduction was that its chief impact would be upon the 'industrial centre' of Canada, where pressure upon resources was greatest. This, then, was another attempt to use a regionalized fiscal policy for macro-economic purposes. In the same vein, deferred depreciation was applied in the commercial buildings industry, but only in centres of over 50,000 population in Ontario, Alberta and British Columbia. The explicitly stated hypothesis was that these centres were the focal points for inflationary pressures in the building industry, with smaller centres and other regions being affected by the cost increases, but not sharing in their actual generation. While stabilization policies with special features to stimulate activity in depressed areas had been used quite often during the 1960s, the attempt to focus measures of restraint in the areas of high employment was an important new step and one that raises some questions. If this type of policy is to be used in the future, experience in the early 1960s with expansionary policies with special features directed at areas of chronic unemployment would seem to suggest that if regionally differentiated stabilization measures are to be successful they must be of a more thorough nature than the decidedly *ad hoc* measures that were adopted in that period.

One essential difficulty was that because of the 'inflationary psychology' that prevailed at the time, investment projects were not generally likely to be postponed. This meant that the impact of the measures was thus mainly to add to costs, and presumably prices, when the construction projects went ahead. It was therefore not a particularly apt measure, if the government's analysis of the causes of the price and cost increases were correct.

A more fundamental problem is that whilst expansionary measures focused on areas of chronic unemployment are likely to be beneficial for long-term growth prospects nationally, the opposite result might well apply in the case of restrictive measures directed towards the most buoyant regions. A regionally differentiated restrictive fiscal policy is thus very much in its infancy, and poses some significant problems if it is to be used in the 1970s.

The Bank of Canada pursued a more restrictive policy in 1969 than in the previous year and total Canadian dollar assets of chartered banks grew at the much slower rate of 5 per cent during the year. In July the bank rate had reached 8 per cent and the interest-rate structure moved to a record high level. As an adjunct to other restrictive measures, moral suasion of the banks was used on a variety of matters during the year; in particular, banks were asked that special attention be paid to borrowers in the less prosperous regions. Although there had often been suggestions in the past that a regional approach to monetary policy be tried, the national nature of the capital markets seemed to provide insurmountable technical problems, and this was probably one of the few ways in which monetary policy could aid in achieving regional balance.

The rate of increase of prices declined somewhat in 1970 and, with more pronounced inflationary pressure appearing in other countries, Canada's performance in respect to price stability was among the best in the industrialized countries. This achievement, however, must be partially discounted, as the underlying rate of increase in costs showed only slight moderation, and special short-run restraining factors, such as the appreciation of the Canadian dollar, played an important role. The growth of output was maintained very well considering the lack of expansion in the United States economy, but with a rapidly increasing labour force, the actual growth was insufficient to stop unemployment rising to the highest level since 1961. With this background, monetary policy and, to a lesser extent, fiscal policy were directed to expansion during the year. The March budget showed very little change but developments throughout the rest of the year resulted in a moderately expansionary impact on the economy. A potentially important measure was the signified intention to introduce certain controls over the consumer credit. These were never introduced, however, as the circumstances leading to the freezing of the exchange rates intervened and the government felt the resulting restrictive effect to be about of the same order as the proposed controls over consumer credit. Considerable criticism was made of the hesitancy of the government in introducing more expansionary measures. By the first quarter of 1971, it appeared that some quickening of economic activity was occurring and many forecasts suggested that a decline in unemployment was likely. But events in the remainder of 1971 did not justify these expectations. The overestimation of the strength of the expansionary forces operating in 1970 and 1971 proved a serious barrier to adequate expansionary measures by the government, but there was also clear evidence of the Canadian predilection to attach a relatively lower weight to the employment objective than in the other countries.

There were particularly significant changes in the external balance in 1970, especially when they are viewed in the context of the important developments in the international sphere the following year. The current account moved to a surplus for the first time since 1952, and it was a large surplus of approximately $1·2 billion. The rapid increase in exports, which was instrumental in producing the surplus, was partially a continuation of the trend to larger surpluses on merchandise trade during the 1960s, but also reflected several special factors, such as the recovery from several important strikes in 1969.

With the reversal of the current account deficit, there were naturally important repercussions upon the capital account. The net inflow of capital declined, but there was still a rapid accretion of official reserves. By May total international reserves had risen by about $850 million above the level reached in December 1969; and, in addition, $US360 million had been acquired for future delivery. Including this $US360 million, the holding of US dollars rose by $1,140 million. This influx of reserves upon an original base of about $3,100 million produced a clear necessity for policy action in order to readjust the structure of capital flows. At the end of May, therefore, the exchange rate was freed to move above the previous limit in relation to the US dollar and the government indicated its desire that borrowing in the USA be reduced. The Canadian dollar moved up sharply in relation to the US dollar during June and, after a momentary pause, continued to rise at a reduced rate for the rest of the year. Canada continued floating the dollar throughout 1971, and (although at times there was official intervention in the foreign exchange market) the previous experience of reasonable stability of the exchange rate with a floating dollar was repeated. After the imposition of the special United States excise tax measures in 1971, this Canadian policy was considered by the countries concerned and agreement reached on the continuation of the floating rate.

Initially, in an atmosphere of general uncertainly the Canadian government asked for special exemption from the United States special excise tax measures. The Canadian reaction was predicated upon an over-estimation of the likely short-run effects upon employment in Canada. The eventual agreement among the countries concerned left Canada's position basically unchanged, although the benefits attained by the US can be expected to have a favourable effect on Canada. The US measures were introduced at a time when the trading arrangements between Canada and the USA were the subject of mutual review, with specific issues of contention such as the automotive agreement receiving special attention. This review is likely to have eventual long-term effects of great importance to Canada, as the final agreements will be important factors in determining the long-run nature of the trade balance between the two countries with attendant implications for capital flows and the degree of foreign ownership.

The establishment of the Prices and Incomes Commission during 1969 heralded a new course in the attempt to temper inflation.

Canada had been very reluctant to adopt an incomes policy of any type, despite the advocacy of such policies by the OECD (among others). The arguments against the establishment of such a body in Canada, besides the generally inconclusive record of such an approach to inflation in other countries, were stated by the Economic Council of Canada in its third Annual Review in 1966. The Council felt that, with the highly decentralized wage-system and with the openness of the economy to external factors, the use of an incomes policy in Canada would be advisable only as a temporary measure in urgent circumstances. The Council's assessment of the difficulties of applying an incomes policy seemed to be proved correct when the initial attempts by the Commission to convene a conference on price stability failed as a result of the decision of labour unions not to attend. At the same time the labour unions indicated that they would not adhere to any announced guidelines. After this initial failure, the Commission adopted a sequential approach, and succeeded in early 1970 in getting an agreement from business firms to minimize the size and number of price increases during the year and also from the Provinces to apply the proposals of the Commission as far as possible in their own jurisdiction. In the light of the refusal by labour unions to co-operate – which was, indeed, foreseeable, especially in the decentralized bargaining framework of the Canadian economy – there seems to be little likelihood of the Prices and Incomes Commission having any more than a marginal impact on the rate of increase of prices and costs. In the United States, experience with guidelines suggested that they could be useful in the early stages of an expansion in slowing the acceleration of price and cost changes, but were unlikely to be successful in a later period, when the cost and price increases were well established. If this reasoning can be applied to Canada, the introduction in 1969 of an incomes policy lacking any means of direct control was unlikely to have any major effect, given the stage that the upsurge of prices had reached. A lack of success would also endanger the credibility of the instrument for use at a more suitable time. Another important objective of the Commission is to study the inflationary process in Canada; to advise the government on problems related to inflation; and generally to improve the public understanding of the nature of the problem. It is in relation to these longer-run aspects that the Prices and Incomes Commission is likely to have the best hope of making a significant contribution to overcoming the problem of inflation.

The scope of regional economic policy was rationalized and enlarged during the year. Major events included the establishment of the Federal Department of Regional Economic Expansion and the passage of the Regional Development Incentives Act. The basic approach adopted with these developments was the making of capital grants for the establishment of new facilities or the expansion or modernization of existing secondary manufacturing in 'designated regions', and development plans for 'special areas'. The 'designated regions' were chosen after consultation with the Provinces and included certain regions (some in each Province) with unusually inadequate employment opportunities, but with good prospects of capital grants making a significant contribution to their economic expansion. 'Special areas' differ from 'designated regions' in that for 'special areas' development plans were to be prepared and possibly also some assistance given in the building up of the infrastructure. With the adoption of this long-term approach to regional expansion, stabilization policy, in so far as it has regional differences, is likely to be increasingly attuned to the problems produced by inflationary pressures developing in the areas of low unemployment. To the extent that this frontal attack on regional imbalances is successful, macro-economic policy will be somewhat easier to frame in the 1970s.

ISSUES FOR FUTURE POLICY

With the exception of prices and incomes policy, the successful use of macro-economic policy in the future is not likely to hinge upon the development or adoption of completely new policy instruments; for the record of the 1960s indicates that there is a full range of instruments available for use. Price and cost stability will, however, continue to be a major problem, and it is here that the existing policy instruments are least useful. Until a more successful approach to prices and incomes policy is developed, the most important contribution to price stability that macro-economic policy in Canada can make is still the avoidance of periods of excessive demand; for the price increases generated in such periods continue for a lengthy period afterwards; and this produces especially difficult problems in the timing of policy changes.

Regional imbalances and other structural problems, as well as federal-Provincial relations, all present special problems in the use of macro-economic policy. The adoption of long-term plans to redress the regional imbalances and to reduce some of the structural rigidities should provide a better environment for the use of stabilization. One important feature of a regionalized stabilization policy requiring special attention is the application of restrictive measures to those regions in which stresses first appear. If this approach is to be used, a set of continuing measures is needed, rather than a series of '*ad hoc*' arrangements.

Finally some of the burden of macro-economic policy will need to be carried by the Provinces if their share of expenditures grows further and if some form of regional approach to stabilization is used. This would not necessarily (or even preferably) be in the form of a decision-making role for the Provinces, but merely of some arrangement to modify their expenditure to an appropriate extent.

Select Bibliography

The following annual publications provide a commentary on changes in various economic sectors and some discussion of policy.

Bank of Canada, *Annual Report of Governor to the Minister of Finance*, Ottawa, Bank of Canada.
Economic Council of Canada, *Annual Review*.

Budget Papers
Organization for Economic Co-operation and Development, *Country Studies, Canada*.

The following selection of articles and books, while by no means a comprehensive listing of books on Canadian macro-economic policy since 1958, provides a cross-section touching upon all the major points in the body of the discussion.

R. E. Artus, 'Canada Pegs its Dollar', *The Banker*, vol. 112, 1962, p. 492.
Clarence L. Barber, 'Canada's Unemployment Problem', *Canadian Journal of Economics and Political Science*, vol. XXVIII, no. 1, February 1962.
H. H. F. Birhammer, 'Canada's Money Muddle in Retrospect', *Dalhousie Review*, vol. 44, no. 2, Summer 1964.
H. H. F. Birhammer, 'Canada's Foreign Exchange Problems: A Review', *Kyklos*, vol. XVII, no. 4, 1964.
J. J. Deutsch, 'Canada's Economic Problems', *Queen's Quarterly*, vol. LXVIII, no. 4, Winter 1962.
H. G. Gordon, *The Economists Versus the Bank of Canada*, Ryerson Press, Toronto, 1961.
H. G. Johnson, 'Economic Nationalism in Canadian Policy', *Lloyds Bank Review*, no. 74, October 1964.
E. P. Neufeld, 'Disowning Canada's Dear Money', *The Banker*, vol. 109, 1959, p. 660.
E. P. Neufeld, 'Canada Tackles its Deficits', *The Banker*, London, August 1962.
W. Pool, 'The Stability of the Canadian Flexible Exchange Rate, 1950–1962', *Canadian Journal of Economics and Political Science*, vol. 33, May 1967.
Royal Commission on Banking and Finance, Queen's Printer, Ottawa, 1964.
David, W. Slater, 'Canada's Troubled Prosperity', *The Banker*, vol. 114, 1964, p. 625.
David W. Slater, 'Capital Flows into Canada', *The Canadian Banker*, vol. 70, no. 4, Winter 1963.
David C. Smith, *Incomes Policies: Some Foreign Experience and Their Relevance for Canada*, 1966.
John H. Young, 'Credit Conditions and the Bank of Canada', *The Canadian Banker*, vol. 74, Spring 1967, pp. 198–207.

Chapter 4

NEW ZEALAND

J. W. ROWE

International transactions are an important potential source of instability for the New Zealand economy, as exports of goods and services make up about a quarter of New Zealand's Gross Domestic Product, and they are predominantly primary products subject to considerable price variations. But since World War II employment and production in New Zealand have fluctuated less than in most countries, and unemployment has been consistently small, if not insignificant.

In terms of economic growth, of external balance, and in more recent years inflation, the record is much less satisfactory. Indeed, early in the 1970s a full employment rate of growth with a reasonably stable price level appears to be much harder to achieve than it would have done a decade earlier; for cost–push inflation has now become – in New Zealand as elsewhere – a serious obstacle to the achievement of internal balance.

The record during the 1960s
In calculating trends over a period (by the terminal year method), or in drawing comparisons (of a non-cyclical nature) between one year and another, it is important to select years that are reasonably comparable in terms of the balance of payments and the general level of activity. As internal fluctuations have been small in New Zealand, the main consideration is that of external influences on the economy. 1959/60 and 1969/70 (April–March years) are, however, fairly closely comparable; for both 1959/60 and 1969/70 were years of uninterrupted expansion, and in both of them (unusually for New Zealand) a balance of payments surplus eventuated.[1]

According to a recent study by the Reserve Bank of New Zealand using reference cycle techniques, the sixties began with the economy recovering from a recession centred on March 1959. This expansion spanned two years, followed by another year-long recession lasting

[1] 1968/9 was even more closely comparable with 1959/60, but not sufficiently so to offset the advantage of dealing with a whole decade.

until April 1962. Then until December 1966 there was a long expansion followed by a short recession up to December 1967. From this trough economic activity expanded continuously until the end of the decade and at an accelerating rate. Indicator analysis does not lend itself well to quantitative interpretation, but this study suggests that in the period 1959–61 the rate of expansion was about twice as strong as in the period 1962–6. That is to say, about the same increase in activity occurred in 1959–61 as in 1962–6, but in 1959–61 it took only half as long. In this respect the most recent upswing (1967–70) resembles that of 1962–6 in being moderate in its rate of expansion as well as in its duration. The decade thus encompasses two complete cycles and most of the upswing portion of a third.

The sixties were notable for the activation of fiscal policy, more or less in step with an acceptance of the view that monetary policy – at least as it had been applied in New Zealand – was relatively ineffective and likely to remain so. There was also some weakening of the confidence of the government in the usefulness of direct controls, particularly import licensing. Generally, the emphasis shifted somewhat from stability to growth, which paralleled the growing recognition that new export markets must be found as well as old ones preserved, even before the National Development Conference emphasized this view in 1968. The sacred cows of full employment and social welfare were still worshipped, but with rather less fervour than in the fifties, and the need for high nominal interest rates became more generally accepted. Overall, economic policy was unadventurous – in keeping with the philosophy of the ruling National Party which retained power from November 1960 onwards, following a (three-year) term in office by the Labour Party, which throughout the post-war period has been the only other political party of any significance.

In terms of growth the decade was undistinguished. GDP per head in real terms rose on the average by 2·3 per cent per annum, or 2·1 per cent per annum if allowance is made for the slight deterioration in the terms of trade over the period as a whole. Since net factor payments abroad increased quite rapidly, GNP grew a little more slowly than did GDP. During the period population growth averaged 1·8 per cent per annum, with natural increase accounting for 1·4 per cent per annum. (The above growth rates are derived from a comparison of decade terminal years, as in Table 4.1 and Table 4.2.)

Growth was by no means regular, with decreases in effective GNP per head occurring in three years, but with increases of over 4 per cent in three other years. But real GDP per head increased in

Table 4.1. *New Zealand: Economic growth 1959/60–1969/70 per cent per annum*

GDP at current prices	7·1
GDP at 1954/5 prices	4·1
GDP per head at 1954/5 prices	2·3
Effective GDP at 1954/5 prices*	3·9
Effective GDP per head at 1954/5 prices*	2·1
Effective GDP per head at 1954/5 prices*	2·0

Source: New Zealand Department of Statistics

* 'Effective' signifies that these items are adjusted for changes in the terms of trade; that is to say, exports of goods and services are revalued at import prices instead of export prices.

Table 4.2. *New Zealand: Price indexes 1959/60–1969/70* (*April–March years*)

	Annual average rate of increase (per cent)
Retail prices	3·3
Wholesale prices	2·5
Wholesale prices: home produced goods only	2·4
Wholesale prices: imported goods only	2·6
Import prices	2·3
Export prices	1·0
GDE implicit deflator	3·1
GDP implicit deflator	2·0

Source: New Zealand Department of Statistics

every year except 1968/9, and increases of more than 4 per cent occurred in five years. Since the labour force rose roughly in line with population, productivity grew at much the same rate as real GDP per head. Although reliable estimates of real GDP, etc., exist only from 1954/5, it seems clear that productivity growth in the sixties was greater than in the fifties; and the essential aim of the National Development Conference exercise (initiated in 1968 and concluded in 1969) is to raise it further to a consistent rate of $2\frac{1}{2}$ per cent per annum. This will not, however, be easy in face of the inevitable trading difficulties that are to be expected in the next few years.

Generally, the decade was characterized by neither the sort of stability conducive to a quiet life nor by dynamic instability conducive to a rapid re-allocation of resources. Exports and other current receipts abroad grew at an average annual rate of 7 per cent, and total current payments at 8 per cent – the latter fluctuating almost as much as the former. Incidentally, the long run of recorded balance of payments deficits up to 1967/8 is a little misleading, as the official estimates do not include as credits most income from portfolio investment overseas, notably that earned in Australia. This is counted only if it accrues to New Zealand companies or if earnings are repatriated. One can only speculate on the magnitude of this bias, but it could amount to $50 million per annum at the present time. During the sixties direct private investment from abroad was modest, commonly amounting to only $40 million, mainly in the form of reinvested profits. Generally the New Zealand balance of payments in this period was seriously out of balance only in a few years, but by 1967 the situation had reached the point where devaluation was necessary to restore confidence in the New Zealand dollar. The spectacular improvement in the following years suggests that a new basis now exists for equilibrium, but at the time of writing it is too soon to be sure.

One of the best historical correlations in the New Zealand economy is that between imports of goods and services on the one hand and gross domestic expenditure plus exports on the other, even when both are measured in terms of first differences, that is to say, annual changes.[2] In view of the high elasticity of demand for imports it is not surprising that New Zealand found difficulty in achieving balance of payments stability, at least prior to devaluation.

Internally the period saw considerable price inflation, but no more than in many countries. As may be seen from Table 4.2, retail prices increased more than wholesale prices (as they have in most countries), and wholesale prices in turn by more than import or export prices, with increases in money income in excess of productivity accounting for about two-thirds of retail price inflation.

The period was notable for a uniformly high degree of employment by world standards, although unemployment figures in New Zealand,

[2] For the period 1954/5–1969/70 the coefficient of determination on this basis is 96 per cent, and the regression restated in terms of GDP points to a 'normal' rise of $128 in imports for every $100 increase in GDP. The constant term is of course negative.

being based on registrations, understate the number of people out of work at any one time. Conditions in the labour market clearly change more sharply than unemployment registrations indicate. Thus in 1968 a higher proportion of children than usual went back to school instead of seeking work, and it seems that some married women and superannuitants simply dropped out of the labour force – the former no doubt only temporarily. By any standard, however, male unemployment in New Zealand was very low in the sixties, as the following comparison shows.

Table 4.3. *Male unemployment*

(*Thousands*)

	Registered unemployed	Census figure	Work force	Registered (per cent)	Census (per cent)
April 1961	0·2	4·7	671	0·3	0·7
April 1966	0·4	5·1	746	0·5	0·7

Source: New Zealand Department of Statistics.

Another New Zealand indicator that is of interest is migration. In the fifties there was usually a net population gain from this source of about 10,000 a year, equivalent to nearly ½ per cent of total population and more in terms of workers. This situation changed sharply in 1968 and 1969, when there was net emigration of roughly the same order, but earlier years also showed that net immigration is sensitive to internal economic conditions.

The foremost constraint on New Zealand's economic development, at least in the short and medium term, is the level of export receipts. Since farm products still account for the great bulk of all exports, this is inseparably linked with freedom of access to markets. With minor exceptions, however, the last decade was not marked by significantly greater difficulties in finding export markets. Agricultural protectionism in Western Europe, North America and Australia showed itself rather in depressed prices for some products. Over the period as a whole prices rose strongly for meat and weakly for dairy produce, but wool prices declined markedly. Exports other than meat, wool and dairy produce fared slightly better than the pastoral average, but the contribution was too small to affect appreciably the price index for total exports.

Import prices are largely determined by factors outside New Zealand. But changes in the pattern of imports, induced by import licensing and other policies and by New Zealand's economic development generally, have during the past decade modified the influence of movements in import prices upon the New Zealand economy. In broad terms, prices of imported raw materials and semi-manufactured goods rose less than those of finished goods, and the pattern of imports changed in the direction of more raw materials and semi-manufactured goods. As a result of this, the rise in import prices did not have a great impact on the domestic price level prior to the devaluation of 1967.

The devaluation of sterling in November 1967 was perhaps the most spectacular outside influence on New Zealand during the 1960s. It came at a time of weakness in internal demand as well as in export prices. It was therefore no surprise that the government took the opportunity to devalue by more than the United Kingdom, to an extent that brought the New Zealand dollar to parity with that of Australia. This is best regarded as being an *ex post* recognition of the state of the economy rather than as a policy initiative, but it facilitated a marked increase in non-traditional exports (particularly to Australia), which had already been encouraged by export tax incentives and a slack level of demand within New Zealand.

Since availability of foreign exchange is one of the main constraints on economic growth in New Zealand, the trend of expenditure abroad in relation to GNP is important. In the sixties expenditure on goods increased much more slowly than other expenditure abroad, particularly servicing charges in respect of public and private borrowing. In this sense, therefore, import substitution did take place; but in real terms there is no evidence of a significant downward trend in total expenditure abroad relative to GNP. Such a trend is evident in money terms, but only because internal prices rose faster than import prices.

The sixties saw a marked change in the distribution of income, with labour gaining at the expense of capital, and farmers losing in relation to other producers. Salaries and wages as a proportion of national income rose fairly consistently from 58 per cent to 63 per cent, whereas the share of farm incomes fell, again fairly consistently, from 14 per cent to 7 per cent. The share of company and public authority earnings and other returns on capital rose by 4 per cent, whereas other earned incomes fell by 2 per cent. On a reasonable apportionment of mixed incomes between labour rewards and capital returns, it appears that the total share of labour in national income rose from 75 per cent in 1959/60 to 77 per cent in 1969/70. By way of comparison, the share of labour in 1949/50 was no more than 73 per cent. These rises are partly attributable to the steady trend towards corporate organization at the expense of self-employment, but the declining share of farmers during the sixties was generally because this was a decade when national income per head rose by 56 per cent, while income per head in farming fell by 5 per cent. Towards the end of the decade wage inflation gathered pace, culminating in a 20 per cent rise in salaries and wages in 1970/1; but this is a problem for the seventies rather than a characteristic of the sixties.

The proportion of the work force engaged in primary industry fell in the sixties from 17 per cent to 13 per cent, in continuation of a long-term trend. This was entirely offset by a rise in the share of tertiary industry, the total of manufacturing, building and construction remaining constant at 38 per cent.

To sum up, the period was characterized by relatively slow growth, a generally buoyant internal market and sharp fluctuations in export receipts. Prices rose quite markedly, but almost everyone had jobs and New Zealand was a comfortable place in which to live. The endemic pressure on the balance of payments culminated in several near crises, which provoked sharp fiscal intervention, stiffer monetary policies and in 1967 devaluation. At no stage were imports or other external transactions entirely freed from controls, but the severity of import licensing and/or exchange control varied with the level of overseas reserves. Currently policy is directed towards increasing the country's export earnings and a higher real growth rate, and there is hope of a more balanced internal demand situation.

As in many other countries, however, these orthodox policy aims are now overshadowed by industrial unrest and excessive wage inflation. The former threatens at any moment to erupt in a major confrontation between militant unions and the government. Wage inflation in 1971 is not as rapid as in 1970 but it is not clear whether this is attributable to the creation of the Remuneration Authority early in 1971. This body is independent of the government, but is charged with the responsibility of ensuring that salary and wage settlements do not normally exceed a 7 per cent legislative guideline. The Authority is evidently an *ad hoc* body necessitated by the breakdown of traditional wage-fixing procedures under the aegis of a Court of Arbitration. A more permanent successor to the Arbitration Court has yet to be agreed upon by the government, the Employers' Association and the Federation of Labour.

FISCAL POLICY

During the sixties official assessments of fiscal and most other economic policies were normally made in the *Annual Economic Survey* immediately preceding the budget (presented in June or July), which articulated policy for the following year. Changes in fiscal instruments were generally made (or at least announced) at budget time, along with major variations in monetary policy, though changes of a minor routine nature (including alterations in charges for public services) were made as and when necessary. But in early 1967 and late 1970 mini-budgets, embodying important changes in budgetary policy, were presented in response to rapidly deteriorating economic conditions. Indeed, since 1967, there have been conscious attempts to spread policy changes more evenly over the year, with a view to minimizing policy-induced fluctuations.

The 1960 *Survey* observed that some reflation was desirable following the 1958/9 recession, and this was reflected in the provision for a fiscal deficit for 1959/60. At the same time there were already signs that economic activity might be expanding too rapidly. The 1960 *Survey* included the following paragraph, which was meant to look back to the fifties, but in fact anticipated the sixties. The last sentence in particular sounds oddly naive at the present time, when unity of purpose is notably lacking.

'The conclusion which emerges from the review of economic policy measures over the past decade is that more might have been done to achieve a steadier trend of economic growth. This would have required the maintenance of a more adequate level of overseas reserves and greater emphasis on policies directed towards the avoidance of inflationary pressures. A greater awareness of these problems would facilitate the adoption of policies likely to lead to their solution with maximum advantage to all sections of the community.'[3]

In considering fiscal policy, a convenient starting point is personal taxation, the most politically sensitive instrument. In the 1960 budget the only significant change was the substantial abolition of the aggregation procedure whereby the incomes of husbands and wives were treated virtually as one income for tax purposes. In the next budget practically nothing was changed, but 1962 saw some minor increases in personal exemptions and minor reductions in

[3] *N.Z. Economic Survey, 1960*, pp. 46–47.

taxation, as well as a modest scheme exempting from tax certain charitable and similar donations. This scheme was extended in the following year and again in 1969, but it is still modest. In 1963 a further reduction in rates of tax by way of an *ad valorem* rebate came into effect, but there were no changes of importance the next year, nor in the following one.

In 1966 the government appointed a taxation review committee, rather than deciding on any significant tax changes, and for the first time the government gave public recognition to the view that 'high' taxation was an inevitable feature of a modern society, and that consequently the basic issue was what should be the tax structure rather than what the quantum of taxes should be. The committee's work was not completed at the time of the 1967 budget, and when it reported in late 1967 the government could not swallow all its recommendations, or indeed the essential one, which was that more emphasis should be placed on indirect taxation. A start with tax reform was none the less made in the 1968 budget with a decision to reduce the steepness of the progression of rates of personal income tax, and to reduce personal exemptions, but in such a way as to yield much the same overall revenue. The budget of 1969 made no change, but 1970 saw a further reduction in the tax progression to a maximum of 50 per cent compared with 65 per cent, and an increase in the tax exemption for a wife. A change of major importance was that dividends were henceforth to be treated as ordinary income in the hands of individual taxpayers. Previously dividend tax rates had been subject to an upper limit at such a rate as to ensure that the combined rate of company tax and dividend tax was no higher than the maximum rate of personal income tax. The political benefits of these changes were considerably offset shortly afterwards by the announcement of a temporary surcharge on personal income but (to the surprise of many people) this was removed eight months later, as originally scheduled. The 1971 budget effected no other substantial change.

Throughout the sixties tax exemptions were allowed for life assurance premiums or other superannuation contributions, the amount exempted rising more or less in step with incomes from $NZ 350 per annum to $NZ 700 per annum, and in more recent years the self-employed have been able to claim rather more than taxpayers belonging to superannuation schemes subsidized by employers. Over the period there was also some increase in the (small) amount of interest income that is exempt from tax. Rates of estate duties and some similar taxes have also been moderated, but the rise of asset values resulting from inflation has offset the effect of this on tax receipts.

The main issue on which the 1966 taxation review committee and the government failed to see eye to eye was indirect taxation. The former proposed that this be raised substantially in order to compensate for reductions in income tax. While not immediately accepting this in principle, the government on various occasions in the decade of the 1960s (notably in 1967 and 1970) raised indirect taxes and/or reduced subsidies: but (as is noted below) over the period as a whole the yield from indirect taxation did not increase as fast as that from direct taxation. Earlier in the period considerations of equity accounted for this emphasis on direct taxation: more recently, increases in indirect tax rates have been thought undesirable as being more likely to lead to price rises than are increases in direct rates.

No significant change in the structure of corporate income tax took place in the sixties – the maximum rate remaining at 50 per cent throughout – but a controversial pay-roll tax was imposed in 1970. This was a flat 2 per cent on nearly all remuneration, and it was not deductible for income-tax purposes, so that for the average company of any size it was equivalent to about 5 per cent of pre-tax profits on a deductible basis. The pattern of incidence naturally differed greatly from industry to industry, and a declared aim of the tax was to encourage labour saving – on the grounds that labour was currently the most scarce resource. It is questionable whether the tax has done much in this direction, but it has certainly yielded a lot of revenue and irritated a lot of people. There has been some ambivalence in official circles about whether it should be viewed as a direct or indirect tax.

Now that the need for extra revenue as a disinflationary measure is less pressing, the government may well consider it appropriate to combine the continuance of the pay-roll tax, possibly at a higher rate, with some reduction in company tax – perhaps to the Australian level, which is marginally lower than in New Zealand. There could be merit in a payroll tax that effectively encouraged economies in the use of labour but the present tax is not much use in this respect.

For many years New Zealand has had a plethora of investment incentives and similar provisions designed to encourage particular industries, regions or sections of the community. Thus in 1960 a special depreciation allowance on plant and machinery of 20 per cent, spread over five years was re-introduced. An analogous provision was implemented for certain farm buildings in the following year and extended in 1962 to cover much capital expenditure on farms as well as tangible investments in industry. Depending on the level of internal economic activity, prospects overseas and the sectoral distribution of income, such incentives were varied from time to time during the decade. Except in farming there is little evidence that they had much effect on production, productivity and employment.

In the 1963 budget the government announced measures to stimulate exports – tax concessions on increases of earnings abroad, promotion of tourism, export development expenditure and export credit insurance. These did not become fully effective until the following year and the key measure – the export tax concession – was liberalized in 1966 and is still operative today. Throughout the period monetary policy was also biased in favour of exports. However, the 1967 devaluation proved to be much more galvanic than these various measures on their own.

Other taxation innovations during the sixties include tighter regulation of trusts; various measures, some in the nature of gimmicks, to encourage saving in the face of artificially low administered rates of interest; and efforts to make government trading departments finance a higher proportion of their capital requirements from revenue. From time to time death duties were reduced, more or less in line with inflation and increases in real wealth. (There is no tax on capital or capital gains in New Zealand.)

Overall assessment

Table 4.4 summarizes the fiscal outcome in the period 1959/60–1969/70 in current prices. (The appendix to this chapter discusses some of the conceptual as well as practical difficulties of any macro-economic appraisal of fiscal policy.) Some immediate observations suggest themselves. 1967/8 resulted in easily the smallest expenditure increase (1%), but 1961/2 was the year of greatest fiscal restraint in terms of the deficit before borrowing. A large internal surplus eventuated in 1964/5, a year in which expenditure (and revenue) rose sharply. Internal borrowing (net) was clearly much more variable than either expenditure or revenue. It will also be noted that the deficit before borrowing and (especially) the internal deficit appear to have fallen in relation to expenditure or revenue during the period. In the case of the former this is an accident of timing; deficits before borrowing in 1959/60 and 1960/1 were high compared with those obtaining in the late fifties. In the case of the internal balance the swing into surplus in 1964/5 and the surpluses achieved in the last three years are largely if not entirely attributable to

Table 4.4. *New Zealand: Fiscal transactions*
($NZ million)

Year ended March	Expenditure	Revenue	Deficit before borrowing	Internal borrowing (net)	Internal deficit (−) or surplus (+)
1960	811	717	94	66	−28
1961	864	785	79	84	+5
1962	901	835	66	32	−34
1963	935	814	121	106	−15
1964	991	878	113	113	—
1965	1,082	993	89	158	+69
1966	1,164	1,055	109	93	−16
1967	1,271	1,138	133	89	−44
1968	1,287	1,173	114	120	+6
1969	1,358	1,237	121	157	+36
1970	1,481	1,388	93	116	+23

Source: New Zealand Treasury.

institutional changes resulting in the activation of idle bank deposits. In 1964/5 the trading banks were allowed to establish savings bank subsidiaries provided that at least 70 per cent of their deposits were invested in government stock. At the same time trustee savings banks were granted more freedom; together these developments activated perhaps $50 NZ million of formerly idle money. More recently trading banks have been permitted to raise their the holdings of government securities and to subscribe to treasury bills (which were formerly just a device to facilitate Reserve Bank lending to the treasury) and a wide range of financial institutions have become subject to compulsory government stock ratios, which greatly facilitated government borrowing – almost certainly without a fully offsetting reduction in private spending. Indeed, the operations of financial institutions generally succeeded in activating idle bank balances, partly by offering higher rates of interest, with dramatic consequences for the velocity of circulation. This rose from 3·7 in 1960 to 6·2 in 1970, measuring velocity in terms of GNP relative to money supply narrowly defined (that is to say notes, coin and trading bank demand deposits).

The definition of the government sector can be wide or narrow, depending on the purposes of the analysis. Generally, the public accounts offer an appropriate coverage. These take in all administrative functions and a considerable proportion of government trading activities but exclude public corporations, which are to some extent responsive to short-run changes in fiscal policy, but generally public corporations behave more like private sector agencies than instruments of government. In some respects the social accounting treatment of central government activities is preferable to that in the public accounts, and in many ways the accounts of the government sector are the best of all. The compilation of the accounts of the public sector is, however, now several years behind schedule and the treatment of central government activities in the social accounts does not embrace capital transfers nor differentiate between internal and external borrowing. A further justification for analysing government activities in terms of the public accounts is that this is how those responsible for fiscal policy and its execution do so. The public accounts as published include some transfers internal to the accounts, but these have been netted out in Table 4.4 and subsequent tables. The public accounts of course include transfers to local authorities but otherwise do not embrace the activities of local government.

Further evaluation of fiscal intervention requires analysis of revenue and expenditure. For the former, the obvious categories are (1) direct taxes; (2) indirect taxes; and (3) miscellaneous receipts, notably profits from trading (which depend basically on charges fixed for publicly provided goods and services). In the absence of policy changes, direct taxes tend to increase faster than incomes because of the progression in income taxation, whereas both indirect taxes and miscellaneous receipts tend to increase at the same rate as outlays. For government expenditure another three-fold classification is indicated: (1) monetary transfers to persons; (2) other current spending; and (3) capital expenditure. These also have a built-in tendency to rise over time (in the absence of policy changes), but in a complex manner, depending *inter alia* on population growth and structure, the timing of public sector works programmes and the level of activity in the private sector.

Expenditure

Table 4.6 analyses expenditure according to the above classification and also shows annual increases in total spending. On the basis of the norm of a 5 per cent per annum rate of growth proposed in the appendix to this chapter, it appears that in only three years did total government spending increase no faster than the trend rate of growth of the economy in real terms plus a minimal allowance for inflation. In 1961/2 all three categories rose roughly in step with one another

Table 4.5. *New Zealand: Analysis of government revenue*
($NZ million)

Year ended March	Direct taxation	Indirect taxation	Miscellaneous revenue	Total
1960	378	221	118	717
1961	445	225	115	785
1962	487	230	118	835
1963	458	227	129	814
1964	491	252	141	884
1965	571	273	149	993
1966	632	286	137	1,055
1967	691	299	148	1,138
1968	699	314	161	1,174
1969	718	340	179	1,237
1970	808	373	207	1,388

Source: New Zealand Treasury

but in the following year a sharp increase in 'other current spending' took place. Only by a virtual standstill in transfers to persons and in capital expenditure was the total increase kept in line with the economy's absorptive capacity (as indicated by the suggested norm). In 1967/8 however, other current spending was effectively checked and capital expenditure was cut substantially in order to permit a big increase in transfers to persons, whilst still holding down the increase in the total to the smallest in the whole post-war period.

A notable feature of fiscal policy in the sixties as a whole was the much greater rise in current spending on goods and services than in capital expenditure which in turn rose more than transfers to persons. The slow growth of the last of these was largely a consequence of holding family benefits unchanged throughout the decade. To some extent the relatively small rise in central government capital expenditure reflects certain transfers to local authorities that are in fact for capital purposes, but which are classed in the public accounts as current expenditure. Major reasons for the greater rise in current than in capital expenditures are the tendency (in New Zealand at least) for government activities to multiply and never die, and the sharp escalation of public service salaries and wages in the last two years, largely as a result of the adoption of automatic six-monthly reviews based on surveys of remuneration in the private sector (but with growing evidence that government salaries are now in many cases heading the field).

In every year in which total expenditure rose rapidly current expenditure rose by more than the norm of 5 per cent, and capital expenditure did so in all but one of these years. On the other hand, transfers to persons exceeded the norm in only one year. Capital expenditure was naturally the most variable of the three broad categories of government spending. But neither it nor transfers to persons was the main factor in making fiscal policy in the sixties generally expansionary. The analysis of current government spending in Table 4.6 shows that education, interest on the public debt,

Table 4.6. *New Zealand: Analysis of government current spending*
($NZ million)

	1960	1970	Per cent change
Education	79	196	149
Health	91	203	123
Other social services	36	52	43
Defence	58	106	83
Administration	62	114	83
Stabilization	25	17	−32
Maintenance of works, etc.	25	42	71
Development of industry	37	81	119
Interest on public debt	58	145	149
Sub-total	470	956	103
less Capital expenditure included in the above item	36	74	106
Current expenditure	435	882	103

Source: New Zealand Treasury.

health and development of industry were the broad categories with the most marked expenditure increases. The only category to show an absolute decrease was 'stabilization', that is to say, consumer subsidies.

The conclusion so far is that fiscal policy was a generally in-flationary influence in the sixties. To complete the story we may ask in what years there was any slack in the economy and whether in these years fiscal policy tended to stimulate activity and thereby minimize the amount of slack. In terms of real GNP the only years in which growth was significantly below the long-term average of 4 per cent per annum were 1962/3, 1967/8 and 1968/9. In the first of these years the rise in government expenditure was well below the norm, but there was also an absolute reduction in revenue, partly attributable to low receipts from taxation and other sources of revenue, so that overall fiscal policy was neutral.

In 1967 the rise in expenditure was also well below average; indeed, the recession of that year was largely attributable to fiscal policy. It may be argued that deflation was carried too far but at the time a fairly severe check seemed necessary to prick the bubble of the preceding years and to give devaluation a change of working. In retrospect it would also seem that fiscal policy could advantageously have been made more expansionary in the following year, and by the same token less expansionary in 1969/70.

Revenue

At the beginning of the sixties direct taxation accounted for 53 per cent of total revenue compared with 31 per cent for indirect taxation. By the end of the decade the corresponding proportions were 58 and 27 per cent. (Indirect taxation in this case is gross; with subsidies netted out the decline is from 28 to 26 per cent.) It should be noted that in Table 4.5 (which is the source for the above comparison)

Table 4.7. *New Zealand: Holdings of government bonds*

($NZ million)

	1960	1970
Government holdings	1072	1445
Financial system	240	934
Other private	314	266
Overseas	273	526
Total	1899	3171

Source: Reserve Bank of New Zealand.

proceeds of the pay-roll tax introduced in 1969 are treated as indirect taxation. But for this the contribution of indirect taxation would have been greatly reduced in that year. The tendency for domestic expenditure to rise faster than imports (both in money terms) coupled with the fact that most customs and related duties are *ad valorem* (though some are specific) is a partial explanation for the relative decline in the contribution of indirect taxation; but for the most part it reflects the steep progression in personal income taxation in this period and the institutionally embodied tendency for wages to be linked to consumer prices including (net) indirect taxes.

Total revenue in the sixties varied in a generally appropriate (inverse) manner to that of activity generally. It is, however, difficult to see that fiscal policy on the revenue side had much effect in promoting economic development or stability in the sixties. It seems to have reacted to changes in activity rather than activated offsetting movements in demand.

MONETARY POLICY

For many years monetary policy in New Zealand has been bedevilled by an odd mixture of socialist-cum-social-credit nonsense which has effectively prevented the evolution of rational and timely policies. It has also inhibited the growth of the most economical and responsible institutions in the field (the commercial banks), with the inevitable result that fringe agencies have flourished by virtue of their being less amendable to controls rather than through any intrinsic comparative advantage.

In respect of money transfers, however, the commercial banks have broken through with a computerized cheque-clearing and credit transfer mechanism linking all branches of all banks in the country. Apart from the general economic advantages of such a system, this has effected a sharp reduction in the trading float – that is, the value of cheques already credited to customers' accounts but not yet debited – and thereby reduced the liquidity of the private sector. In consequence, monetary policy in the change-over period was more restrictive than is indicated by statistics of advances and deposits.

A basic tenet of monetary policy in New Zealand has been, and still is to a lesser degree, that variations in trading bank advances (overdrafts) are a major cause of fluctuations in economic activity. From this simple hypothesis, and the fact that in the post-war period economic activity has almost always been excessive, it would follow that a prime aim of policy should be to hold down increases in advances. This was, indeed, the case for most of the sixties, and it is therefore not surprising that advances declined over the period in relation to GNP from about 14 per cent to about 12 per cent.

There is, however, little evidence that this policy did much to minimize fluctuations, and it was certainly not conducive to growth or price stability. It is possible, of course, that economic activity would have fluctuated more had bank advances not been so constrained; but it is equally plausible that the velocity of circulation increased *pari passu* with cuts in bank lending. This latter view seems especially likely to be valid for New Zealand in view of the strenuous official efforts to hold down interest rates well below market levels. On the other hand, it might be argued that the relatively undeveloped capital market in New Zealand would limit the extent to which a bank credit squeeze could be offset by increased lending through other financial institutions: but the nature of the controls (where they exist) on such institutions, the rapid rate of growth of their lendings, and the consequent rise in the velocity of circulation, are strong evidence against this counter-argument. Until satisfactory official estimates of national income and expenditure aggregates are available on a quarterly basis, it will be difficult to persuade the government that bank advances may be merely a lagged indicator of economic activity. Even if such data do show that rises in economic activity generally ante-date rises in bank lending, no conclusive judgment will of course be possible, but it would tend to increase doubts about the direction of the causation being inevitably from advances to the level of demand.

In the early sixties monetary policy was focused on the trading banks, although capital issues regulations affecting all companies were in force until 1952, and there was an 'interest-on-deposits' order in force which limited interest paid by all firms with such liabilities, whilst savings banks were subject to various restrictions. Other financial institutions were subsequently brought within the ambit of direct control in one way or another, but at no stage were open-market operations undertaken on a significant scale. Presumably the official justification for this was the undeveloped nature of the capital market; but unwillingness to see interest rates rise would be an equally plausible reason for the avoidance of open market sales; and a general preference for direct controls over market mechanisms was probably the most cogent factor of all.

At first bank advances were constrained by a variable reserve ratio system. Under this arrangement the banks as a group were obliged to maintain on deposit with the central bank balances earning no interest, on a scale that depended on the relationship between the prevailing level of advances and the official view of their desirable level. The object of this exercise was primarily to prevent advances rising more rapidly than was felt to be desirable in the light of considerations of internal and external balance, because bank advances were seen as the primary causal or permissive factor in spending at home and abroad. The much less questionable connection between bank advances and the money supply (in a narrow sense) was also in the official mind.

Various other regulatory devices were necessary to make the control of advances effective, including controls over the extent to which banks could hold liquid assets abroad, an embargo on investment in government or local authority securities in New Zealand and a prohibition of lending other than on overdraft. At this stage there was no regulation of overdraft limits as distinct from drawings against these limits, and (perversely in a period of enforced scarcity) the maximum (average) overdraft interest rate was rigidly held down – for political reasons. Bank liabilities were also straight-jacketed through the denial to the banks of savings bank facilities and official discouragement of term deposits through the unrealistically low level of interest rates that was permitted.

Some measure of lagged response to official injunctions was secured from the banks, by forcing them into a position where they had to borrow from the central bank in order to maintain statutory deposits whenever their level of advances was thought too high, and by charging penal rates of interest on these loans from the central bank. The longer such controls were resorted to, however, the greater the scope for expansion by non-bank financial institutions, which were much less effectively constrained by limitations on capital issues and maximum deposit interest rates, as these controls were abolished for non-bank intermediaries in 1962. Direct controls on hire purchase terms had hardly any more success in checking the growth of fringe financial institutions. The government also endeavoured to control savings banks in a direct manner, but they were controlled much less stringently than the trading banks, and the controls over savings banks operated mainly through portfolio requirements and limitations on deposit interest rates. In this situation a rapid expansion was easily achieved by life assurance companies (which incidentally benefited greatly from tax concessions to policy holders on premiums paid), by building societies, especially those of the terminating type, and all financial institutions that were politically or administratively difficult to control.

Early in the sixties capital issues controls, which were not specifically directed against financial institutions, were relaxed and greater freedom was allowed in their deposit interest rates, matched by a belated recognition that interest on government loans was too low. Of more significance was an official admission that a short-term money market existed, followed in 1962 by its official recognition, when the usual lender-of-last resort facilities were made available to it from the central bank. The various measures consummated in that year were not, however, matched by any significant easing of the pressure on the trading banks. They were permitted in 1963 to administer themselves the details of selective advance control, by which effect was given to priorities laid down by the government for bank loans within the total that they were enjoined to observe; and term loans were authorized, though they were thereafter effectively discouraged from growing in line with demand by the unrealistic limitation on their total amount.

The 1963 budget admitted that the effectiveness of monetary policy, largely exercised through control of bank advances, had been weakened by the development of borrowing and lending outside the banking system. Banks were therefore to be encouraged to compete for term deposits by being allowed to invest in government securities an amount equal to any increase in these bonds. The effectiveness of this measure was, however, minimized by the then low rate of return on government stock and by the subsequent limitation placed on the extent of the investment permitted. In the same budget the banks were enjoined to reduce overdraft limits more or less *pro rata*, but this achieved little. Generally speaking, there was some improvement during the mid-sixties in the communication between the central bank and the trading banks on the details of what was expected of the latter.

Towards the end of 1965 the government took steps to extend the coverage of monetary policy, 'encouraging' a wide range of non-bank financial institutions to divert part of their funds into government securities. In the 1967 budget this encouragement was reinforced by applying capital issues controls to finance companies, but it would appear from the figures that these controls were effectively avoided in most cases. In the following year insurance companies and savings banks were permitted to substitute (to some extent) support of the local authority borrowing market and the housing market for additional investment in government securities.

Capital issues controls over finance companies were abolished in 1969 and a government stock ratio requirement substituted, as part of a package designed to improve the functioning of the financial system. At the same time treasury bills (3 months and 6 months) were introduced; these were meant to reduce the difficulties long experienced by financial institutions arising from the severe liquidity drain of the economy due to an abnormally large proportion of tax revenue being collected in March. The introduction (in the fifties) of Pay-As-You-Earn for new companies had not removed this problem entirely, because existing companies were allowed to continue paying tax on an annual basis. The introduction of treasury bills has had less effect than expected, mainly because the rates offered on them were not competitive and the trading banks have been the only significant users.

The 1969 budget gave trading banks much greater freedom in soliciting term deposits and investing the proceeds, coupled with greater responsibility for handling seasonal ebbs and flows of funds. At the same time the central bank indicated that it would change the basic reserve ratio requirements much less frequently than in the past. In short, a liquidity convention was on the way. Like so many other aspects of monetary policy, however, subsequent experience has to some extent belied early promise. In various ways the monetary authorities have been unwilling to face the consequences of a more freely operating system. In particular, the (average) interest rate permitted on overdrafts is still ridiculously low, and deposit interest rates are held too low for bank competition to be really effective. There are also still ceilings for non-priority advances and specific penalties on banks where loans to such borrowers exceed these ceilings.

A few years earlier the trading banks had been allowed to offer savings bank facilities once the trustee savings bank network spanned the country, and a little later banks were permitted to have finance company affiliates. The 1969 budget foreshadowed efforts to vary the asset structure of trustee savings banks in such a way as to conform with the increasing desire of the government to have a captive market for government securities – itself a consequence of unwillingness to raise interest rates to anything approaching market levels. The 1970 budget further extended public sector security requirements, notably to bring in building societies and private superannuation funds, and some prescribed ratios were increased, notably those applying to finance companies and life insurance companies. The 1971 budget announced approval of merchant banks operating in New Zealand, but it is not yet clear what this will mean in practice.

The upshot of all the changes in monetary policy in the last decade has been some easing of controls over trading banks and a great strengthening of control over a wide range of non-bank financial institutions, so that the system as a whole is now much more regulated than formerly. This has not so far appeared to check the growth of non-bank financial institutions, nor the rise in those interest rates that are not subject to direct controls. Some of the basic weaknesses evident in 1960 are still present. In particular, the unattractiveness of yields on public sector securities would make it impossible for the government to cover its deficits before borrowing if the captive market for government bonds did not exist. The preceding table indicates the extent of 'public' disenchantment with government securities in the sixties; the figures refer to holdings as at March 31st.

The sixties also saw sharply divergent trends in money supply and liquid assets which may be summed up as follows – the figures referring again to the end of March.

The velocity of circulation of the means of payment (effectively the first two categories in Table 4.8) during the decade varied greatly

Table 4.8. *New Zealand: Money supply*

	1960 $NZ m.	1970 $NZ m.
Notes and coin	142	169
Cheque deposits	523	595
Savings deposits	567	1125
Other demand deposits	40	110
Time and fixed deposits	253	864
Total	1633	2863
Increase of total over period (per cent)		75
Increase of GNP over period (per cent)		95

Source: Reserve Bank of New Zealand.

in relation to GNP, which itself rose less than the value of transactions. (GNP rose by 95 per cent, whereas the money supply rose by only 15 per cent, resulting in a 70 per cent increase in velocity.) By 1971 there were some signs of this process slowing down, but of course there is no mechanical constraint on the growth of liquid assets. Trade credit (often involuntary) appears to be the latest category to take off into rapid growth, partly in consequence of an increasing shortage of the means of payment. It is too soon yet to determine how much the efforts being made to 'lock in' bank deposits will slow down the growth of the business of non-bank financial institutions, but this must be a major factor leading the non-bank intermediaries to offer and charge much higher interest rates recently.

During the latter part of the sixties a two-tier system of classifying bank advances came into being, with farming and exports as the main elements of the top tier, which was virtually exempt from official restraint. The predictable result was that more and more advances found their way into this category, and the distinction between the two tiers has now been largely abandoned. This experience sums up in miniature the basic problem of monetary policy in the last decade. The failure to arrive at a full system of liquidity control over trading bank assets and liabilities, coupled with the prevailing official constraints on interest rates in the controlled segment of the financial system, has led inexorably to increasingly complex and pervasive constraints, exhortatory as well as effectual, on the financial system as a whole. In the process competition has been stifled, and the country may well have thereby suffered an ineffective and heavily lagged responsiveness to real needs (including the imposition of serious obstacles to technological innovation and adaption), and at the same time saddled itself with a system that has largely failed to achieve the control over demand that was intended.

THE DEVALUATION OF 1971

The New Zealand government's reaction to the various currency realignments of December 1971 was to devalue by $1\frac{3}{4}$ per cent against sterling. This brought about an overall devaluation of the same order, for the value of New Zealand's trade with the USA and with other countries whose currencies devalued with the US dollar against gold is of about the same value as that of trade with countries whose currencies appreciated in terms of gold.

In fact, New Zealand simply followed Australia's decision about the exchange rate parity; and it was clear that the New Zealand government was prepared to take almost any action to preserve the parity of the New Zealand dollar with the Australian dollar – which had been established in 1967 after the New Zealand pound has stood at a substantial premium against the Australian pound for over twenty years. There was not much public discussion of the New Zealand decision – partly, no doubt, because the announcement of it occurred on the eve of the Christmas holidays.

The wisdom of the decision to devalue was questionable. On the one hand (as was true also for Australia) the stimulus that it gave to the incomes of exporters – mainly farmers in New Zealand – was welcome because of the current problems of the pastoral industry. On the other hand, the further inflationary pressure that would result from a devaluation could only hamper the government's so far largely ineffectual efforts to reduce cost–push inflation to a tolerable rate.

The officially notified par value against gold (and so the official relationship between sterling and the Australian and the New Zealand dollars) remained unchanged, because New Zealand and Australia both took advantage of the new IMF procedure of allowing a band of 2¼ per cent either side of the official par value to quote a rate for day-to-day transactions that was at the lower end of the permitted range. It was also decided that New Zealand – again like Australia – would henceforth quote the rate of exchange for her currency in terms of US dollars instead of sterling (which might perhaps be seen as symbolic of a further weakening of the ties between the United Kingdom and the antipodean members of the Commonwealth).

OTHER AREAS OF POLICY

This section examines a number of macro-economic policies wholly or partly outside the fields of monetary or fiscal policy.

Immigration

It is arguable whether the term 'macro-economic' embraces overall immigration policies or not, but a brief consideration of them seems justified. Table 4.9 sets out the relevant data, with the corresponding rates of natural increase for comparison. The most striking observation is the close parallelism between the number of assisted immigrants and total net immigration, of which the former is normally only a minor part. It appears, therefore, that the government has not endeavoured to use the assistance programmes to counteract other influences on migration. It is apparent that the overall net immigration is sensitive to economic conditions in New Zealand, and to a lesser extent to those in Australia, from which many people arriving in New Zealand come and to which most people leaving the country go. The years ending in March 1960 and 1961, and again 1968 and 1969, were characterized by much less buoyant conditions in the labour market in New Zealand than at any other time since World War II. The government reacted by cutting back the assisted immigration programme, and more people left of their own accord than usual or failed to come in their accustomed numbers. As one would expect, there are time lags in migration, both administrative and informational, so that movements persist after changes have occurred in the circumstances that called them into

Table 4.9. *New Zealand: Net immigration and natural increase*

Year ended March	Net immigration Thousands	Per cent*	Assisted immigrants Thousands	Natural increase Per cent†
1960	2·8	0·14	2·5	1·75
1961	1·9	0·09	2·2	1·77
1962	19·6	0·80	3·6	1·80
1963	13·7	0·55	4·5	1·73
1964	16·9	0·66	4·3	1·67
1965	11·7	0·45	4·4	1·53
1966	13·0	0·51	4·0	1·41
1967	14·0	0·52	4·1	1·36
1968	− 10·6	− 0·39	2·8	1·40
1969	− 11·2	− 0·41	0·5	1·37
1970	0·8	0·30	0·4	1·38
1971	8·5	0·30	0·5	1·32

* Per cent of mean population in preceding calendar year.
† For preceding calendar years as percentage of corresponding mean population.

Source: New Zealand Department of Statistics.

being. But generally the assisted immigration programme has seldom been on a scale sufficient to influence the level of demand in either direction.

Farm income stabilization

Farm income stabilization policies are potentially important means of stabilizing the New Zealand economy, because almost all exports still originate with farmers and most farm exports are prone to marked price fluctuations. Strong inventory cycles may also be generated by the efforts of marketing authorities to minimize the price consequences of major changes in world supply and demand. By 1960 there were three schemes in operation – for wool, for meat, and for butter and cheese respectively. As to wool (which is subject to greater price variations than New Zealand's other major exports), there was a support price scheme supplemented by powers vested in the Wool Commission to buy wool at auction, and to store and sell it later when prices rose above the support price level. Until the late sixties the Wool Commission elected to intervene directly in the market rather than to make deficiency payments. It set conservative support prices and was not often called upon to intervene. In this period the arrangement probably helped to improve the operation of the auction system and gave farmers confidence, but it contributed little to the stability of farmers' incomes and still less to the overall stability of the economy.

The situation changed dramatically in 1967 when the Wool Commission substantially raised its support price and the market collapsed. Within a very short time the Commission found itself holding a large proportion of the clip, with its reserve funds (most of which dated back to World War II) almost exhausted. At this stage the Commission lowered the support price and changed over to making deficiency payments. Soon afterwards New Zealand devalued, and this further reduced the foreign currency equivalent of the support price. As a result of these changes, the drain on the Commission's reserve funds largely ceased, and more recently much of the wool stockpile has been disposed of at prices that appear reasonably satisfactory in terms of the devalued New Zealand currency.

However justifiable they may have been as a means of maintaining farmers' incomes, the substantial cash payouts and stockpiling that took place in 1967 had the effect of buoying up internal incomes while simultaneously depleting external receipts at a time when New Zealand faced its worst post-war balance of payments crisis. Much of the blame for this external de-stabilizing effect is attributable to the fact that almost all of the Wool Commission's reserves, in common with other farm stabilization reserves, were invested in New Zealand Government stock and not overseas.

To complete the story for wool, a half-hearted stabilization measure was introduced in 1964, when wool prices were briefly buoyant, whereby farmers were allowed to spread their incomes over several years for tax purposes so far as they opened blocked accounts at the trading banks for this purpose. This arrangement had only limited success.

In respect of meat, stabilization arrangements were superficially successful at the expense of being in reality ineffectual. It is relevant that meat prices in general have fluctuated less, and about a more strongly rising trend, than have those of wool, butter or cheese. The Meat Producers' Board sets support prices, mostly on a very conservative basis, and deficiency payments have seldom been necessary. As a consequence, the reserve funds of the Meat Producers' Board are still substantial; in fact, interest earned on them has generally exceeded deficiency payments, so that the reserves of the Board have more or less steadily increased since World War II, when they originated. The Meat Producers' Board has no power to purchase, although a subsidiary handles the marketing of lamb in North America. In general, however, slaughtering and processing is in the hands of individual meat export houses which are strongly competitive, although they have to agree among themselves on livestock purchase prices, which the Meat Producers' Board compares with its support price in order to determine whether or not deficiency payments are desirable.

The record of the dairy product stabilization scheme (for butter and cheese only) has been chequered. In response to pressure from farmers, the government in the early fifties agreed that any increase in export prices should be passed on to them. More recently power was taken to reduce the prices paid out to farmers, but by only 5 per cent in any year. Not surprisingly, reductions limited to this maximum have not been as sharp as would have been appropriate in some years, and the dairy industry reserve funds have now disappeared. But, in the light of the favourable prospects for dairy products in the early seventies, it may not be a bad thing that surpluses in earlier years were used to buoy up the incomes of dairy farmers in the latter part of the sixties, and thereby ensure an adequate level of investment.

The various stabilization arrangements have to some extent smoothed out the fluctuations in gross farm income, but have not done so very effectively. Furthermore, the amounts sequestered in good years have been inadequate to cover drawings in lean years, except for meat, so that the schemes have on the average buoyed up internal demand. This is, of course, closely related to the observation above about the reserve funds being invested internally rather than abroad. In general, farm income stabilization policies were of no more than marginal effect during the sixties. Looking to the future, it is hard to see their being more effective, if only because wool prices seem most unlikely to bounce back sufficiently to build up reserve funds to any significant extent, and internal inflation has lately been so rapid that producers of other staple products need higher returns if they are to maintain a reasonable level of personal spending and at the same time to feel confident enough to undertake further capital formation.

At the end of 1971 the government outlined a measure of assistance for the beleaguered pastoral industry, which was confronted with low lamb and wool prices, and at the same time with high and rising costs of operation (including labour costs). This assistance will take the form of suspensory loans for development (which are in effect gifts), and outright bounties based on sheep numbers. The scheme is to be financed partly from taxation and partly from Meat Industry reserve funds.

Import controls
At no time in the sixties were imports completely free from quantitative restrictions, but the severity of these restrictions varied considerably. The avowed policy of the National Party (which has been in power since the end of 1960), is to replace import licensing by a tariff system, but progress in this direction has been negligible for imported goods of types competing closely with those produced internally. Imports of raw materials and capital goods had by 1971 become freer, and in the 1971 budget the government evinced greater practical determination than formerly to dispense with licensing as a protective device. Another sign of a more enlightened official attitude towards import licensing is that by 1971 virtually no one any longer pretended that it was retained mainly to protect the balance of payments.

Apart from the natural unwillingness of less efficient producers to be exposed to competition from abroad, there are a number of reasons for the slow dismantling of import controls. One is the inadequacy of the Tariff and Development Board, as it is at present constituted and manned, to handle the volume of work that would be needed for such a change of policy. Another is the fact that tariffs in New Zealand are typically lower than in many other countries and afford considerable preference for goods imported from Britain and from certain other countries whose exports to New Zealand also benefit from British preferential tariff rates. Until the question of British entry into the EEC was resolved there was understandable unwillingness in official circles to undertake a wide-ranging tariff review, but it is now almost certain that both contractual and non-contractual margins in favour of British goods will disappear when Britain does enter the EEC. A third reason for the failure to eliminate import controls was the inadequacy of anti-dumping regulations prior to the end of 1971; and the Emergency Tariff Authority which was supposed to handle this problem is probably still inadequate for the task.

Underlying these inhibitions was an administrative, and to a lesser extent political, preference for control by regulation, stemming from a distrust of market mechanisms. But continued protection for a wide range of manufacturing activities by means of quantitative restrictions would accord oddly with the new emphasis now being placed upon the need for exports – a change of emphasis ushered in by export tax incentives, carried further through the stimulus of

121

devaluation, and officially blessed by the National Development Conference. There is therefore now some reason to believe that the government intends to dispense with quantitative restrictions on a wide range of goods, although with some prior increase in tariff protection.

Despite weak export prices, some excess of internal demand, and the virtual removal of exchange controls on foreign exchange for travel, the balance of payments remained healthy in 1971, so that anxiety on this score was no longer a relevant reason for not liberalizing imports. With wage–price inflation proceeding faster in New Zealand than in most other countries, there is special justification for providing more competition for domestic industry by allowing a freer choice of suppliers, as one way of restraining domestic inflation.

Planning

The 1966 budget pointed to a more systematic approach to the planning of central government activities and of government expenditure in particular. In the following years the treasury developed programme-budgeting of a sort, and made some progress in the direction of extending it to public corporations. A reorganization of the public accounts was another step in the direction of more rational decision-making in the public sector.

Other foretastes of indicative planning were a series of sector conferences – on industrial development at the beginning of the decade, on export promotion a little later, then on agricultural development in the mid-sixties, and on forestry and tourism towards the end of the decade. The more recent of these conferences were associated with the National Development Conference itself, which held two sessions, one in late 1968 and the other in early 1969. At these sessions leading industrialists, public servants, academics and others met to consider the economic future of New Zealand in broad terms, and the place of particular sectors in the economy. The outcome was a series of sector councils, which meet from time to time and proffer advice to the government.

The National Development Conference, like the sector conferences preceding it, was essentially a high-level public relations exercise. The conclusions stemming from it hardly constituted an indicative plan in the usual sense, but agreement was reached upon broad targets in macro-economic terms. At the same time, the nucleus was established of a permanent planning bureau centred in the treasury; but this is so under-staffed that no more detailed plan seems likely to emerge in the foreseeable future. As in the past, economic problems of a narrowly contemporaneous sort have had a prior claim on official attention – notably the problems that will arise out of Britain's accession to the EEC, and domestic wage inflation. A deep-seated preference for the determination of policy by pressure groups is another reason for doubting whether planning will ever become fashionable in New Zealand.

Wage inflation

For most of the post-war period New Zealand experienced no more wage–cost and price inflation than most countries – in fact less than many others, despite the ubiquity of excess demand on a scale almost without parallel elsewhere. Indeed, full employment was almost literally achieved without intolerable inflation. A major factor in this was the successful functioning of the Court of Arbitration which (among other things) issued general wage orders from time to time, in the light of such factors as movements in the price level, changes in productivity, and variations in the terms of trade. When the principal orders were made, the system of general wage orders was frequently assailed as inflationary, but in retrospect it is clear that the Court was conservative in both its awards and their timing.

Wage drift did, however, occur, and towards the end of the sixties there was a wide margin between minimum award rates of pay (which were nominally the Court's responsibility) and actual remuneration. In due course unions sought a narrowing of these margins, which employers generally resisted – unwisely as it now seems. The turning-point in industrial relations, as in comparative wage stability, came in 1968 when the Court issued a nil order, which it was virtually forced to supersede ignominiously some months later. From then onwards the more militant unions espoused direct industry-wide or plant bargaining, commonly invoking the strike weapon or other 'direct actions' such as working to rule.

This dangerous situation was aggravated by some aspects of public sector wage-fixing. The principle that public servants should be paid as if they worked in the private sector was translated into action by means of periodic surveys of tradesmen's wages and of salaries and wages generally. Unfortunately these mechanisms for one reason or another incorporated built-in inflationary devices, with the result that the state's decisions on its own wages and salaries compounded the rate of wage increase elsewhere in the economy. Furthermore, many employers, especially those producing for the domestic market behind the protective wall afforded by import licensing, preferred excessive wage settlements to work stoppages.

Between April 1970 and April 1971 salaries and wages rose on the average by 19 per cent and consumer prices by 10 cent. The government's answer to such inflation was the Remuneration Authority – a five-man body independent of the government – set up to administer a new Act, the main object of which was to limit salary or wage increases in 1971 to 7 per cent, but with provision for the approval of greater increases for workers who had not fully participated in the previous year's wage gallop or in defined special circumstances. The Act was not welcomed by the Federation of Labour, and its mandatory provisions were soon implemented when it became clear that the guidelines would not be voluntarily achieved in many cases. The Authority has wide powers, but has so far proved unwilling to exercise them to the full, no doubt for fear of provoking confrontations. As might have been expected, the 7 per cent maximum guideline has become a minimum goal of most unions and average wages rose by much more than 7 per cent during 1971 because of adjustments being allowed in the many cases of wages that had, at the time the Act came into force, lagged behind the general rate of increase.

Although the Authority has effectively superseded the Arbitration Court in some respects, this is of little immediate importance because unions had virtually boycotted the Court prior to the passage of the Stabilization of Remuneration Act. What is still an open question is whether the Authority can moderate wage increases, or whether a major industrial stoppage on the scale of the 1951 waterfront strike will eventuate sooner or later. Of greater importance is the probable nature of the 'industrial commission' which is at present (early 1972) being discussed by the government, the Employers' Association and the Federation of Labour, as a possible successor to the Remuneration Authority.

Since wage–cost–price inflation appears at the start of the seventies to be New Zealand's most pressing problem, this is an appropriate issue on which to close the present review. Without doubt the key to success in controlling this sort of inflation in New Zealand lies in recreating acceptable wage-fixing machinery covering public servants, as well as local authority employees and workers in the private sector. It is neither necessary nor desirable that the new machinery should take over all aspects of industrial conciliation and arbitration, but it must effectively regulate remuneration in a broad sense. In particular, it will need power to intervene in wage negotiations prior to settlement, so as to avoid being always confronted with agreements which, however, inimical to the national interest, represent the will of both parties. The inability to intercede in the national interest during the bargaining process has been a crucial weakness of the Remuneration Authority.

But naturally no new agency will succeed unless price increases can be moderated and workers have confidence in steady growth of real wages in the long run. Up to the present, however, there is little sign of New Zealand being any more successful in this matter than other countries have been. Massive unemployment is politically unacceptable, as well as being of questionable efficacy for checking inflation; but there is at least a possibility that a combination of greater competition from imports, short-term subsidization of publicly provided goods and services, lower company taxation, and more effective price control may work. There is, however, no assurance that the government will exercise effective leadership in this area of macro-economic policy any more than that it will do so in facilitating structural reorganization, the other urgent economic issue, which results from the continued deterioration in the terms of trade and from the prospect of further problems arising in the marketing overseas of New Zealand's exports.

Appendix to Chapter 4

ASSESSING THE EFFECTS OF A BUDGET

There are conceptual as well as empirical difficulties in assessing the impact and outcome of fiscal intervention at the macro-economic level, even if one makes no distinction between transfer payments and expenditure on goods and services, or between current and capital outlays. Ideally, the relevant aggregates are: (1) expenditure; (2) revenue; (3) the difference between them (that is the deficit before borrowing); (4) borrowing; and (5) the resulting overall surplus or deficit. Each of these should be analysed into internal and external transactions, because only their internal components directly affect the domestic economy. (It is true that overseas borrowing enables a country to sustain a higher level of internal activity than would otherwise be possible, but it is not an initiating influence, any more than are government transactions abroad).

In practice, however, it is very difficult systematically to analyse government receipts and payments into transactions at home and abroad. For one thing, statistics of government imports are not available. Government imports may be obtained either from local merchants or directly from abroad, and the stringency of import licensing at any given time largely determines which of these alternative sources is used. It is therefore usually necessary to assume that changes in the external components of these variables are relatively small in relation to changes in their internal components. On this assumption the deficit before borrowing minus net internal borrowing (from the private sector) measures the overall fiscal effect on domestic spending and may be termed the internal deficit. This is formally equal to net borrowing abroad minus the overall surplus. In symbols:

$$(E-R)-B = A-S$$

where E denotes total expenditure
R denotes total revenue
B denotes internal borrowing (net)
A denotes borrowing abroad (net)
S denotes the overall surplus.

The left-hand side is the internal deficit (I) and the bracketed expression is the deficit before borrowing (D).

A fundamental problem in exercises of this sort is to distinguish initiating influences from their consequences. With quarterly data it is reasonable to ignore, for example, the effect on revenue or borrowing of an increase in expenditure, but with annual data it is not legitimate to ignore such induced effects. Changes in expenditure may generally be taken as affecting revenue and borrowing, and not vice versa, because no New Zealand government in recent years has felt constrained to vary its expenditure merely because of changes in its receipts. A substantial increase in current expenditure and/or planned capital expenditure may, however, so raise the general level of economic activity that the government works programme falls behind schedule through shortage of resources. *Ex post* total government spending will thus be less than planned, and the expansionary (or inflationary) impact of the budget will therefore appear to be less than was intended. In New Zealand this possibility is particularly important because the economy is normally maintained at such a level of activity that there are virtually no resources free to cope with any abnormal expansion. Similarly, a policy-induced rise in revenue, such as occurs through an increase in tax rates, may so reduce private spending that the consequent breaking of bottlenecks enables the government works programme to be accelerated, and this would make fiscal policy turn out to be less deflationary than was intended. Moreover, the general level of activity – which is itself greatly influenced by government spending – reacts back on revenue, just as it does on certain types of government expenditure.

Of course, fiscal policy is seldom the only or the main exogenous influence on the economy, as other expansionary or deflationary factors are almost always present. But the point remains that changes in fiscal variables are likely to reflect feedback effects as well as policy decisions and economic growth generally. But within a single accounting period no induced change can more than partially offset an initiating change, so that fiscal aggregates may be taken as overall expressions of policy. In other words, the direction and order of magnitude of changes in fiscal aggregates will still indicate broadly how policy has changed. The effect of the negative feedback into the budget from changes in tax receipts is merely to reduce (not to eliminate) the effect on demand of changes in fiscal policy.

Government revenue, expenditure and borrowing naturally tend to vary more or less automatically with population and prices. This might seem to suggest that if one wishes to identify the year-to-year changes in fiscal policy one should calculate the main budgetary variables in terms of constant prices and per head of population. But an expansionary fiscal policy may itself tend to raise prices, and some forms of restrictive policies – higher indirect taxes, lower subsidies and higher charges for government services – also have a tendency to raise certain prices. In any event, even if one adjusts the budgetary variables by prices and population this would not remove that part of the trend in them that is associated with growth in productivity of the economy.

These considerations suggest that the appropriate standard of comparison is the growth of GNP at current prices, as no other variable sums up equally well the effects of changes in population, productivity and prices. But an objection to this is that changes in the constituents of the budget are themselves important determinants of GNP, and that this inter-relationship makes it inappropriate to use GNP as the benchmark when one is trying to identify year-to-year variations in fiscal policy.

A convenient compromise, therefore, is to compare annual changes in revenue and expenditure with a norm based on the growth of GNP at constant prices, plus an allowance for the minimum feasible rise in the price level. New Zealand's GNP at constant prices rose during the 1960s at an average annual rate of almost 4 per cent. To this one might add 1 per cent for the minimum amount of inflation that would have been feasible. This may appear to be a small allowance in view of the actual rate of inflation of some 3 per cent a year (on the basis of the implicit GNP deflator); but much of this increase was avoidable, as it resulted from excess demand, which was prevented from working itself out through the balance of payments, because of import controls, and therefore had most of its effect on the domestic price level. If taxation and government spending – as well as monetary policy – had been less expansionary, price inflation could well have been reduced without this leading to a significantly higher level of unemployment. The 'Phillips' curve in New Zealand is not clearly identifiable, largely because of inadequate (total) unemployment statistics, but until the end of the sixties at least it was arguable that near-stability in prices could have been achieved without appreciable unemployment.

It therefore seems reasonable to compare year-to-year changes in the budget with an average annual rate of growth in GNP (including a very small allowance for inflation) of 5 per cent. This is the basis for the discussion of short-term budgetary policy used in the text of this chapter.

Select Bibliography

New Zealand Economic Survey, annually until 1970.

New Zealand Budgets, annually.

Reserve Bank of New Zealand, monthly bulletins.

New Zealand Official Year Book, annually.

Monetary and Economic Council, various reports, especially 2, 10, 21, 22 and 23.

New Zealand Institute of Economic Research, *Quarterly Predictions*.

A. R. Low, 'Indicative Planning—The New Zealand Experience', *Australian Economic Review*, 3rd quarter 1970.

Chapter 5

SOUTH AFRICA*

J. P. NIEUWENHUYSEN

The South African economy grew at the high average rate of about 6 per cent in real terms in the decade 1960–70 as may be seen from Table 5.1. It therefore more than fulfilled the hopes of its Economic Development Programme.[1] The Development Programme estimated that South Africa's resources were adequate to maintain real growth at a rate of $5\frac{1}{2}$ per cent a year, but that a rate exceeding this would encounter a shortage of skilled labour and balance of payments difficulties. Even a lower growth rate would (as suggested later) no doubt have left South Africa, with existing policies, short of skilled labour. But the Development Programme was certainly correct in its fears about the balance of payments, and South Africa ended the decade as it began it – with a balance of payments problem (see Table 5.2).

Probably the most notable feature of South Africa's growth rate in the sixties (as in the fifties) was its stability relative to growth rates in the past. Table 5.1 (showing growth rates in the sixties) can be contrasted with the annual growth rates in the twenties (which varied between a fall of 6·6 per cent and a rise of 18·4 per cent), and the thirties (when growth rates varied from a fall of 10·0 per cent to a rise of 24·0 per cent.)[2] But steady growth at a strong rate in the sixties has been accompanied by a creeping inflation (see Table 5.3) which, although moderate by some standards, has been one of the chief concerns of those responsible for economic policy. While the purchasing power of the rand declined at an average rate of about 3 per cent per year between 1963 and 1969, there were signs of

* Because of the scattered references to tables in this chapter, a statistical appendix is included in which all the tables will be found.

[1] *Economic Development Programme for the Republic of South Africa 1964–1969*, Pretoria, 1965. This (continuing) programme attempts to quantify the average growth rate the country can maintain without serious bottlenecks in the capital and labour markets, and with a healthy balance of payments.

[2] Quoted from the *Third Report of the Commission of Enquiry into Fiscal and Monetary Policy in South Africa* (the Franzen Commission) Pretoria, November 1970, R.P. 87/1970, p.5.

acceleration in the rate of inflation towards the end of the decade (see Table 5.3), and the 1971 rise in the consumer price index turned out to be a record 6·9 per cent.

Inflation is of particular significance to South Africa because of the fixed price of gold in the official market, and because gold continues to be of basic importance in South Africa's exports (33 per cent of the total value of all exports in 1961, and 30 per cent in 1970). Whilst gold production reached a new record level in 1970 (when output from the 44 producing mines rose from 973 to 1000 tons), inflation affects new mines especially adversely; for example, the costs of new housing provided by mines for their employees rose especially rapidly. From the balance of payments viewpoint, the problem is, however, partly mitigated by the prospect that the expansion of other mineral sales, such as platinum, asbestos, diamonds, coal, copper and iron ore, may plug the hole left by gold. (This may be seen from Table 5.17.) Table 5.2 shows that gold exports increased from R. 576 million to R. 837 million between 1961 and 1970 (about 45 per cent). Table 5.10 (showing Gross Domestic Product by kind of economic activity, 1963–9) indicates that the value of mining and quarrying increased from R. 790 million in 1963 to R. 1,231 million in 1969 (about 56 per cent). But the marked rise in the free market price of gold early in 1972 raises the possibility of a substantial increase in the importance of the metal for South Africa.

Tables 5.15 and 5.18 show the extent to which South Africa's exports consist of primary products, and the importance of the UK market. Table 5.10 indicates some changes in the relative importance of different sectors in the economy. Sectors that increased in relative importance included construction (from 3·0 per cent to 4·5 per cent of GDP between 1963 and 1969), manufacturing (from 22·1 per cent to 22·7 per cent, after reaching 23·5 per cent in 1965), and general government (from 8·6 per cent to 9·1 per cent). Both agriculture, forestry and fishing, and mining and quarrying, were somewhat erratic, though tending to decline in relative importance. The implications of some of these sectoral changes are, however, more forcefully displayed by Table 5·6, which shows employment in the non-agricultural sectors from 1963–70. In particular, employment in the construction industry more than doubled, whilst total non-agricultural employment rose by just over a quarter. Employment in the non-agricultural sector as a whole grew by nearly 27 per cent between 1963 and 1969, as may be seen from Table 5.6.

Macro-economic policy in South Africa during the sixties has therefore to be seen against a background of economic growth and structural change. In Table 5.4 an indication of the size of the components of aggregate demand and supply in South Africa is given for 1969. From these statistics, some idea of the nature of the problem facing the authorities may be gauged. (Table 5.4 may be compared with Table 5.13, where some similar data – at 1963 prices – are given for 1961–70.)

Table 5.4 shows that, in 1969, about 62 per cent of gross domestic expenditure consisted of private consumption expenditure. Current government expenditure and that part of total capital expenditure over which the authorities have direct or indirect control amounted to more than R. 2,700 million in 1969, or about 23 per cent of total domestic spending. Exports and imports in 1969 were each equal to about 22 per cent of aggregate domestic spending.

INSTRUMENTS OF CONTROL

Monetary and fiscal measures employed in managing the South African economy in the sixties have been varied, and have been accompanied by controls over foreign exchange and imports. Perhaps the main internal control has been the range of monetary measures which, in the mid-1960s, had to cope with the problems resulting from what some observers have regarded as a degree of fiscal irresponsibility. Interest-rate policy has been used, though some critics have suggested that it ought to have been more extensively employed. At various times there have been extensions of the controls over bank discounts, loans and advances to the private sector, and (in the fight against inflation since 1964) the imposition of additional liquidity requirements on merchant, hire-purchase, general and savings banks. Fiscal policy, in the shape of flexible tax and expenditure policies and appropriate financing of government deficits, has not visibly been a stabilizing influence in the South African economy. Expenditure on the infra-structure required for the future in a rapidly developing economy (and a racially segregated society) has not been counterbalanced by restraints in the growth of other forms of public expenditure, and the rapidly rising increases in government projects have naturally not assisted in the fight against inflation. (In Table 5.5b are set out the current Revenue and Expenditure of General Government in South Africa, 1963–70. The increase in current expenditure was from R. 898 million in 1963 to R. 1,932 million in 1970.) On the side of taxation, the government announced in 1969 some changes in the taxation structure, with the problem of checking inflation at least partly in view, and followed the recommendations of the *First Report* of the Franzen Commission.[3] These changes (which are discussed later) shifted the emphasis from direct to indirect taxation, although in 1971 income tax was raised.

Whilst South Africa has used a variety of devices in an attempt to control inflation, there has been no incomes policy of the kind that has characterized post-war measures in many industrialized market economies. The extent of wage–push elements in inflation would, in any event, be even more difficult than usual to determine in the South African context because of the complexity of the country's labour market. This is an important point. For although South African macro-economic policy can be discussed in the usual terminology of a developed economy, the South African economy is itself essentially dualistic. This is in the traditional sense of there being both a subsistence and an advanced sector of the economy,[4] and also in the sense of dualism within the modern sector. This dualism in the modern sector is portrayed in Table 5.8, which shows wages and employment for different racial groups in South Africa in mining, manufacturing and construction. The relatively very wide wage differentials (which are not always differentials for skill so much as differentials for race) distinguish the South African wage structure from that of most economically developed countries. As may be seen from Table 5.8, in 1970 the ratios of average wages earned by white employees in mining, manufacturing and construction to those of Africans in the same industries were roughly 21:1, 6·1:1 and 6·3:1 respectively. These differentials, and the economic forces and social policies that have produced them, have complex but important implications for macro-economic policy, where shortage of skilled labour[5] is increasingly recognized as a serious bottleneck to growth (an issue that is discussed later). Another related and important aspect is that the unemployment figures for South Africa are far from complete. Table 5.7 shows a heavy decline in registered un-

[3] *Taxation in South Africa: First Report of the Commission into Fiscal and Monetary Policy in South Africa*, R.P. 24/1969, November 1968.

[4] The African Reserves (or 'Homelands') comprise 13 per cent of South Africa's total surface area, and include 46 per cent of the African population, or 33 per cent of South Africa's total population. Yet these areas in 1966/7 produced only 1·9 per cent of South Africa's total domestic product. Output per head in the Reserves was one-eighteenth that in the rest of the country. (*Economic and Demographic Characteristics of the South African Bantu Areas*, J. Stadler, *Agrekon*, Department of Agricultural Economics and Marketing, vol. 1, Jan. 1970, table 10.)

[5] On the other hand, South Africa's population growth rate is relatively high (over 2 per cent per year in the 1960s).

employment between 1963–70. But there appears to be no official details of African unemployment: Table 5.7 is restricted to racial groups other than Africans.

One of the influences of gold on the South African economy has probably been to assist in stabilizing exports, details of which are given in Table 5.14. This has meant that some of the chief problems of instability faced by the authorities (at least before 1970) have come from capital inflow and outflow rather than from export fluctuations. The capital outflow after 1960, and the capital inflow after the 1967 devaluation of sterling, are good illustrations of this. In the latter case, as mentioned below, a distinction had been drawn in the Washington Communiqué in March 1968, betwen private and official gold sales. Because it thought the official gold price would be raised in spite of the attitude of the United States, the South African government held out against a compromise. By so doing it attracted speculative foreign capital into gold shares. This increased the money supply and led to responses in most components of gross domestic expenditure. In fact, throughout the decade of the sixties fluctuations in short-term capital movements sharply influenced South Africa's gold and foreign exchange reserves: during the five years from 1960 to 1964 South Africa lost more than R. 500 million on a net basis to foreign sources, but in the following five years attracted more than R. 1,200 million from overseas. These changes in gold and foreign exchange reserves altered the liquidity of South Africa's banking sector and produced destabilizing effects on money supply, interest rates, share prices and mortgage loans, and spelled important consequences for the co-ordination of monetary, fiscal and other policy measures. The relatively large import component of South Africa's gross domestic expenditure (see Table 5.4) has also had important balance of payments implications. During periods of high business activity in South Africa in the sixties, imports showed a propensity to increase at a rate that has given concern to economic policy makers. (Payments for services allied to the import of goods also naturally increased at these times, and some goods normally available for export were used domestically.)

During the sixties, balance of payments policy in South Africa has been largely concerned with coping with the somewhat random instability caused by the above factors. As described below, import and exchange control measures, as well as controls over capital movements, were adopted to meet short-term changes of circumstances in the balance of payments. In the opinion of the Franzen Commission in its *Third Report* (p. 236) the South African balance of payments also presents a structural problem, and in formulating a balance of payments policy more attention should be given to the medium and long-term tendencies of the balance of payments. It recommended that 'priorities should also be specified in respect of the balance of payments and that the available foreign exchange should be applied to those purposes that will offer the greatest advantage to the country'.

THE BALANCE OF PAYMENTS PROBLEM OF THE EARLY 1960s

The main feature of the South African economic scene at the start of the 1960s was a sharp increase in capital outflow which was responsible for an appreciable net deficit in the balance of payments in 1960. (On capital account, there was a net outflow of R. 153 million.) The severe outflow of capital was due mainly to sales by foreigners of securities listed on the Johannesburg stock exchange. This followed the collapse of overseas investment confidence after the political disturbances (centred on the shooting of African demonstrators at Sharpeville) in March 1960. During May and June 1961 the government and Reserve Bank were forced to take corrective measures: bank rate was raised; the minimum reserve balances that commercial banks are required to maintain with the Reserve Bank against demand liabilities were increased; import control was intensified and extended; and increased customs and excise duties were imposed on imported and locally assembled motor cars. Furthermore, exchange control was tightened in respect of allowances for tourists and emigrants and transfers of legacies. South African residents were prohibited from remitting funds abroad for the purchase of securities. The proceeds of sales on the Johannesburg stock exchange by non-residents were blocked and could be re-invested only in securities quoted on that exchange. Control was also tightened on capital transfers by foreign subsidiaries and branches in South Africa, while South African residents were called upon to render returns to the Reserve Bank of all their foreign assets and liabilities. The Reserve Bank action of imposing restrictions on the repatriation of non-residents' funds went against the grain of all its previous reassurances. But the governor of the Bank mentioned that, apart from its unfavourable impact on the reserves, the outflow of capital through net sales of South African securities by non-residents had dampened new enterprise by absorbing the available supply of equity capital and had depressed local stock market prices, thus increasing 'the yields on existing securities which naturally tended to render new investment less attractive'.[6]

These restrictions, however, served only to limit capital outflow, which remained substantial in 1961 (R. 120 million) and 1962 (R. 88 million). None the less, South Africa's gold and foreign exchange reserves increased by R. 86 million in 1961 and R. 229 million in 1962. This was attributable to the highly favourable relation between imports and net current invisible payments on the one hand, and merchandise exports and gold production on the other. It was fortunate for the balance of payments situation at this time that a good performance by merchandise exports was bolstered by increasing output from the new Orange Free State goldfields. Before levelling off after 1965, net gold exports had increased steadily from R. 504 million in 1959 to R. 775 million in 1965 (see Table 5.2).

Between 1961 and 1963, the accumulated surplus on the current account of the balance of payments was R. 698 million. During each of these years, South Africa achieved a current account surplus. The strength shown by the balance of payments on current account, and the increase in the country's gold and foreign exchange reserves, permitted the relaxation in 1962 of the exchange control measures imposed the year before. Non-residents were permitted, for example, to utilize blocked funds to subscribe to a special issue of five-year non-negotiable government bonds, bearing interest at 5 per cent and repayable in five equal annual instalments, and freely transferable in foreign currency on the expiry of each instalment. Secondly, under a 'permit' scheme and an 'arbitrage' scheme, the government aimed at furnishing additional scope for the overseas investor to realize his investments in South African shares, as well as to provide for a controlled repatriation of South African securities held overseas and to narrow the gap between foreign and local prices of South African shares.[7] In addition to the further liberalization of exchange control, import control was relaxed in certain respects during 1962 and 1963.

TRANSITION, 1963/4

The strength of the balance of payments on current account in 1962 and 1963, and expansion in foreign exchange reserves, had the effect of increasing internal liquidity in the South African economy

[6] 'Review of the Financial and Economic Situation in South Africa, *S.A.J.E.*, September 1961, p. 180.

[7] See South African Reserve Bank, *Annual Economic Report*, 1963, p. 39.

in 1963, and of exerting a downward pressure on money rates, despite an increase in the rate of economic growth. (See Table 5.1a.) Moreover, this downward trend in money rates occurred in spite of various measures that were taken with a view to countering excessive liquidity in the interests of monetary stability. One of these measures, adopted as a temporary expedient to reduce the local supply of investable funds to the commercial banks, concerned a 'swap' arrangement between the Reserve Bank and the commercial banks.[8] In addition to the swap arrangement (and the relaxation of exchange control in various ways already mentioned), there were larger domestic borrowings by the treasury than required by the government. This, together with the initial effects of a PAYE income tax system introduced on 1 March 1963, raised the government's credit balances with the Reserve Bank to R. 145 million on 30 June 1963, compared with only R. 15 million two years earlier. These measures were intended, in the words of the governor of the Reserve Bank

'to relieve the excessive liquidity and to avoid undue disturbances in the financial structure as a whole. In the absence of inflationary pressure, the principal objective of monetary policy continued, therefore, to be that of trying to effect a more orderly increase in the supply of money and near-money and a more orderly downward adjustment of money rates than would otherwise have been the case. . . . This was also the motive for the further reduction in the bank rate in November (1962)'.[9]

While fiscal policy had already been employed to some extent as an expansionary measure during 1962, more positive action was taken in the 1963 budget. Various tax concessions were made, such as a discount of 5 per cent on income tax payable by individuals, a reduction in customs and excise duties on petrol and diesoline, and increased income tax concessions for exporters. There was also a substantial increase in expenditure on the Revenue and Loan Accounts.

The moderate expansionary phase marked by the 1963 budget lasted roughly until the fourth quarter of that year. During this phase, the monetary authorities held to the view that it was desirable to assist the recovery in economic activity, and welcomed the more expansionary monetary and banking environment which was

[8] See M. H. de Kock, 'Review of the Financial and Economic Situation in South Africa', *South African Journal of Economics*, September 1963, p. 190.

[9] *Ibid.*, pp. 179–80.

conducive to an increase in total investment and consumer spending. It is true that measures were taken during 1963 to ease the pressure of rising liquidity. But in the Reserve Bank's *Annual Economic Report* for 1964 it was claimed that 'these measures were merely intended to moderate the downward tendency in the treasury bill and other related short-term interest rates and to prevent undue disturbances in the financial structure; they were not aimed at restraining the expansion of investment or consumption in any way'.[10]

Before the end of 1963, however, the opinion was formed among policy-makers that the upswing no longer needed any special encouragement but could be relied upon to look after itself. This view was reached in the light of an upturn in gross private fixed investment (which increased by about 20 per cent in 1964, as shown in Table 5.13) and because of skilled labour shortages and other bottlenecks that seemed to be developing. But while the authorities saw no reason to continue to give any special encouragement to the upswing, they also saw no need to apply a brake in the 1964/5 budget, partly in view of such factors as the relatively high gold and foreign exchange reserves at the time (see Table 5.2), as well as the scope for a further rise in imports, and the high level of inventories. Accordingly, the 1964/5 budget did not include any special disinflationary measures: the 5 per cent rebate on personal income tax was retained and no important tax changes were made. The Minister's speech stressed the shift from the stimulation of growth to the maintenance of stability. Had it not been for a liberal import policy, however, the need for a more restrictive monetary and fiscal policy might have arisen in the early months of 1964: as it was, substantial relaxations in import control were announced from time to time, and care was taken to ensure an adequate supply of goods in the economy.

Nevertheless, towards the middle of the second quarter of 1964, a more cautious attitude to credit creation was deemed necessary, in view of the rise in consumer spending, in government outlays and in fixed investment. Apart from increasing bank rate from $3\frac{1}{2}$ to 4 per cent in July 1964, however, the Reserve Bank felt that little other action was necessary, since there had been a significant decline in the liquidity ratios of commercial banks and other banking institutions.

POLICY FROM 1964 TO 1971: CONTROLLING INFLATION

The more cautious attitude in monetary and fiscal policy which had become apparent during 1964 was by the middle of 1965 fully

[10] Pretoria, 1964, p. 37

confirmed as a policy requirement. Indeed the story of policy in the period 1964–71 is largely one of the various attempts to counter inflationary tendencies in the economy. One of the recurring problems in these attempts has been that of credit control. At the start, there was an 'excessively high rate of investment' (a rise of 24 per cent in private fixed investment in 1964/5) and an increase in personal consumption spending (by 9 per cent in the same year). The Reserve Bank judged that these increases were greatly facilitated by the easy availability of credit. Although the Bank urged credit restraint on the main financial institutions in October 1964, there was a poor response, probably owing to the 'keen competition to expand credit business under the prevailing boom conditions which was probably increased by the greater number of financial institutions operating in the credit field'.[11] During 1964, a report was submitted by a Technical Committee of Banking and Building Society Legislation.[12] The committee had been asked to suggest methods of achieving efficiency of monetary stabilization policy, greater equity in competition among the various classes of banking institutions and greater protection for the depositor in the light of the growth of the 'near-bank' intermediaries.[13] The committee argued that there was a difference of degree, rather than principle, between the variety of institutions competing for deposits and lending. A functional approach was therefore suggested, to bring all institutions under the same set of rules, particularly as to maintaining the same capital and liquidity ratios, and keeping a minimum reserve balance with the Reserve Bank based on short-term liabilities. It was also suggested by the committee that the Building Societies Act be amended so as to make the requirements for the Societies more nearly comparable with those of the banks. These, the committee's chief proposals, were made effective in March 1965 by legislation which provided for deposit rate control for all institutions falling under the Banks Act (No. 23 of 1965). As illustrated in Table 5.14, the relative growth of the building societies, which had exceeded the growth of the commercial banks between 1953 and 1964, did not keep pace with the growth of registered banks and deposit receiving institutions after 1965. The reasons for this, according to the *Third Report* of the Franzen Commission (p. 179) include

[11] G. Rissik, 'Review of the Financial and Economic Situation in South Africa', *S.A.J.E.*, September 1965, p. 197.

[12] R.P. 50/1964, Pretoria.

[13] See A. B. Dickman, 'The South African Money Market', *S.A.J.E.*, September 1965.

'more intense competition for interest-bearing deposits from the side of the "new" banking institutions as well as the commercial banks, the availability of a greater variety of saving instruments, and the restrictions imposed by the Building Societies Act (Act 24 of 1965) on the accepting of saving deposits and the issuance of subscription shares to companies with limited liability.'

The rapid growth of unit trusts between 1965 and 1969 also adversely affected the growth of building societies.

However, despite the extensions of control under the 1965 legislation, evidence submitted to the Franzen Commission suggested strongly that, for the purposes of dealing with excess liquidity, the powers at the disposal of the monetary authority were inadequate.[14] Certainly, in the fight against inflation in the mid and late sixties, there appeared to be a need to use all available methods of monetary control. In December 1964 bank rate was raised by $\frac{1}{2}$ per cent to $4\frac{1}{2}$ per cent and the Reserve Bank's pattern of rates for government stock was increased by $\frac{1}{4}$ per cent as a supplementary restrictive measure. In March 1965 bank rate was increased further to 5 per cent and rates for government stock were increased to $5\frac{1}{4}$ per cent for maturities in excess of $10\frac{1}{2}$ years. Later in 1965 the supplementary liquidity requirements for the commercial banks were raised to the maximum of 10 per cent, and rates for government stock were increased to 6 per cent for maturities in excess of $10\frac{1}{2}$ years, and roughly in proportion for other government stock.

These measures were not by themselves sufficient, however, and in September 1965 the Minister of Finance announced further steps which it was hoped would assist in curbing excessive monetary demand. These comprised the reduction of government expenditure, especially on capital works, and the submission of important tenders for government purchases to a special Cabinet Committee. Furthermore, the Provincial authorities, municipalities and public corporations were requested to reduce expenditure and invest the funds thus saved with the government. It was also decided that essential government expenditure that could not be postponed would be financed as far as possible in a non-inflationary manner, and a 20-year 6 per cent loan was issued which it was hoped would be supported by financial institutions. The increase in the current surplus of general government between 1966 and 1967 is shown in

[14] The Commission also pointed out in its *Third Report* (p. 145) that at the end of January 1970 all registered banking institutions, with the exception of discount houses, were subject to certain supplements to the powers of the 1965 Act.

Table 5.5b. It will be noticed from this table that although the current surplus of general government rose quite strongly, from R. 258 million in 1966 to R. 474 million in 1967, the expansion of current expenditure over the whole period from 1963 to 1970 was consistent and substantial.

Despite the decision to reduce government expenditure (which was regarded in some circles as overdue) and the measures designed to restrict the domestic availability of credit, further anti-inflationary actions were deemed necessary in the latter half of 1966 and the first quarter of 1967. There had been a substantial increase in exports, and in fixed and inventory investment (see Table 5.13), accompanied by an upward movement in a variety of economic activities and transactions. The response of the authorities was to relax import control and to tighten fiscal and monetary policy. Import control was relaxed in three stages, in July and December 1966, and in May 1967. In the hope of increasing the degree of competition in the economy and of assisting the reduction of excessive liquidity, two budgets were introduced. In the August 1966 budget, the main anti-inflationary moves were an increase in various taxes, the introduction of a new tax-exempt savings bond, and the imposition of an obligation upon unit trusts to hold more government stock. Previously, in July, the interest rate on long-term government stock had been raised from 6 to 6½ per cent. This was followed by an increase in company tax and customs and excise duty on motor cars, and an increase in the loan levy on companies and individuals, in a budget introduced in March 1967. In monetary policy there were upward adjustments in the Reserve Bank's pattern of rates for government stock, the extension and tightening of direct control over bank discounts, loans and advances to the private sector, and the imposition of additional (higher) liquidity requirements upon merchant, hire-purchase, general and savings banks.[15]

The relaxation of import control appeared justified in 1966/7 because of the large surpluses in the current account of the balance of payments and a large and sustained inflow of private foreign capital from the second quarter of 1965 onwards (see Table 5.2). South Africa's gold and foreign exchange reserves increased very rapidly, from R. 340 million at the end of September 1965 to R. 604 million at the end of July 1966. This sudden change in the balance of payments position complicated the anti-inflationary measures. It contributed substantially to the rapid rise in the quantity of money

[15] See T. W. de Jongh, 'Review of the Financial and Economic Situation in South Africa', *South African Journal of Economics*, September 1967.

and near money in the hands of the private sector, and also stimulated internal fixed investment and consumer spending (by partly shifting the demand for imports to local products).[16] International influences were, however, to complicate policy even further in the remaining years of the sixties.

INTERNATIONAL INFLUENCES IN 1967/8:
THE BRITISH DEVALUATION

The Reserve Bank's *Annual Economic Report* for 1967/8[17] showed that there had been some success in eliminating excess demand, whilst a rise of 6 per cent in real GNP had occurred. Total Gross Domestic Expenditure had increased sharply from the middle of 1966 up to the third quarter of 1967, but declined in the fourth quarter and rose only moderately in the first half of 1968. Inventory investment and investment by public and private corporations declined during 1967/8. On the other hand, private consumption expenditure increased substantially during the first half of 1968. But after the middle of 1967 most of the available monthly indicators of economic activity either increased more slowly, levelled out, or declined temporarily, and the governor of the Reserve Bank felt that 'the inflationary increase in total demand was relatively well contained after the middle of 1967'.[18] The consumer price index rose at an annual rate of 3·5 per cent during the first half of 1967, but rose in the second half at the much lower annual rate of 0·3 per cent, and then at the higher rate of 2·0 per cent during the first half of 1968. Wholesale price indexes showed a similar trend.

After June 1967 there was also an improvement in the current account of the balance of payments, a surplus of R. 75 millions at the end of 1968 being the result mainly of increased merchandise exports, and to a lesser extent of a decline in imports. There was, however, as Table 5.2 shows, a decline in gold and foreign exchange reserves in 1967, and this may have helped to explain why the quantity of money and near-money in the hands of the private sector 'actually declined appreciably in relation to the gross domestic product'.[19] During the first nine months of 1967 a second factor responsible for this decline was a moderate downward trend in the net claims of the monetary banking sector on the government sector, which was 'the outcome of restraints on government expenditure,

---

[16] *Ibid.*, p. 190.   [17] Pretoria, 1968.
[18] T. W. de Jongh, 'Review of the Financial and Economic Situation in South Africa', *S.A.J.E.*, September 1968, p. 187.   [19] *Ibid.*, p. 187.

increased taxes and loan levies, and the Treasury's success in raising loans from the non-bank private sector through government issues including tax-free Savings and Treasury bonds'.[20]

The devaluation of the pound sterling in November 1967, by 14·3 per cent, altered the monetary and financial scene in South Africa, giving rise in ensuing months to widespread currency uncertainty and speculation, and to an abnormal demand for gold and gold shares. This was followed by the Washington communiqué of March 1968, the broad intention of which was that newly produced gold would be channelled to private markets for sale at ruling prices, and that there should be a closed circuit for gold transactions at the official price among the central banks responsible for the Washington communiqué, and among others that decided to cooperate. This arrangement created difficulties for the marketing of South African gold, which will not be discussed here. But the decisions announced in the communiqué led indirectly to a rise in internal liquidity in South Africa, as the relaxation of exchange and import controls that would otherwise have come sooner was consequently delayed until July 1968.[21]

South Africa did not devalue the rand, but an abnormally large capital inflow occurred, which was reflected in an increase in gold and foreign exchange reserves from R. 527 million at the end of October 1967 to a record level of R. 960 million at the end of July 1968 (a net increase of R. 534 million for 1968, as shown in Table 5.2). The expansionary effects of these developments were offset only partially by the continuing decline of the banking sector's net claims on the government sector. Total money and near-money, which had increased by R. 42 million (or 1·6 per cent) during the first three-quarters of 1967, increased by no less than R. 390 million (or 14·5 per cent) during the nine months ended June 1968. (For end-of-year total, see Table 5.9.) The ratio of money and near money to gross domestic product rose from 26 per cent during the second quarter of 1967 to 30 per cent during the second quarter of 1968, and the liquidity of private businesses and individuals increased sharply. Moreover, the excessive level of liquid assets held by the banking sector 'increased still further and eased the money market, thereby exerting downward pressure on short-term interest rates'.[22] The

[20] *Ibid.*, p. 187.
[21] The government relaxed exchange control selectively and authorized some import allocations in regard to certain capital and consumer goods from 31 July 1968. (See South Africa Reserve Bank, *Annual Economic Report*, 1968, p. 25.)
[22] T. W. de Jongh, *ibid.*, p. 189.

Reserve Bank, concerned at the prospect of an inordinate easing of the money market and of a fall in short-term interest rates, took various measures to absorb funds from the market, including an increase in the minimum balances to be held by monetary banks with the Reserve Bank, and the issue of government stock and more treasury bills.

One of the most important indirect consequences of the British devaluation for South Africa was the impact of the large inflow of foreign capital on the stock exchange. Part of the inflow of capital was directed through the exchange, while local investors were also encouraged to switch from fixed-interest-bearing securities to equities and other growth investments. The index of gold mining share prices increased by 44 per cent between October 1967 and June 1968, and that of commercial and industrial shares by 39 per cent. In the following twelve-month period, up to June 1969, an atmosphere of speculation continued to prevail (with unusually low levels of dividend yields). For example, the average monthly rate of turnover on the stock exchange during the first five months of 1969 was roughly five times as great as that of the year 1967, whilst the prices of shares other than gold shares more than doubled between October 1967 and May 1969. Some indication of these developments is given in Table 5.11. Unit trusts experienced spectacular expansion at this time, and insurance companies and private pension funds also entered the market on a substantial scale. The net investment of unit trusts, for example, as shown in Table 5.12, increased from R. 1 million in 1965 to R. 409·5 million in 1969. The governor of the Reserve Bank remarked that

'The extraordinary conditions which developed on the share and property markets caused various distortions, not only in savings flow, but also in the production sphere of the economy. The flow of funds to the security and property markets was so great, for example, that considerable difficulty was experienced by the building societies in meeting the strong demand for housing loans, and other savings institutions suffered in a similar fashion.'[23]

At the start of the 1968/9 financial year, the main issue causing concern to the authorities has been

'the abnormally high level of private sector liquidity as indicated, *inter alia*, by the high ratio of money and near money to gross domestic product. . . . This new build up of excess liquidity in the

[23] *Ibid.*, p. 190.

144

hands of private businesses and individuals over the past year was largely the internal counterpart of the large overall surplus on the balance of payments and not, as in 1963–6, mainly the result of excessive credit extended by the monetary banking sector to the private and/or the government sector.'[24]

But the problem of excess liquidity remained at the end of the 1968/9 financial year also, and this time the governor ascribed the increase in money and near-money to

'the large expansion in bank credit . . . [which] is explained in part by the raising of the ceiling on discounts and advances from 92½ per cent to 100 per cent of the March 1965 level and by the concession granted to smaller business undertakings.'[25]

One of the main reasons why 1968/9 was a difficult year for the financial authorities related to the problems experienced in the marketing of gold. This hampered attempts to reduce the excessive liquidity of the private sector until, in April 1969, South Africa was able to sell larger quantities of gold overseas, and could therefore further relax exchange control in June. In December 1969 an agreement was reached between South Africa and the IMF to the effect that South Africa would have the right to sell to the IMF or to other monetary authorities all the gold it might need to sell for balance of payments purposes at the official price of 35 US dollars per fine ounce, whenever the price on the private market was not above the official price. South Africa was also given the right to sell gold to the IMF or to other monetary authorities (irrespective of the price on the private market), in the case of specified international transactions, for example to finance an overall balance of payments deficit.[26] This agreement thus removed some of the uncertainty for South Africa that had followed the Washington communiqué.

As in previous years, both the Reserve Bank and the South African government continued in 1969/70 to show concern at the rate of increase in prices (which may be seen from Table 5.3). During 1969/70 the economy grew at a highly satisfactory rate, GDP at constant prices increasing by 7 per cent in 1969; but fears were again expressed that the imbalances and bottle-necks caused by rapid growth would threaten sustained economic expansion in the future. At the start of the 1970s, three problems loomed for economic policy. They were (probably in ascending order of intractability): (1)

[24] *Ibid.*, p. 190.   [25] *S.A.J.E.*, September 1969, p. 189.
[26] See T. W. de Jongh, 'Review of the Financial and Economic Situation in South Africa , *S.A.J.E.*, September 1970, p. 211.

the rapid increase in domestic spending (shown in Table 5.4) which resulted during 1969/70 in an imbalance between the supply of and demand for capital, and was part of the problem of inflation; (2) the serious deterioration in the current account of the balance of payments; and (3) the imbalance between the supply of and demand for labour, especially skilled labour (also part of the inflationary problem).

In presenting the 1970/1 budget, the Minister of Finance mentioned these and other difficulties. First, during 1969/70, consumption had increased too rapidly and savings too slowly. Secondly, there had been an imbalance in the growth of fixed investment in the sense that investment in building and construction received particular attention, whilst investment in manufacturing lagged (as may be seen from Table 5.10). Thirdly, stresses and strains had developed in the monetary and banking system as evidenced, for example, by the upward pressure on interest rates. Finally, the threat of inflation had become more ominous, partly because of some of the factors already mentioned, but also because the government, owing to its less successful borrowing operations, had been forced to finance its deficit in an inflationary manner in the year up to June 1970. With some of these problems in mind, the August 1970 budget imposed increased sales tax on certain luxury items and an increased excise and sales duty on cars above a retail value of R. 3,000. A new treasury bond savings scheme was announced, and banks and building societies were released from their obligation to keep their interest rate on deposits at not more than 7 per cent. During 1970/1, however, the rate of increase in private consumption expenditure remained high (6 per cent in real terms), though this was less than the rise in 1969/70 (7 per cent in real terms).[27]

As to the second major problem mentioned – the substantial deficit in the current account of the balance of payments – the 1970 budget took some measures intended to improve exports. First, there was an increase in the existing allowance granted in respect of expenditure incurred in the development of export markets. Secondly, manufacturers were permitted to deduct 15 per cent of the cost of new machinery and plant and 10 per cent of the cost of new factory buildings, or of additions to them, from taxable income. Despite these and other (later) incentives, however, merchandise exports actually declined by 4 per cent in the year ending 30 June 1971. This was mainly because of poor export performance in diamonds, wool and fruit. Even a record net inflow of overseas capital (R. 725

[27] See South African Reserve Bank, *Annual Economic Report*, 1971, p. 9.

million) in 1970/1 was not enough to prevent a deficit in the overall balance of payments deficit from reaching the record figure of R. 1,084 million.

The balance of payments deficit for the two previous years occurred despite a substantial net inflow of capital. It had been caused, according to the official diagnosis, by the 'excessive total demand for consumer and capital goods and for services for more than two years past. This exerted undue pressure on scarce resources of skilled labour and other factors of production, and thereby raised costs, led to an excessive rise in imports of capital goods, raw materials and consumer goods, and detrimentally affected exports'. It was felt in the early part of 1971 that the policy of applying restrictive monetary and fiscal measures was having some effect in restraining excess demand: imports ceased to show a pronounced upward trend from the beginning of 1971 and exports tended to recover, though not as much as desired.[28]

International developments again exacerbated South Africa's balance of payments position, however – this time in the shape of the action of the USA on 15th August 1971 in suspending the convertibility of the dollar and imposing a 10 per cent surcharge on imports. The deterioration in the international economic situation following President Nixon's announcement had a detrimental effect on South Africa's already weak exports. Also, because of the expectation of some form of devaluation of the rand, there were after August 1971 'leads' in import and other payments and 'lags' in export and other foreign receipts and the witholding of foreign capital. Because of these factors, and the underlying balance of payments deficit, South Africa's total gold and foreign reserves declined to a level of R. 603 million at the end of September 1971, compared with R. 906 million a year earlier and a peak of R. 1,235 million at the end of April 1969.

As a result of these developments, the South African government decided on 26 November 1971 to tighten import control very substantially over a wide range of goods.[29] A month later, on 21 December 1971, following the realignment of exchange rates in other countries, the South African government announced that the rand was to be devalued by 12·28 per cent in terms of gold. This amounted to a 14 per cent increase in the official rand price of gold from R. 25 per fine ounce to R. 28·50 per fine ounce. It was thought that this devaluation would naturally assist the balance of payments

[28] See South African Reserve Bank, *Annual Economic Report*, 1971, p. 5.
[29] See *South African Reserve Bank Quarterly Bulletin*, December 1971, pp. 24–5.

position by encouraging exports, increasing gold-mining receipts, restraining imports and eliminating the 'leads' and 'lags' mentioned above. In order to attempt to reap the benefits of devaluation without excessive price increases, the government Price Controller acted to freeze temporarily the prices of some goods, though an early relaxation of the freeze seemed likely, and some substantial price increases (for example, of about 20 per cent for fuel and clothing) seemed inevitable.

While the effects on the balance of payments of the substantial 1971 devaluation of the rand remain uncertain, the third general probelm mentioned in the 1970 budget – the shortage of skilled labour – seems likely to increase in severity, especially in view of the declining rate of white immigration to South Africa. The 1970 budget provided for the limited (and questionably relevant) action of granting tax concessions on donations by companies and individuals to universities and other institutions for higher education. Increased government financial assistance to these institutions was also proposed as part of an endeavour to alleviate the shortage of skilled manpower. These measures do not, however, seem even remotely to match the urgency of the situation. Even in the slow-down in economic activity which occurred in 1970/1 (an increase of only 4 per cent in GDP at constant prices) there was only a slight easing of the tight labour market conditions in South Africa. In June 1971, the only figures available for registered unemployed (those covering White, Asians and Coloureds) showed a mere 8,900 or $\frac{1}{2}$ per cent, unemployed:[30] and according to the Economic Development Programme, which assumes a $5\frac{1}{2}$ per cent growth rate, the total demand for labour will grow at an average rate of 190,200 per annum between 1970 and 1975. Making its (obviously oversimplified) calculations in terms of white and non-white, the Programme suggests that by 1975 there will be an (annual) excess of demand over the supply of white labour of 1,000 persons.

WAGES DETERMINATION IN SOUTH AFRICA

The tight labour market conditions in South Africa – and their implications for policy – have a confused background. In South Africa, as elsewhere, it is, of course, extremely difficult to assess how far the 'pushfulness' of a tight labour market, and how far the 'pull' of excess demand, have each been responsible for price rises. In his report on the financial situation for 1968/9, the governor of the

[30] See South African Reserve Bank, *Annual Economic Report*, 1971, p. 15.

Reserve Bank, Dr de Jongh, mentioned that tight labour market conditions required 'the special attention of the authorities'. He suggested that 'although there was little evidence of general demand inflation, wages and salaries nevertheless increased considerably and significant upward adjustments were made to the prices of certain services'.[31] The difficulties caused by the shortage of skilled labour were also regularly referred to in the Economic Development Programme. On the other hand, a conference on inflation and the South African economy held in 1967, and addressed by a number of leading economists, showed little concern for the role of wage–push or cost–push inflation. In summarizing the proceedings of the conference, Dr G. de Kock suggested that 'the South African inflation during 1964–1967, has probably been one of the best examples ever witnessed in peace-time of classical demand–pull inflation. It is true, of course, that costs have risen sharply during this period and that in many sectors of the economy money wages have risen faster than average productivity. But this proves nothing as to cause and effect'.[32]

While the literature appears to contain no thoroughgoing econometric studies of the relative importance of wage–push or cost–push, compared with demand–pull, influences in South African inflation,[33] such studies are likely to be even more difficult in South Africa than elsewhere. This is because the impact of wage fixation on price formation in South Africa is complicated by diffuse bargaining processes; by highly organized white union organizations; by their weak African counterparts; and by the control of the structure and flow of the labour force through the 'job reservation' and 'pass law' system.

The main wage-fixing instruments are the Industrial Conciliation Act, (1924, 1956) and the Wages Act (1925). The former provided in 1924 for consultation between employers' organizations and trade unions for the determination of wages and conditions of work by collective bargaining, and for arbitration in the event of disputes.

[31] 'Review of the Financial and Economic Situation in South Africa', *S.A.J.E.*, September 1969, p. 191.
[32] 'Conference of Inflation and the S.A. Economy. Summary of the Proceedings', G. de Kock, *S.A.J.E.*, December 1967, p. 361.
[33] The article by I. Hume ('Notes on South African Wage Movements', *S.A.J.E.*, September 1970, p. 240) is the closest to this approach, but has the more limited objective of discussing the likely impact of African wage increases on prices. On this score, Hume is implicitly an adherent of a demand–pull explanation of inflation, as he argues that his findings 'show quite unequivocally the groundlessness of the argument that autonomous increase in black money wages would be self-defeating' (p. 253).

The Act was restricted, applying only to 'organized' industries (i.e. where unions represented more than half of white or non-African workers in the industry). By its definition of an employee, the Act also excluded Africans, the predominant group in the labour force, as Table 5.8 shows. White workers were thus empowered to negotiate with employers for an industrial agreement which was binding on African workers. Complementing the Industrial Conciliation Act, the Wages Act of 1925 operates in those industries where workers are not sufficiently organized to engage in collective bargaining with employers. This Act set up a Wage Board consisting of three members, appointed by the Minister of Labour, to investigate conditions of work and rates of pay where this was deemed desirable. If the minister consented, these minimum wage determinations had the force of law.

The 1956 amendments to the Industrial Conciliation Act contained two highly contentious provisions. One concerned 'job reservation', whereby the Minister of Labour was given wide power to reserve certain jobs for members of a particular race to be employed. Another concerned the enforced racial separation of the trade unions. While Africans had previously been excluded from collective bargaining machinery, the 1956 Act provided that no trade union might be registered for both white and 'coloured' workers.

The general effect on the labour market and on wage pressures in the economy of the legislation governing job reservation and the control over the urban influx of Africans is confused. In terms of the Industrial Conciliation Act new determinations concerning jobs reserved for whites only are continually being made, but others, affecting more people, are being relaxed on a 'temporary exemption' basis. The rapid expansion of industry has meant that the white line that the government has drawn is being daily breached. Whilst there have been increased 'job reservation' powers at the government's disposal, it has been forced to turn a blind eye on a steady influx of non-whites into spheres of activity formerly labelled 'whites only'. This is not a process that the government relishes, but economic expansion seems to demand it. The skills necessary for rapid economic development in South Africa cannot be squeezed from the whites alone, who (although their numbers are being swollen by immigration), are less than one-fifth of the population and a declining proportion of the total (as may be seen from Table 5.9). Thus non-white advance in industry is occurring willy-nilly. In view of the 'civilized labour' policy of earlier years, it is rather surprising that even in the government-operated railways large numbers of non-whites have recently been employed, not only in unskilled jobs that were previously strictly reserved for the diminishing pool of 'poor white' labour. The dominance of Africans in mining, manufacturing, and construction is shown in Table 5.8.

The impact on the labour market that might be expected from job reservation (i.e. the artificially tight labour market conditions resulting from enforcement of a 'non-competing labour group' structure) has thus been attenuated by the widespread breaches of the job reservation code in the decades of rising industrial employment.

WAGE PRESSURES AND POLICY

In recent years, wage policy in many countries has become an important part of aggregate regulation of the economy. From this viewpoint, the South African government faces a dichotomous situation.[34] For a complex of reasons, the pressures to increase African wages are muted. Static or declining average agricultural productivity in the African rural 'reserves' has meant that a pool of surplus labour from these areas has been prepared to work at a relatively cheap wage rate. Control over the influx of African labour might have created an artificial shortage of unskilled labour and so raised its wage rate. But this possibility has been counteracted by the absence of a viable or legal base for African union organization, while job reservation and the fear of 'endorsement out' of urban areas has also hampered the competitive bidding up of wage rates. Furthermore, there is a large supply of foreign unskilled labour employed in South Africa, and this competes with domestic labour to delay any increase in the unskilled wage rate. (While labour immigration means a gain to foreign workers at the direct expense of South African labour, it is sometimes argued that cheap labour is essential for gold production and hence for an important proportion of exports.) But perhaps the main reason for relatively low incomes and bargaining power among Africans is the social, economic, educational and legislative colour bar. It should not be forgotten, however, that the effects of this policy have fallen with differing degrees of severity on different sectors. In the 1960s, for example, there was a relatively greater rise in African wage levels in industry and construction than in mining, which was probably due to the increased activity of the Wage Board in setting effective minimum

[34] See J. B. Knight, 'A Theory of Income Distribution in South Africa', *Bulletin of the Oxford Institute of Economics and Statistics*, vol. 26, 1964, p. 308.

wages in individual industries and a new attitude on the part of employers.

In contrast to the African labour situation, the South African government fosters and faces the bargaining strength of white labour. A period of full employment for white labour since the war and bargaining processes under the Industrial Conciliation Act have permitted successive negotiated wage increases across a broad front. (Other non-African employees appear to have been carried along in varying degrees with the advance of white wages.) At those times when inflation has threatened the economy, however, the government has made no efforts to undertake the type of controls over the labour market that in other countries fall under the heading of incomes policy. Rather, as other sections of this chapter describe, the government has relied on 'traditional' fiscal and monetary devices (especially the latter), though admonitions and requests for wage restraint have at times been made by those responsible for economic policy.

It is now customary to discuss inflation by reference to the 'Phillips curve' device of plotting wage changes against the level of unemployment. The ordinary difficulties of this 'trade-off' analysis are compounded in the South African context by the absence of data on African unemployment. The only data available – as shown in Table 5.7 – indicate merely the substantial decline in registered unemployment for population groups other than Africans between 1963 and 1970. Judging from the study by Hume, it seems likely that the relationship between wage increases and unemployment varies between the 'white' and 'black' labour markets in South Africa, the former displaying the traditional expectations of the Phillips curve (with most above-average wage increases occurring at below-average unemployment levels, and vice versa). In the 'black' labour market, however, Hume's finding was the direct opposite of this.[35] With bargaining power concentrated in the politically dominant white portion of the labour market, any attempts at incomes policy in South Africa would most probably meet with more than ordinary difficulties.

PRICES POLICY

Attempts to ease the rate of price increase through a deliberate 'prices policy' have, like an incomes policy, been absent from South Africa, though in theory the government Price Controller has power

[35] *S.A.J.E.*, September 1970, pp. 242-3.

to freeze prices. It is also true that South Africa has had comprehensive legislation restricting the scope of monopolistic practices since 1955 when the Monopolistic Conditions Act was passed. This Act was based on a 1952 Report by the Board of Trade and Industry, which found that, although 'as a whole, the existing system of competition works satisfactorily, there definitely are harmful conditions and practices [in South Africa in which] with its limited market, monopolistic situations are a frequent occurrence'.[36] In terms of the 1955 Act, the Minister of Economic Affairs might direct the Board of Trade and Industries to investigate any practice which, over a wide field of activity, 'restricts competition'. The Minister is given powers to control restrictive practices through publicity, through the potential suspension of custom tariff protection, and by other means such as direct penalties. The Act operated on the principle of the later United Kingdom legislation that restrictive practices should not be condemned *per se* and should be curtailed only where it could be shown that they were against the public interest. The measure has been sparingly used and seems designed mainly as a deterrent to more obvious and harmful abuses. As is usual with trade practices legislation, the Act excluded the operations of agricultural control boards and employees' organizations. The main point about the Act (for our purposes) is, however, that it has never been used as part of an 'incomes and prices policy', and, more particularly, it was not passed as anything like a *quid pro quo* for wage restraint on the part of unions.

THE FRANZEN COMMISSION

The *Third Report of the* (Franzen) *Commission on Fiscal and Monetary Policy*[37] emphasized the view that South African macroeconomic policies during the decade of the 1960s stressed monetary rather than fiscal controls. The Commission concluded (p. 9) that 'a strong case can be made out (in South Africa) for the more purposeful use of fiscal policy as a weapon against inflation. Fiscal policy can be employed in such a way as to act as a brake specifically on the increase of private consumption and unproductive government expenditure'. In this Report, the Commission (p. 6) recommended 'stricter control over the growth of public expenditure and the manner in which the budgetary deficit is financed'. It made several specific recommendations (Chapter 2) on the control of spending in

[36] Report No. 327 of the Board, para. 255.
[37] RP 87/1970, Pretoria.

the public sector, including the programming of government expenditure, forward planning over a number of years, and cost–benefit studies in respect of larger projects. 'This would enable a central guiding body, such as the proposed Cabinet Committee for Finance, to determine priorities.' The Commission also argued that the government should consider the introduction of a unitary budget to replace the division between revenue and loan accounts. 'This would help to focus attention more especially on the size of the annual deficit in the accounts of the central government'. In Chapters 3 and 4, the Commission considered the influence of fiscal policy on private saving, consumption and investment. It recommended (p. 71) that 'use should be made of indirect taxes as the main instrument in a fiscal stabilization policy, because the economic side-effects of taxes of this kind are smaller than are the side-effects of other taxes'. The Commission also recommended (p. 87) that 'through relevant tax legislation the Minister of Finance should be authorized to adjust the paths of certain taxes and the loan levy between budgets, if and when the course of economic activity demands . . .' and (p. 76) 'that the practice of using the surcharge-discount method as a stabilization instrument should be continued'.[38]

On monetary policy, the Commission distinguished (p. 10) three main factors: (1) the credit-creating activities of the banking institutions; (2) the financing practices of the State; and (3) developments in the balance of payments. It noted that 'during the past decade control over bank credit has indicated that during any particular year at least one of these three factors has had a disruptive influence on monetary stability. Consequently, in spite of the adoption of drastic measures such as the credit ceiling, the money supply in South Africa has increased much faster than production'. In Chapters 6 and 7 the Commission made proposals for strengthening the instruments of control at the disposal of the Reserve Bank. These proposals included a narrowing of the definition of liquid assets which, in the Commission's words (p. 14) would 'have a far-reaching influence on the existing money market and the financing practices of the Land Bank as well as those of certain other institutions'. The relevant findings of the Franzen Commission are now being studied by a Technical Committee on Bank and Building Society Legislation with the object of redrafting the present Banks Act. One of the findings of the Commission that will no doubt receive attention is that concerning the proliferation of deposit-taking institutions –

[38] Between 1960 and 1971, there were three discounts and one surcharge on income tax on individuals in South Africa.

some of which have country-wide branch systems – which all compete for the same pool of savings. 'The question arises whether it has become necessary for the legislature to reserve particular "areas" for the activities of banks and insurers.'

An area not covered by the Franzen Commission's terms of reference was that of incomes policy. But the Commission did mention (p. 15) the efforts being made in other countries to influence wage determination directly, in contrast to the 'traditional independent negotiation between employers and employees in South Africa'. The Commission also warned that 'the timing of salary adjustments in the public sector is a matter of national importance and is not divorced from other measures which the state adopts against inflation'.

Potentially one of the most important issues considered by the Franzen Commission was South Africa's exchange rate policy. The question was raised (p. 256) of whether the tying of the rand to sterling and the resulting cross rates with other currencies that resulted from this coupling remained in South Africa's best interest.

'When the British pound is under pressure because of the continuing balance of payments problems encountered in the British economy, the result is that unfavourable rates between sterling and other currencies, especially in respect of forward exchange contracts, arise . . . South Africa thus experiences the same difficulty as do other small countries, namely that they cannot readily follow an independent exchange rate policy. . . . It would appear to the Commission that it has become necessary for the South African monetary authorities to have a thorough study made of the exchange rate arrangements that are likely to suit South Africa's special purpose best . . . with a view to the extension of South Africa's export trade there will have to be an investigation into the possibilities of having a direct forward quotation between the rand and the most important non-sterling currencies.'

Another possibility mentioned by the Commission (p. 257) was the establishment of a national exchange market like that of Canada.

'This would mean that there would have to be direct quotations daily for sterling and dollars in such a market. The market requirements of other currencies would have to be met by purchasing the relative currencies in other exchange markets by offering sterling or dollars.'

The Commission (p. 117) doubted, however, whether it would be possible to create such an exchange market in South Africa 'under present circumstances'.

CONCLUSION

At the start of the 1970s, the South African economy is on the threshold of important changes. These include the possibility of a shift in emphasis from a macro-economic policy stressing monetary controls to one which, as suggested by the Franzen Commission, places more emphasis on fiscal policy (including the containment of unjustifiably high levels of public expenditure).

On fiscal policy, the South African Government has accepted the recommendation of the Commission that a special Cabinet Committee for Finance under the chairmanship of the Minister of Finance be appointed. This will seek to attain a larger measure of central direction, priority determination and co-ordination of expenditure incurred by all bodies in the public sector. The dilemma of restraining public sector expenditure is, however, well portrayed by a remark of the Minister of Finance made in July 1971. He stated that 'the expenditure of the (public) authorities has recently increased more rapidly than I should like to see, though nearly all this increase has been for very essential services'.[39] The problem of the co-ordination of monetary and fiscal policy is likely to remain during the seventies, though the 'lesson' of 1965/6 may have been well learned. At that time, as mentioned above, when the monetary authorities were applying a large array of other measures to control demand, expenditure in the public sector was actually allowed to increase rapidly.[40] Apart from the ordinary pressures for increased public expenditure in an expanding economy, the problem of containing the level and growth of public expenditure in South Africa is compounded by growing defence budgets and by the (often duplicated) provision of facilities in a racially segregated society, which practises also the costly and wasteful system of migrant labour. Moreover, an industrial decentralization policy for reasons of racial ideology has been undertaken over the last ten years.[41]

[39] Address to the South African Institute of Public Administration.

[40] J. J. Cloete has also pointed out that at this time the government 'engaged in large-scale short-term borrowing from the banking system, and also shortened the maturity of the public debt instead of lengthening it as necessitated by anti-inflationary debt management'. See 'The Implications for Monetary Policy of Post-War Developments in the Market for Bank Deposits', *S.A.J.E.*, September 1970, p. 279.

[41] See J. P. Nieuwenhuysen. 'Prospects and Issues in the Development of the Reserves', *S.A.J.E.*, June 1964.

(This policy has, however, despite substantial incentives to industrialists, had very limited success. By the end of 1970, only 68,500 Africans had been employed in 'border' (decentralized) areas since the start of the programme.[42] No doubt some of this employment would have occurred even in the absence of the incentives.)

Judgment of the complex consequences of stressing indirect over direct taxation, as recommended by the Franzen Commission, has also to be seen in the context of South Africa's racial structure, and the severe inequalities in income distribution previously mentioned. Even if the object of changing tax rates is to restrain or stimulate spending (rather than alter the basic structure of taxation), the use of variations in indirect taxation for this purpose is open to question. The Franzen Commission (*Third Report*, p. 17) was 'convinced that a more considerable change in the level of consumer spending can be brought about by means of indirect than can be brought about by direct taxation, especially in the event of an upward adjustment in the relevant rates. The Commission recommends that use should be made of indirect taxes as the main instrument in a fiscal stabilization policy, because the economic side-effects of taxes of this kind are smaller than are the side-effects of other taxes'. So forceful a conclusion may be unjustified in the light of the criticisms sometimes made that indirect taxes are often less useful than progressive income taxes as policy instruments since they are too directional, too slow to respond, and have little 'built-in' stabilization effect.[43] The Commission's conviction that initiative and productivity are likely to be diminished by increases in progressive income tax is also open to question, especially since, by international standards, the marginal tax rate at given income levels in South Africa is by no means high. The 1969 changes in taxation structure in South Africa, which followed the *First Report* of the Franzen Commission, basically reflected the view that, since higher income taxes would be at the expense of saving and not consumption, any increases in income tax would not be likely to be anti-inflationary and might even tend to increase inflation. Against this, however, it could be argued that the use of indirect taxes results in an increase in prices which may generate wage increases and aggravate inflationary conditions. But whatever the merits or drawbacks of using indirect tax as an economic stabilizer in South

[42] *Permanent Committee for the Location of Industry, Report for 1970, Government Printer, Pretoria, p. 5.*

[43] See F. S. Simpson, 'The Concept of "Fiscal Drag" and its Relevance to the the Tax Bulge in South Africa', *S.A.J.E.*, September 1968, p. 143.

Africa in the future, the 1971 tax changes include increases in income tax and are aimed at combating inflation.[44]

As to the weapons of monetary policy, the authorities have since March 1965 found it necessary to supplement the powers they already had under the Banks Act. This was done through the use of controls exercisable under proclamations in terms of the Currency and Exchanges Act (no. 9 of 1933). At the end of 1970, all registered banking institutions (except discount houses) were subject to the following control measures not provided for in the Banks Act: (a) maxima or 'ceilings' on certain investments in, and on discounts and advances to, the private sector; (b) a supplementary reserve requirement (in addition to the requirement of a reserve equal to 8 per cent of their short-term liabilities to the public); and (c) additional liquid asset requirements against the short-term liabilities of the banks.

The ceiling method of control has been an important aspect of recent monetary policy in South Africa. Opinions expressed before the Franzen Commission (see the *Third Report*, p. 146) were critical of the use of the method, and argued that the 'traditional' method of control through open market operations had been under-utilized. The Commission was, however (p. 146) 'quite convinced that the use of credit ceilings as a monetary policy measure in South Africa and elsewhere should be attributed to the fact that in the exceptional monetary circumstances experienced during recent years the traditional indirect measures have not been effective enough. The inflationary financing of a large inflow of capital from abroad not only creates large quantities of liquidity in the form of money and quasi-money in the possession of the private non-bank sector, but also supplies the banking system with considerable excess liquidity. Under these circumstances a restrictive policy based on liquidity or cash requirements for banking institutions might be ineffective. It then becomes necessary to employ as a temporary measure direct control over the credit granted by banks until such time as the liquidity of the banking system becomes normal . . . in the circumstances that arose in South Africa (during 1965–70) the monetary authorities had little other choice than to subject some credit granted by banking institutions to ceilings'. None the less, as the Commission notes elsewhere in the same report (p. 148), the ceilings were applied leniently by the Reserve Bank. This is shown by the fact that on a calendar year basis, bank credit granted to private institutions in

[44] See E. Spiro, 'The 1971 Income Tax Changes in South Africa', *Bulletin for International Fiscal Documentation*, September 1971, p. 327.

South Africa increased by 3 per cent in 1966, 4 per cent in 1967, 16 per cent in 1968, 19 per cent in 1969 and 13 per cent in 1970.

In its recommendations, the Commission stated that it definitely preferred the indirect measures of controlling bank credit by variable cash reserve and liquid asset requirements, but felt that it was sometimes necessary to supplement these with further measures on a temporary basis. The Commission therefore recommended (p. 149) 'that the banking legislation should be amended by the insertion of a section granting the Reserve Bank the power to issue credit directives to banking institutions and also to lay down penalties when its directives are not complied with'. It will be interesting to see how far any changes actually made in the banking legislation are able to cope with any future sudden (externally induced) changes in the commercial banks' cash and liquid reserves due, for example, to balance of payments surpluses.

As to its interest rate structure, South Africa has shared with money and capital markets elsewhere an unusually high level of interest rates in the late 1960s, though rates of interest in South Africa's public sector have not reached the record levels experienced in Britain, the United States, Canada and elsewhere. One of the reasons for this has been that exchange control has isolated South Africa to a certain extent from overseas interest rate movements. But the main explanation of relatively low public sector interest rates is the substantial use made in South Africa of a 'captive market'. In particular, the investment freedom of the Public Debt Commissioners is severely circumscribed, and in 1970 they owned 60 per cent of the outstanding marketable public debt.[45] On the other hand, the Franzen Commission (*Third Report*, p. 158) heard evidence that manufacturing industry could not expand sufficiently at the high levels of interest rates in the late 1960s. The Commission concluded that the level of interest rates and the allocation of funds in South Africa's money and capital markets 'show a decided lack of balance'. But this did not lead it to advocate legal deposit rate control: it could not 'recommend deposit rate control by legislation as a means of countering excessive competition for the public's funds'. Yet it was recommended that 'the Reserve Bank Act be amended by the insertion of a section enabling the Bank to control interest rates as well as to impose penalties for non-observance of its directives' (p. 167).

As it was, the authorities had exercised legal control over deposit rates in 1965 (in terms of a proclamation under the 1933 Currency

[45] See the Franzen Commission, *Third Report*, p. 56.

and Exchanges Act). This control laid down maximum rates for deposits of varying maturities, and was rescinded in 1966. In 1969 moral suasion was employed to keep the interest rate on 12-month deposits with commercial banks at 7 per cent. This was withdrawn in August 1970. But South African governments have thus far not regarded deposit rate control or any other form of interest rate control as an integral part of official interest-rate policy (unlike Australia, New Zealand and – previously – Canada). The scope for this control remains to be considered by the Technical Committee appointed by the government. Another issue receiving consideration at present is the possibility of more extensive employment of open-market operations, which have been limited by various factors, including the fairly small secondary market in government stock. The Franzen Commission's view (*Third Report*, p. 167) was that 'the Reserve Bank's present inability to carry out an effective open market policy is . . . a serious shortcoming in the existing instruments of monetary control'.

In all, therefore, it seems likely that during the 1970s, South African macro-economic policy will attempt to improve the means of controlling the money supply and to effect more flexibility and co-ordination in fiscal and monetary policy. If, however, the external uncertainties of the 1970s are as great as those in the 1960s, it would be optimistic to expect a substantially improved ability in the achievement of economic stability. External unpredictabilities have been related to South Africa's role as a major gold producer and the large share of foreign trade in its gross national product. More particularly, the country has had a proclivity to become depleted of overseas investment in times of internal political strain, and to become a haven for foreign funds in times of international currency crisis.

Internally, the dualism of the economy, and the attempt to squeeze the skills necessary for growth from a minority of the population, may prove to be a serious barrier to stable growth. There is certainly a growing awareness of the skilled labour shortage in South Africa, perhaps most ably expressed by the chairman of the Anglo-American Corporation, Mr H. F. Oppenheimer, in his 1971 (annual) address. 'To my mind', he said,

'it is quite wrong to represent South Africa's economic difficulties as merely superficial . . . South Africa's undoubted potential for rapid, long-term economic growth requires major changes in the whole economy for its realization. What has been achieved in

South Africa is very remarkable, so remarkable indeed that we are approaching the stage where the full potential of the economy, as it is at present organized, will have been realized, so that if structural changes are not made, we will have to content ourselves with a much lower rate of growth . . . South African industry has not been able to make full and effective use of the large reservoir of labour that is available to it. . . . Prospects for economic growth will not be attained so long as a large majority of the population is prevented by lack of formal education and technical training or by positive prohibition from playing the full part of which it is capable in the national development.'[46]

This problem prompts the suggestion that improvements in productivity performance in South Africa will depend not so much on more efficiency in overall demand management as on eradicating general inefficiencies at the micro level. One study of indices of productivity per labour unit in manufacturing in various countries, including South Africa, emphasizes this view.[47]

Other clouds hang over the more immediate prospects of the South African economy. In the great variety of discussions about safeguarding particular interests in the context of the British negotiations for entry into the European Economic Community, South Africa has been an area of conspicuous silence. Although South Africa, as an industrial and primary-producing country, will be as fully affected as, say, Australia by the alteration of trading patterns that will follow the enlargement of the EEC, none of the principal participants has shown any serious inclination to defend, or even to state, South Africa's interests.[48] The change in South Africa's position will come with the ending of 'Commonwealth' preferences, from which certain exports have continued to benefit, even since South Africa ceased to be a member of the Commonwealth. Britain has continued to be the largest single market for South Africa's

[46] (London) *Times*, June 9, 1971, p. 23.

[47] See *Standard Bank Review*, November 1971, p. 10. According to this study, South Africa's rate of productivity increase was well behind that of Britain, the USA and West Germany, and very substantially behind that of Japan, for the period 1953–70.

[48] The Franzen Commission in its *Third Report* (p. 248) also argued strongly that South Africa's needs – especially for providing industrial employment for a rapidly expanding population – were not properly served by the large extent to which it has 'bound' tariffs (that is, agreed not to increase them) under GATT. The Commission suggested that South Africa has much less room for manoeuvre than Australia or Canada in trying to provide tariff protection for new sectors of industry.

visible exports, and the buoyant level of these exports has been assisted by the preferences. The prospect of being 'left out in the cold' after the negotiations is clearly of concern to South Africa, whose political isolation must make associate status with the expanded Community inconceivable. To what extent this prospective deterioration in South Africa's trading position will be alleviated by the devaluation of the rand in December 1971 is one of the crucial issues for the economy in the early 1970s.

Select Bibliography

Annual Economic Report of the Reserve Bank of South Africa, Pretoria.
'Annual Review of the Financial and Economic Situation in South Africa', by the governor of the Reserve Bank; Reprinted in successive September issues of the *South African Journal of Economics* (S.A.J.E.).
R. N. Brown, 'South African Gold Sales to the I.M.F.', *S.A.J.E.*, June 1971.
J. J. Cloete, 'The Implications for Monetary Policy of Post-War Developments in the Market for Bank Deposits', *S.A.J.E.*, September 1971.
Conference on 'Inflation and the South African Economy', *S.A.J.E.*, December 1967.
A. B. Dickman, 'The South African Money Market—Progress and Problems since 1960', *S.A.J.E.*, September 1965.
Economic Development Programme for the Republic of South Africa (various years since 1964), Government Printer, Pretoria.
J. de V. Graaf, 'Alternative Models of South African Growth', *S.A.J.E.*, March 1962.
I. Hume, 'Notes on South African Wage Movements,' *S.A.J.E.*, September 1970.
B. Kantor, 'The Money Supply and the Inflationary Process', *S.A.J.E.*, December 1968.
J. B. Knight, 'A Theory of Income Distribution in South Africa', *Bulletin of the Oxford Institute of Economics and Statistics*, vol. 26, 1964.
J. P. Nieuwenhuysen, 'Prospects and Issues in the Development of the Reserves', *S.A.J.E.*, June 1964.
Reports of the (Franzen) *Commission of Enquiry into Fiscal and Monetary Policy in South Africa.*
    a. *First Report: Taxation in South Africa*, R.P. 24/1969
    b. *Second Report: Taxation in South Africa*, R.P. 86/1970
    c. *Third Report: Fiscal and Monetary Policy in South Africa*, R.P. 87/1970.
C. S. Richards, 'Problems of Economic Development in South Africa', *S.A.J.E.*, March 1962.
South Africa: A Survey, *The Banker*, September 1971.
South Africa: A Survey, *Financial Times* (London), 14 June 1971.
R. D. Stacey, 'The Accuracy of the Stellenbosch Forecasts', *S.A.J.E.*, September 1968.
Under the Green Bay Tree (A Survey of South Africa), *The Economist*, 29 June 1968.

Statistical Appendix to Chapter 5

LIST OF TABLES

163

Table 5.1. *South Africa: Change in gross domestic product as at constant prices**

(Per cent)

1960	5·9
1961	5·6
1962	5·8
1963	8·1
1964	6·7
1965	6·6
1966	4·7
1967	7·6
1968	3·8
1969	7·0
1970	5·2

* The figures for 1960–2 are at 1958 prices, and those for 1963–70 at 1963 prices.

Source: *South African Reserve Bank Quarterly Bulletin.*

Table 5.2. *South Africa: Balance of payments*
(R. million)

	1961	1962	1963	1964	1965	1966	1967	1968	1969	1970
Current Account										
Merchandise exports, f.o.b.	923	948	1,024	1,074	1,067	1,216	1,323	1,513	1,484	1,413
Net gold output	576	632	688	736	775	769	775	769	847	837
Service receipts	236	253	262	305	319	350	433	486	501	534
Merchandise imports, f.o.b.	−1,017	−1,041	−1,283	−1,578	−1,799	−1,645	−1,942	−1,885	−2,199	−2,578
Service payments	−490	−484	−538	−603	−681	−723	−811	−880	−1,003	−1,055
Total goods and services (net receipts+)	228	309	153	−66	−319	−33	−222	3	−320	−849
Transfers (net receipts+)	−13	9	13	18	23	32	41	72	58	61
Balance on current account	215	317	166	−48	−296	−1	−181	75	−262	−788
Capital Movements										
Private sector	−100	−69	−95	−56	170	160	241	389	203	403
Central government and banking	−29	−19	15	15	85	−19	−79	70	−6	98
Total capital movements (net inflow+)	−129	−88	−80	−41	255	141	162	459	197	501
Total change in gold and foreign exchange reserves	86	229	86	−89	−38	140	−27	534	−58	−263

Source: South African Reserve Bank Quarterly Bulletin.

Table 5.3. *South Africa: Consumer price index*

	1958 = 100	1963 = 100
1961	104·6	n.a.
1962	106·1	n.a.
1963	107·5	100·0
1964	110·1	102·6
1965	114·1	106·7
1966	118·2	110·6
1967	122·2	114·4
1968	124·3	115·7
1969	n.a.	120·5
1970	n.a.	125·4

'n.a.' signifies 'not available'.

Source: South African Reserve Bank Quarterly Bulletin.

Table 5.4. *South Africa: Demand for and the supply of goods and services, 1969*

(R. million)

Demand		
Private consumption expenditure		7,186
Current expenditure by general government		1,457
Gross domestic fixed investment		2,613
Public authorities	966	
Public corporations	271	
Private businesses	1,376	
Changes in inventories		286
Residual		72
Gross domestic expenditure		11,614
Exports		2,632
Aggregate demand		14,246
Supply		
Gross domestic product		11,635
Imports		2,611
Aggregate supply		14,246

Source: Franzen Commission, Third Report, p. 4.

166

Table 5.5a. *South Africa: Personal income and expenditure*
(R. million)

	1963	1964	1965	1966	1967	1968	1969	1970
Remuneration of employees	3,301	3,642	4,074	4,509	4,887	5,393	5,907	6,657
Income from property by households	1,370	1,373	1,532	1,703	1,931	1,802	1,896	1,979
Current transfers received from general government	154	167	187	197	211	230	273	330
Transfers received from rest of world	47	49	44	53	60	84	81	71
Current income	4,872	5,231	5,837	6,462	7,089	7,509	8,157	9,037
Less direct taxes	275	308	362	425	482	534	539	578
Disposable personal income	4,597	4,923	5,475	6,037	6,607	6,975	7,618	8,459
Less private consumption expenditure	3,974	4,463	4,857	5,267	5,684	6,252	6,889	7,649
Less current transfers to general government	15	17	19	22	25	27	30	35
Less transfers to the rest of the world	39	36	28	29	32	35	39	46
Personal saving	569	407	571	719	865	661	660	729

Source: South African Reserve Bank Quarterly Bulletin.

Table 5.5b. *South Africa: Current revenue and expenditure of general government*

(R. million)

	1963	1964	1965	1966	1967	1968	1969	1970
Income from property	136	161	151	117	216	186	198	201
Less interest on public debt	48	50	66	77	97	122	178	168
Net income from property	88	111	85	40	119	64	20	33
Indirect taxes	428	496	518	562	644	714	916	1,017
Direct taxes	659	682	780	873	1,017	1,113	1,229	1,361
Current transfers received from households	15	17	19	22	25	27	30	35
Transfers received from rest of world	14	14	15	17	24	36	31	41
Current revenue	1,204	1,320	1,421	1,514	1,829	1,954	2,226	2,487
Consumption expenditure	690	779	868	978	1,041	1,146	1,301	1,455
Subsidies	51	59	69	80	102	102	117	145
Current transfers to households	154	167	187	197	211	230	273	330
Transfers to the rest of the world	3	2	1	1	1	1	1	1
Current expenditure	898	1,007	1,125	1,256	1,355	1,479	1,692	1,932
Current surplus of general government	306	313	296	258	474	475	534	556

Source: South African Reserve Bank Quarterly Bulletin.

Table 5.6. South Africa: Employment of labour in non-agricultural sectors

	Private manufacturing	Gold	Trade	Railways	Central government	Provincial administration	Local authorities	Private construction	Private service	Post Office	Other	Total
Number in 1963	760,724	444,477	376·128	219,833	217·750	156·565	151·325	133,293	58,179	43,679	146,230	2,796,905
Index number (1963 = 100)												
1963	100·0	100·0	100·0	100·0	100·0	100·0	100·0	100·0	100·0	100·0	100·0	100·0
1964	109·4	99·1	n.a.	101·4	103·7	98·8	104·2	113·2	106·6	100·3	111·4	104·9
1965	121·2	97·2	n.a.	102·7	105·6	99·0	108·3	152·4	113·2	100·6	119·9	111·8
1966	127·0	95·8	106·9	101·9	124·2	102·9	110·7	167·8	114·6	105·0	127·0	115·8
1967	132·2	93·1	110·4	100·2	125·5	103·8	110·8	189·4	114·0	107·2	124·7	118·2
1968	135·5	94·2	114·2	101·2	125·3	108·2	115·6	205·0	112·9	110·6	130·1	121·8
1969	144·0	92·9	117·5	101·5	128·0	113·8	115·6	234·6	117·2	118·6	133·9	126·9
1970	n.a.	95·7	n.a.	n.a.	n.a.	n.a.	n.a.	n.a.	n.a.	n.a.	146·1	n.a.

'n.a.' signifies 'not available'.

Source: *South African Reserve Bank Quarterly Bulletin.*

169

Table 5.7. *South Africa: Registered unemployed (excluding Africans)*

	Index number (1963 = 100)
1963	100·0
1964	75·1
1965	58·6
1966	68·1
1967	69·9
1968	68·8
1969	54·8
1970	42·7

Source: *South African Reserve Bank Quarterly Bulletin.*

Table 5.8. *South Africa: Wages and employment*

	Wages (R. million)		Numbers employed		Annual wage per head (R.)	
	1965	1970	1965	1970	1965	1970
Mining						
Whites	186·7	264·9	63,800	61,700	2,926	4,293
Coloureds	2·8	5·3	4,500	5,500	567	914
Asians			440	300		
Africans	93·3	121·7	538,300	573,500	173	212
Manufacturing						
Whites	545·9	996·4	233,900	277,000	2,334	3,597
Coloureds	97·3	166·6	150,100	195,800	648	851
Asians	34·6	66·4	50,900	74,200	680	895
Africans	220·4	380·7	494,600	617,200	440	617
Construction						
Whites	83·0	226·4	36,600	59,500	2,227	3,805
Coloureds	19·7	57·5	21,500	44,600	916	1,289
Asians	0·9	7·8	1,100	4,500	818	1,733
Africans	49·3	144·9	122,300	247,000	403	587

Source: Department of Labour, Pretoria.

Table 5.9. *South Africa: Size and composition of population*

| | 1960 | | 1970* | |
	Number	%	Number	%
Whites	3,080,000	18·4	3,779,000	17·6
Coloureds	1,528,000	9·1	2,036,000	9·5
Asians	494,000	3·0	633,000	3·0
Africans	11,627,000	69·5	14,975,000	69·9
Total	16,729,000	100·0	21,423,000	100·0

* Preliminary figures.

Source: Population Census.

Table 5.10. South Africa: Gross domestic product by kind of economic activity

	1963		1964		1965		1966		1967		1968		1969	
	R. million	%	R. million	%	R. million	%	R. million	%	R. million	%	R. million	%	R. million	%
Agriculture, forestry and fishing	753	12·2	711	10·5	760	10·2	834	10·3	1,047	11·7	963	10·1	1,005	9·5
Mining and quarrying	790	12·8	882	13·0	947	12·7	1,024	12·7	1,050	11·8	1,114	11·7	1,231	11·7
Manufacturing	1,363	22·1	1,542	22·8	1,745	23·5	1,875	23·2	2,010	22·5	2,143	22·5	2,143	22·7
Electricity, gas and water	157	2·5	169	2·5	181	2·4	200	2·5	228	2·6	253	2·7	281	2·7
Construction	184	3·0	237	3·5	299	4·0	325	4·0	353	3·6	395	4·1	470	4·5
Wholesale and retail trade, catering and accommodation	869	14·1	962	14·2	1,055	14·2	1,116	13·8	1,241	13·9	1,378	14·4	1,509	14·3
Transport, storage and communication	613	9·9	677	10·0	710	9·6	756	9·4	861	9·7	910	9·5	993	9·4
Financing, insurance services, real estate and business	560	9·1	621	9·2	683	9·2	751	9·3	827	9·3	946	9·9	1,093	10·4
Community social and personal services	115	1·9	127	1·9	136	1·8	151	1·9	165	1·9	183	1·9	201	1·9
Sub-Total	5,403	87·5	5,928	87·5	6,515	87·7	7,033	87·1	7,781	87·3	8,285	86·8	9,172	87·0
General government	530	8·6	577	8·5	624	8·4	722	8·9	793	8·9	883	9·3	961	9·1
Other producers (domestic servants etc.)	245	4·0	267	3·9	291	3·9	318	3·9	344	3·9	373	3·9	408	3·9
Gross domestic product at factor cost	6,178	100	6,772	100	7,430	100	8,073	100	8,917	100	9,540	100	10,540	100

Source: South African Reserve Bank Quarterly Bulletin.

Table 5.11. *South Africa: Stock exchange activity, share prices and yields*

Period	Index of Number of shares traded 1963 = 100	Selling price of units Index 1966 = 100	Yield %
1961	44	n.a.	n.a.
1962	66	n.a.	n.a.
1963	100	n.a.	n.a.
1964	110	n.a.	n.a.
1965	77	90	4·21
1966	76	100	3·82
1967	89	114	3·45
1968	186	164	2·40
1969	270	220	1·79
1970	151	144	3·10

'n.a.' signifies 'not available'.

Source: *South African Reserve Bank Quarterly Bulletin.*

Table 5.12. *South Africa: Unit trusts, purchases, sales and assets*

(R. million)

Year	Transactions in securities Purchases	Sales	Net investment	Total assets
1965	1·0		1·0	2·7
1966	20·4	1·2	19·3	24·6
1967	44·9	6·0	39·1	71·2
1968	190·6	30·6	160·0	284·9
1969	482·1	72·5	409·5	719·8
1970	36·0	122·2	− 86·3	579·6

Source: *South African Reserve Bank Quarterly Bulletin.*

Table 5.13. *South Africa: Expenditure on gross domestic product at 1963 prices*

(R. million)

	1963	1964	1965	1966	1967	1968	1969	1970
Private consumption expenditure	3,974	4,335	4,548	4,748	4,964	5,327	5,679	6,073
Consumption expenditure by general government	690	749	819	853	882	937	992	1,033
Gross domestic fixed investment	1,302	1,574	1,872	1,896	1,972	2,012	2,198	2,445
Change in inventories	203	146	207	8	424	6	260	487
Residual item	−25	2	−26	−77	−75	15	61	38
Gross domestic expenditure	6,144	6,806	7,420	7,428	8,167	8,297	9,190	10,076
Exports of goods and non-factor services	1,921	2,007	2,025	2,160	2,354	2,565	2,502	2,459
Expenditure on gross domestic product	6,547	6,986	7,448	7,799	8,391	8,712	9,326	9,807

Source: South African Reserve Bank Quarterly Bulletin.

Table 5.14. *South Africa: Absolute and relative size of various banking institutions*

	Total assets (R million)			Shares in total assets (per cent)		
Registered banking institutions:	End 1953	End 1964	End 1970	End 1953	End 1964	End 1970
Commercial banks	901	2,044	3,827	92·1	62·9	58·7
Merchant banks	—	264	542	—	8·1	8·3
Hire-purchase, savings and general banks	77	744	1,792	7·9	22·9	27·5
Discount houses	—	200	363	—	6·1	5·5
	978	3,252	6,524	100·0	100·0	100·0

Source: Third Report of the (Franzen) *Commission on Fiscal and Monetary Policy,* R.P. 87/1970, p. 178.

Table 5.15. *South Africa: Direction of trade*

(R. thousand)

| | Imports | | Exports | |
	1968	1969	1968	1969
Africa (unspecified)	120,462	111,026	249,085	255,322
UK	449,498	499,562	476,064	510,723
West Germany	253,698	292,913	101,310	102,829
France	67,015	61,196	37,517	42,992
Italy	73,038	84,857	42,961	44,536
Canada	44,557	53,064	24,290	28,281
USA	332,808	370,487	104,162	108,243
Brazil	7,750	12,070	510	2,505
Ceylon	12,455	11,610	1,543	707
Hong Kong	12,281	16,037	15,436	22,436
Japan	123,960	188,425	204,451	151,240
Australia	28,098	39,251	13,091	13,211
Total world trade	1,884,363	2,137,221	1,507,308	1,532,741
(of which Europe)	1,029,676	1,143,498	797,937	859,419

Source: Department of Customs and Excise.

Table 5.16. *South Africa: Selected imports and exports, 1969*

(R. million)

	Imports	Exports
Vegetable products and prepared foodstuffs	92·8	276·9
Mineral products	140·3	205·7
Chemical and allied products	133·7	53·3
Textiles and articles thereof	231·3	130·9
Precious and semi-precious stones, etc.	19·6	286·5
Base metals and articles thereof	139·2	250·8
Machinery and equipment	556·3	74·6
Vehicles and transport equipment	408·2	27·6

Source: Department of Customs and Excise.

Table 5.17. *South Africa. Mineral production*

Mineral	1968	1969
Antimony (metric tons)	27,367	29,608
Asbestos (metric tons)	236,301	258,120
Chrome (metric tons)	1,152,495	1,197,424
Coal (metric tons)	51,644,170	52,741,524
Copper (metric tons)	128,205	126,159
Fluorspar (metric tons)	108,537	150,245
Iron ore (metric tons)	8,231,055	8,785,890
Manganese (metric tons)	2,426,697	2,642,673
Phosphates, crude (metric tons)	1,565,097	1,678,162
Diamonds (metric carats)	6,742,019	7,131,593
Gold (Kf)	881,512	886,824

Source: Department of Mines.

Table 5.18. *South Africa: Percentage of public sector expenditure in total gross domestic product*

	Per cent of GDP			Average annual rate of growth (per cent)	
	1938	1960	1969	1938–60	1960–9
Central government sector	7·8	7·5	11·2	8·3	13·9
Provincial administrations	4·2	5·6	6·3	9·9	10·5
Local authorities	3·6	3·6	3·4	8·5	5·8
Public corporations	0·8	1·2	2·6	10·5	19·0
Total	16·4	17·9	23·5	8·9	12·3

Source: *Third Report* of the Franzen Commission, p. 21.

Table 5.19. *South Africa: Total money and near-money*
(R. million)

End of	
1965	2470·3
1966	2623·7
1967	2832·6
1968	3421·9
1969	3774·5

Source: *South African Reserve Bank Quarterly Bulletin.*

176

Chapter 6*

MACRO-ECONOMIC POLICIES IN THE FOUR COUNTRIES

J. O. N. PERKINS and J. P. NIEUWENHUYSEN

The four preceding chapters have discussed macro-economic policy in each of the four countries individually. In this final chapter an attempt is made to contrast and compare the use that each of them has made of the principal measures of macro-economic policy, and to assess the relevance of their experience for all four of them, and to some extent also for other countries.

As a background to the discussion it seems appropriate to ask how successful these four countries have been in achieving the aims of macro-economic policy.

There are no unambiguous indicators of how successful a country has been in achieving these objectives. Perhaps it might be argued that the rate of economic growth or the absolute living standard of a country would be to some extent a relevant indicator; and it is certainly true that a country that maintains full employment and avoids serious inflation, whilst maintaining adequate but not excessive reserves, could be expected to have higher living standards and a faster rate of growth over a period than an otherwise similar country that is less successful. But the rate of economic growth and living standards are affected by many other influences, and by many other aspects of economic policy in addition to those discussed in this book. There are, moreover, numerous serious statistical limitations and difficulties in the way of using the available data to make international comparisons of rates of growth or living standards.

The population and work force of all four countries have been growing fairly rapidly by comparison with those of most other countries of comparable living standards (such as Western Europe or the USA). So far as the faster growth of the work force is an element tending to increase the overall rate of growth this has been a principal factor responsible for their attainment of real rates of growth as high as some 4–6 per cent per annum (so far as one may estimate them from the available data, with all their well-known deficiencies as

* The section on Incomes Policies on pp. 197–9 is by J. P. Nieuwenhuysen; the remainder is by J. O. N. Perkins.

177

indicators of growth rates). On the other hand, their rapidly expanding work force has necessitated 'capital-widening' investment, to equip their populations with social and industrial capital, and this requirement has therefore absorbed savings that might otherwise have been devoted to raising output per head ('capital-deepening' investment). This may help to account for the fairly slow rate of growth of productivity in the four countries (of the order of 2–3% per annum) by comparison at any rate with Continental Western Europe or Japan, though at a rate that does not differ greatly from that of the USA or Britain. At the same time, the fairly high rate of growth of their work force and their population probably served to attract capital to these countries, and to that extent to increase the available resources at their disposal for providing real investment goods. It is also possible that the fairly high immigration into these countries tended to raise their output per head of population, partly because migrants tend to be concentrated into the productive age groups, and partly because recent immigrants may work particularly hard in order to become established in a new country, whilst they may also bring with them more energetic attitudes to work than are typical in the country of immigration. Recent immigrants may also tend to save at a fairly high rate in the years immediately after their arrival; and so far as this is true additional savings would be available to help provide the real investment goods required to equip the immigrants. Furthermore, the relative youth of the capital stock of such countries of high population growth and high capital inflow in recent years is a factor making for relatively high and rising productivity. But even when all due allowance is made for these considerations, it seems likely that the rate of growth of productivity in these countries has been somewhat held down by the need to provide real capital at a rate appropriate for their rapidly rising population at a high standard of living. At the same time the fairly rapid growth of their work force has almost certainly tended to raise the rate of growth of their total output (compared with what it would have been with lower or no net immigration), even when all due allowance is made for the possibly slower consequential rate of increase in their productivity.

If the rate of economic growth and of output per head at a high standard of living is considered to be even a partial indicator of success in macro-economic policy, this group of countries could be placed somewhat above Britain, and probably also the USA; but certainly below Japan, at any rate in terms of rate of growth of GNP or productivity, though perhaps not yet in terms of living standards. They would rank below West Germany, France and Italy in their rate of growth of output, and certainly that of output per head, though their performance would be broadly comparable to that of a number of other Western European countries. But it is hard to assess at all exactly the economic performance of our four countries compared with that of the countries of Western Europe by a straight comparison of annual rates of growth of GNP or of output per head, because it is difficult to decide what account one should take of the probability that the overall growth rates in the four countries were considerably raised by the much more rapid growth in their work force compared with those of Western Europe, and that the rate of growth of output per head in the four countries might well have been held down to some extent by the need to devote much of their capital resources to equipping the rapidly growing population.

More relevant indicators of the success of macro-economic policies are those relating to the labour market. But international comparisons of such indicators are notoriously unreliable, mainly because of the different methods adopted by different countries in calculating unemployment (and unfilled vacancies). There are also special problems involved in such comparisons as a consequence of the widely differing degrees of structural and regional unemployment as between one country and another; for such unemployment is not readily susceptible to treatment by overall macro-economic measures such as have been discussed in this book.

If all due allowance is made for the difficulties of such international comparisons, one may still assert (however tentatively) that New Zealand's record of maintaining full employment – on a very ambitious definition – is probably second to none. On this count Australia also compares well with virtually all other countries except for a few in Western Europe, but it must be borne in mind that Australia has no serious regional unemployment problems, even though rural unemployment in the last few years does present, on a small scale, a problem of a somewhat similar type, although spread over a number of geographical areas of the country. By contrast, Canada has major regional unemployment problems, as well as a considerable seasonal unemployment problem, and these facts make comparisons between Canada and the other countries difficult. Probably – even after all due allowance has been made for these special difficulties in Canada – that country could be said to have had rather less success in maintaining full employment than did New Zealand or Australia over the period covered in this book.

Comparisons with South Africa are virtually impossible, because of the absence of adequate data on African employment and unemployment; but full employment for the white population appears to have been very successfully achieved. Taking the four countries as a group (and inevitably omitting the African population of South Africa), it is clear that none of them suffered unemployment as severe as that of the USA, nor as severe as that of Britain in the early 1970s.

The macro-economic policies of these countries played a considerable role in maintaining something close to full employment, and the principles on which their full employment policies were based were much the same as in most of the developed countries of the world. If any special degree of success was achieved in these four countries it seems unlikely that their approach to these problems was appreciably more enlightened or better administered than that of, say, Britain or the USA. Their sharing of a common English-speaking tradition of Keynesian economics did, however, probably facilitate the acceptance and application of modern macro-economic ideas: many – perhaps most – of their leading economists and administrators have undergone some part of their training in Britain or the USA, and the influence of British and American thought on their politicians and on economic thought and training has been considerable. But these ideas had by the 1950s become a common tradition of the Western world as a whole, and no particular weight should therefore be attached to the English-speaking tradition of economics shared by the four countries as an explanation of their general success in maintaining full employment.

The maintenance of full employment in these four countries was probably facilitated by the high rate of growth of their populations, and the considerable potential of their unexploited natural resources. This underlying potential for a high rate of growth encouraged, and was itself sustained by, considerable capital inflow into all of them, especially in the form of direct investment, with its accompanying inflow of knowhow. It was also facilitated by the reasonably good markets that all of them enjoyed for some, at least, of their main primary exports. It is true that New Zealand, in particular, was handicapped by considerable balance of payment difficulties for much of the period; but, in general, the balance of payments of all four was assisted by fairly strong world demand for many of their exports, as well as by capital inflow (which was itself attracted by the export prospects of prospective mineral developments in Australia, Canada and South Africa, and to a much smaller extent in New

Zealand). These considerations are relevant to any explanation of why their macro-economic policies were fairly successful in maintaining full employment, for a country with a consistently weak balance of payments is more likely to feel it necessary to tolerate higher levels of unemployment.

Despite the generally high level of economic activity, these countries did not suffer more inflation than other comparable developed and industrialized countries (as Table 6.1 shows). It is

Table 6.1. *Annual rate of increase in consumer prices indexes, various countries*

(Per cent)

	Average of annual increases 1960–70	1971
Australia	2·4	6·0
Canada	2·8	2·9
New Zealand	3·6	8·6
South Africa	2·7	6·9
W. Germany	2·8	6·2
USA	2·9	4·0
France	3·7	4·6
UK	4·1	8·3
Japan	5·8	5·2

Source: OECD, *Consumer Prices Indexes; U.N. Monthly Bulletin of Statistics.*

true that all of them shared in the sharp increase in inflation, even at less than full employment as normally defined, that became prevalent in the developed world in the late 1960s and early 1970s, and that New Zealand, in particular, showed a rate of inflation in 1970/1 that was about as high as that of any comparable country.[1] But it does not appear to be true that their generally greater success in maintaining full employment over the period as a whole brought with it greater inflation than prevailed elsewhere. Indeed, Australia and South Africa, and until 1970/1 New Zealand, had rather less inflation than did most countries with a similar degree of industrialization or similar living standards during the 1960s.

[1] South Africa's rate of inflation of nearly 7 per cent in 1971 must also have been among the highest in industrialized countries.

It is possible that the relatively rapid growth of their work force helped to make it possible for these four countries to reconcile a high level of employment with a tolerable level of inflation, for a rapid growth of the work force facilitates the allocation of labour to the areas where there are bottlenecks; and in countries with a high rate of immigration additions to the work force are probably more likely to go where they are most needed than in countries where any necessary re-allocation involves re-settling workers already in the country. A high rate of immigration may also tend to limit the bargaining-power of wage-earners, and so restrain wage inflation.[2]

If some weight can be given to influences facilitating the maintenance of full employment without serious inflation in these countries, one might reasonably argue that their governments need not have been superior in their judgment and administration of macro-economic policy to those of other countries in order to meet with more success in maintaining full employment without serious inflation. The crucial role was probably played by good fortune – or, more exactly, a favourable combination of those economic circumstances outside the control of these countries, notably their endowment of natural resources, and their consequent attractiveness to immigrants and to overseas capital.

BUDGETARY AND MONETARY POLICY

In considering the various macro-economic measures it is important to bear in mind that each of them has a bearing upon both internal and external balance. Perhaps changes in budgetary and monetary measures are more usually thought of by policy-makers as being directed at maintaining full employment without inflation, whilst alterations of the exchange rate or of import controls or tariffs on imports are normally made principally with the aim of affecting the balance of payments. But any change in the setting of any one of these measures has effects on both internal and external balance. It is therefore appropriate to discuss each of the main types of measures with an eye to both its internal and external effects. The order in which they are treated is not a matter of any great importance. But the order chosen here is influenced by the fact that monetary measures are probably the most frequently varied, with budgetary measures being changed somewhat less readily,

[2] In South Africa the readily available indigenous labour force may have performed a similar function – 'immigration from within', as it has been called.

whereas exchange-rate policy and other special 'balance of payments measures' (as we may call them – though still bearing in mind that they affect internal as well as external balance) such as import taxes and export subsidies are generally altered only rarely. Long-term planning for growth has not been a major force in these countries, nor have prices and incomes policies. The National Development programmes in New Zealand and South Africa have, however, acted as a forum in which government and business views on long-term prospects can be co-ordinated, and been something of a focus for public discussion. The projections of the Economic Council of Canada have played the latter role to some extent, but are not drawn up within a framework of formal consultation between government and industry.

Monetary policy
The monetary measures used in the four countries can be classified under the following main headings: first, policy on the purchase and sale of government securities, including open-market operations and policy on the terms of the issue and the redemption of government bonds; secondly, policy towards the short-term money market; thirdly, policy for controlling the total and direction of bank lending, including the interest rates charged the banks for borrowing from the central bank as well as direct controls (both statutory and informal) over the level of bank lending and the cash or liquidity ratios to be observed by them; fourthly, direct controls over bank interest rates; and, finally, controls over non-bank financial institutions and over the terms of hire-purchase credit (which it is convenient to consider here under the heading of monetary policy, although it is not always thought of as such).

The four countries may be thought of as spanning a sort of spectrum in their choice among these measures. At the one extreme, in Canada measures of market control – open-market operations and operations in the money market – have been overwhelmingly the predominant ones: at the other extreme, in New Zealand, there have been direct controls over the total and direction of bank lending, together with controls that kept interest rates on bank lending and on bank interest-bearing deposits, and also those on government securities, artificially low: whilst there was a progressive movement towards controlling – at first informally and then by law – the asset structures of the principal non-bank financial intermediaries. Pressure on the banks to keep down their lending to the level required by the authorities was reinforced by the charging of a high rate of interest to banks that had to borrow from the central bank in order to maintain the required cash ratios.

Australia and South Africa occupied intermediate positions in this spectrum. Up to about 1960 Australia was fairly close to the New Zealand end of it, with direct controls over the total of bank lending being the main measure of monetary control, and with the interest rates on government securities and those of banks often kept down artificially well below the rates that would have been appropriate in periods of boom. But from about 1963/4 onwards much more use was made of open-market operations, mainly in the short-term bonds held by money market dealers, whilst those interest rates under direct official influence and control were generally kept at much more appropriate levels than in the past. In Australia there has not at any time been a published bank rate, the rates charged to banks borrowing from the central bank not being divulged. The possibility therefore does not exist of using it for its psychological or 'announcement' effects on business activity, as has been done in many countries. Changes in government bond rates in Australia do, however, play this role to some extent.

In South Africa the bond market has not developed to the point where it can be a useful channel for open-market operations, but variations in interest rates, including bank rate, were used as part of macro-economic policy, and officially controlled interest rates were never held down artificially to an extent in any way comparable to what happened in New Zealand. But direct controls were maintained over bank liquidity, by the use of both fixed and supplementary reserve requirements and by imposing ceilings on bank lending. Furthermore, direct controls were imposed over the asset structures of some of the principal types of non-bank intermediaries and (as also in New Zealand) the terms of hire-purchase contracts were controlled. On the other hand, South African monetary measures did not generally include one type of control that continued to be used in Australia: namely, the upper limit imposed on bank interest rates, although for two brief periods South Africa had such a control (on the first occasion a formal control and on the second an informal one). But South Africa did impose a control over interest rates paid on their borrowing by building societies; and this naturally led to a very rapid expansion of borrowing by those intermediaries whose borrowing rate was not held down. In exactly the same way, in Australia the upper limit imposed on bank fixed-term deposit rates led to a rapid expansion of borrowing by building societies (whose rates were not controlled in this way) and by other borrowers; and in

New Zealand the low upper limit imposed on bank interest rates for most of the period led to a very rapid growth of borrowing by those intermediaries that were not restricted in this manner.

But in South Africa, as also in a much more extreme form in New Zealand, and to a smaller extent in Australia, there was a 'captive' bond market, in the sense of a substantial demand for government bonds on the part of institutional investors that were under statutory, or sometimes less formal, pressure to hold such securities, virtually irrespective of the return on them. In Australia there was a strong tax incentive (strong enough to have the same effect as a statutory compulsion) for life insurance companies and pension funds to hold at least 30 per cent of their assets in Common-wealth and State government securities, within which total at least 20 per cent of their assets would be Commonwealth government securities.

Such captive bond markets greatly restrict the scope for using the bond market as a channel for monetary policy. For the essence of an appropriate anti-cyclical policy should be to encourage lenders – including the institutional lenders that represent the 'captive' part of the bond market – to lend more freely to the private sector in periods of recession, and to buy relatively more government bonds in periods of excess demand. Such a policy requires the yields on government securities to be varied appropriately in relation to claims issued by the private sector. But where statutory controls keep the holdings of certain major investors above the level that these would reach in a free market these institutional investors are unlikely to increase their holdings of government bonds above the prescribed minima – unless, of course, the returns on them are subsequently made attractive (in which case, of course, the bond market is no longer 'captive'); nor can they reduce their holdings below these minima in periods when it would be an appropriate policy to increase the share of their lending that is being made available to the private sector.

It is worth asking how far these differences of approach were inevitable in the light of dissimilarities in the economies of the four countries, and how far they resulted from diverse governmental attitudes and approaches.

One clear institutional difference between Canada and the other three countries is the much more advanced stage of development of Canada's capital market, including the government bond market and the money market. The close connections between the Canadian capital market and that of the USA also represented a situation that was not closely paralleled in the other countries. The broader bond market in Canada facilitated the use of open-market operations as a means of affecting the liquidity of the banks and the public; but the close connections between the Canadian capital market and that of the USA meant that it was not possible to bring about large changes in domestic demand by variations in the level of Canadian interest rates, as any substantial difference between these and the interest rates prevailing in the USA would call forth equilibrating capital movements and so speedily remove the differential. This limited the use of interest-rate variations as a means of influencing domestic activity in Canada (at any rate so far as the exchange rate was not free to vary).

But other countries have been increasingly exposed in recent years to changes in net capital flows in response to changes in the relationship between their interest rates and those in other countries. Australia, in particular, has found it difficult to pursue an interest-rate policy that makes the general level of her interest rates diverge greatly from those in Britain and the USA; for if that happens there tends to be a considerable change in net capital inflow, with Australian companies borrowing more or less of their requirements overseas, and overseas firms with subsidiaries or branches in Australia speeding up or delaying the remittance of their dividends to their overseas parent companies. South Africa, too, is exposed to the effects of international capital movements, especially through the international mining companies operating there, and has been reluctant to impose very tight controls over capital outflows except in periods of very severe balance of payments difficulty. Nevertheless, the extent to which South Africa has controlled capital outflows has left some scope for her capital market to be insulated from movements in interest rates overseas. Again, New Zealand is at the opposite extreme to Canada, since the close control that has been maintained over capital outflows from New Zealand has meant that official interest rates there have still been able to diverge appreciably from those in other countries.

But the relative stage of the development of the bond markets of the four countries, and the relative extent to which their capital markets are affected by external capital markets, cannot be considered as a complete explanation for the different approaches of the four governments to monetary policy. For the policies of the governments themselves have important effects on the development of the markets for bonds, according to the degree of encouragement they give to the development of the bond and money markets, and according to whether the prevailing pattern of interest rates on government securities conforms to the level of market rates generally. In Canada the development of both the bond market and the money market were encouraged by government initiatives, and yields on government securities have generally been at levels that encouraged active dealings in them. At the other extreme, in New Zealand the level of interest rates has not been adequate to facilitate the development of such markets, despite the official recognition there of a short-term money market. In Australia, the official recognition of the short-term money market was somewhat belated and perhaps a little grudging, and the market was certainly not actively encouraged in its early stages by official action; but government operations in the bond and money markets in recent years and the level of interest rates have been such as to facilitate the expansion of these markets. In South Africa, despite the limitations on the development of the bond market resulting from the controls that led to a 'captive' demand for bonds, the interest-rate policy pursued has been reasonably flexible, and certainly not such as to keep the level of yields out of touch with the market in the manner that has occurred in New Zealand. But the secondary market in government bonds in South Africa is not yet broad enough to make it a useful avenue for open-market operations.

It probably remains true that in Australia, and certainly in New Zealand and South Africa, the bond markets have not reached the stage (and even with every official encouragement could probably not yet have reached the stage), where the scale of official operations in them could suffice to achieve all the effects on bank liquidity and so on bank lending that are necessary as part of monetary policy. But in Australia and New Zealand, and to a somewhat lesser extent in South Africa, the means exist to affect bank liquidity directly, so that it is probably not necessary to develop the bond markets in these countries to the point at which they can be the medium through which monetary policy can achieve the whole of any desired effect upon bank liquidity, and so on bank lending. Australia's experience during the 1960s does, however, suggest that it is possible for medium-sized economies such as these to develop their bond markets to the point where official operations in them can have a useful effect in influencing the general level of interest rates, and so the flow of funds between private and official borrowers, in a manner that can play a helpful role in influencing domestic activity. Where the authorities are able and willing to use the market for government securities in this way, allowing officially controlled interest rates to vary in an appropriate direction in relation to interest rates in the rest of the capital market, even the somewhat limited market for short-term and long-term government securities in a medium-sized economy can be developed into a helpful medium for implementing macro-economic policy. At the same time, such economies may well need to continue to make some use of direct controls over bank liquidity and so over bank lending, as a complementary arm of monetary policy. But to judge from recent developments in Australia, the degree of emphasis that needs to be placed upon direct measures of control over bank lending can be greatly reduced when the development of the bond market enables open-market operations to play a larger role in the operation of monetary policy.

The development of more general measures of monetary policy is especially desirable in view of the difficulties of relying mainly on direct measures of control over banks for influencing demand.

In the first place, the banks may be unwilling to observe the cash or liquidity ratios set by the authorities, or agreed with the banks.

Secondly, even when firm conventions or regulations are established, attempts to reduce the level of bank lending may, under the overdraft system, be met by customers making greater use than in the past of their unused overdrafts. Both Australia and New Zealand have imposed certain commitment fees on unused overdrafts, with a view to reducing the risk of this occurring, that in New Zealand being on total overdraft limits. But whilst such charges may reduce the scale of overdraft limits arranged by customers, under the Australian version once the charges exist they actually act as an encouragement to a customer to make full use of his limits, since the *additional* charge that he incurs by doing this will then be smaller than when his unused overdraft limits were costing him nothing.

Thirdly, the agreed conventions may sometimes leave room for banks to increase their lending to the private sector by holding commercial bills, or by lending to money-market dealers who are thus enabled to hold more commercial bills. In Australia these problems – which arose in Britain in the past, but which may have been solved by the new regulations introduced in 1971 – have not arisen, as banks have not been permitted to include either commercial bills or their loans to the short-term money market as part of the liquid assets included in their governing ('LGS') ratio. Countries where a money market is developed might do well to adopt a similar arrangement. Alternatively, if the money-market dealers are permitted to hold claims on the private sector it may be as well to limit the scale on which they can do this, and, similarly, if banks are allowed to count commercial bills as liquid assets it may be best to limit the scale on which they can count such assets as part of their governing ratio (as is done under the 1971 regulations in Britain). Australia originally prevented the officially backed money-market dealers from holding any claims on the private sector, but more recently has permitted them to hold limited proportions of their assets in this form. It seems desirable that they should be allowed to hold claims on the private sector to some extent, since variations in these holdings in response to variations in the relative yields on them compared with those on government securities may provide a useful means of influencing the economy if a government follows an appropriately flexible interest rate policy.

Even if all these special difficulties in the way of controlling bank lending to the private sector can be overcome, there remain more general objections to trying to reduce excess demand mainly through controls over bank lending. Reductions in bank lending will tend to stimulate the search for other sources of finance, and this will generally distort the flow of funds into less economic channels – not, of course, that banks are necessarily always inherently superior channels for this purpose, but simply because the direct controls over part of the system lead borrowers and lenders to find forms of financing that they would not have chosen in the absence of the control, and which are therefore presumably inferior. It is true that it may take some time for these other, inferior, channels to be devised, and during that period the curtailment of bank credit may serve to restrain demand. But the tighter the rein over bank lending, and the less the extent to which bank and other officially controlled interest rates are permitted to rise, the greater the extent to which non-bank borrowing and lending will expand relative to lending by the banks. In all the four countries the capital markets are sufficiently well developed for monetary measures applied merely through direct control over the banks to be relatively easily offset by an expansion either of lending by other intermediaries or by direct lending from saver to spender. It is very important, therefore, that in future monetary measures to reduce demand should be implemented by a proper use of market measures of control, rather than by direct controls over parts of the capital market – whether over banks or other financial intermediaries – since the effects of such direct measures can be only partial and temporary.

Budgetary policy
Each of the four countries has endeavoured to some extent to vary

the setting of its budgetary instruments in ways that seemed appropriate for achieving or maintaining internal and external balance,
though the extent of their success has varied greatly. But in all of
them it has been hard to restrain the growth of government spending
largely because of the rapid growth of population (rapid, that is, for
countries at such a high standard of living), coupled with the special
demand for capital associated with separate development in South
Africa. The consequently strong demand for social as well as
industrial capital made it easy to maintain something close to full
employment, but hard to reduce the growth of government spending
as a means of checking excess demand.

In these countries, as in many others, it was often difficult to
vary budgetary measures speedily even when the government (or
at least its advisers) was convinced of the need to do so; for the
publicity that attends major changes of budgetary policy often makes
the political objections to such changes considerable. There has
also been some tendency for supplementary budgets to be regarded
as appropriate only to conditions of serious crisis; though the very
frequent changes of budgetary measures in Canada in more recent
years suggest that this obstacle to budgetary flexibility is no longer a
serious one there. South Africa and New Zealand have also had
supplementary budgets fairly often in more recent years. It will
become increasingly important for all of these countries to find ways
of operating their budgets in a flexible manner if (as seems likely)
monetary policy becomes more and more difficult to use to maintain
internal balance, as they become increasingly integrated into the
world capital market; though the adoption of more flexible exchange
rates could also help to make monetary measures more useful. But
it is unlikely that the best time to vary the setting of budgetary
measures will always be in the same month each year, and it seems
thoroughly desirable for all countries to accept as normal the
practice of making budgetary changes at various times during the
year. So far as variations in income-tax rates are used as a measure
of macro-economic policy it may be felt that frequent changes are
difficult. But it is worth remembering that no less than three different
Pay-As-You-Earn rates of tax deduction were operated in Australia
within the space of five months in 1961/2, which suggests that
this measure is more flexible than it is usually believed to be. (Unfortunately, this commendable degree of flexibility has not been
paralleled in Australian income-tax rates in more recent years – nor,
so far as the present writer is aware – in any other country at any
time.)

The convention of drawing up a budget at one particular time of the year and sticking to it even if its main outlines have become inappropriate can have thoroughly undesirable effects in the direction of reducing budgetary flexibility. The budget of 1971 in Australia had clearly become too deflationary within a few months, yet the government continued to try to defend it instead of varying its budgetary measures as conditions changed. This sort of false pride can have undesirable consequences, especially if it leads, as it did in Australia, to an attempt to offset the deflationary effect of the budget by placing a disproportionate emphasis on expansionary monetary measures (which, as we have seen, have serious limitations in a world of generally fixed exchange rates and free capital flows, and which, as we shall argue below, may be more likely to stimulate price rises than would be a tax reduction having similar effects on demand).

Especially if monetary flexibility and variations in government expenditure (and perhaps also in practice income-tax rates) are severely limited as macro-economic measures in countries such as the four we are discussing, what is the scope for using anti-cyclical variations in indirect tax rates?

All these countries have in fact made some use of variations in indirect taxes as macro-economic measures. But an important disadvantage of using them in this way is that when such taxes are applied to durable products, expectations of future changes in these taxes often give rise to variations in demand that operate in a direction that works against the desired aims of macro-economic policy. If the custom has been to increase the tax on purchases of motor vehicles in a boom (or to tighten controls over hire-purchase for these and other goods, as in New Zealand) the expectation that this may be done again may further intensify demand for such products during the next period of high demand until the tax is in fact increased (or the controls tightened). Australia's experience with such taxes at the end of the 1950s and at the beginning of the 1960s led one Prime Minister, Harold Holt (a former Treasurer who had previously varied the sales tax on cars as an anti-cyclical measure), to try to avoid using such taxes as a means of anti-cyclical control, and in fact relatively little use was made of them in Australia in more recent periods. Variations of tax rates on less durable items of general consumption may, however, be a useful means of affecting the overall level of demand, especially as many of these items are in relatively inelastic demand. But as countries become richer it becomes more and more likely that people will be able to maintain the total level of their expenditure by drawing on their savings to pay the extra indirect taxes.

It is important that the choice between variations in direct and indirect tax rates should not be confused with the general case for and against such taxes. But the choice of which taxes to vary is inevitably considered at any given time in the light of the debate on whether the relative weight of either of them should be gradually reduced. It is often argued that high income-tax rates reduce incentives, and that increases in such taxes in periods of boom will thus tend to curb the willingness of people to work hard and efficiently, and may in this way increase inflation. It may also encourage avoidance (finding legal ways of not paying taxes) and evasion, thus diverting people's efforts to these socially unproductive activities. It is, however, by no means certain that high income-tax rates will on balance reduce the incentive for people to work hard. For whilst it is true that high marginal income-tax rates mean that extra effort brings less (post-tax) reward, and to that extent seems less worth while and leisure correspondingly more attractive (the 'substitution' effect), on the other hand the lower level of a person's total post-tax income that results from high income-tax rates makes him more eager to earn a higher income in order to purchase a given volume of goods and services (the 'income' effect): and there is no general presumption about which of these two conflicting considerations is dominant. There is certainly no general presumption that either marginal or total income-tax rates in any of the four countries are unusually high by world standards. Such considerations should therefore not be a serious obstacle to appropriate anti-cyclical variations in income-tax rates. Moreover, even if a country decides to move gradually in the direction of changing the share of either direct or indirect tax receipts in the total, this need not prevent it from varying either of them anti-cyclically about the desired long-term trend.

It is also difficult to say for certain which taxes are the most regressive, although personal income taxes are usually held to be the most progressive. But whatever one's views on this matter it is generally true that those taxes that reduce the real income of the relatively poor will be the ones that can most usefully be increased when the aim is to restrain the level of demand (as they are least likely to be paid out of savings), and which are therefore also the most appropriate ones to reduce when a stimulus is required. In other words, if the aim is to reduce those taxes that bear most heavily on the poor, this can best be done in periods when a stimulus to demand is thought desirable.

There are also considerations relating to the mix of tax measures and budgetary measures generally that arise out of the special problems of 'stagflation' – rising prices at less than full employment. These will be considered in the following section.

'Stagflation'
At the beginning of the 1970s the four countries under review all shared – with one another and with most comparable countries – the problem of 'stagflation': that is to say, an uncomfortably rapid rate of inflation at a time when there was also 'stagnation' in the sense that their economies were operating at less than a full employment rate of growth as normally defined. As in several other countries, including Britain and the USA, the hope was sometimes expressed that operating the economies of these countries at rather less than full employment would, as often in the past, help to check inflation: but in the early 1970s most countries found this was no longer a feasible solution – at least within the limits of what they had come to regard as a socially and politically acceptable level of unemployment. In any case, the consequent sacrifice of potential output is a wasteful way of trying to solve the problem, even if it succeeds, and it is therefore desirable to find better ways of meeting the problem.

One possible line of approach is by way of some form of prices and incomes policy. The four countries in question have not, however, attempted anything that could be described as a general prices and incomes policy; whilst the attempts of Canada and New Zealand in this direction have been only partial and confined to particular periods. (Prices and incomes policies as such are discussed below.)

A hopeful line of approach for countries with a strong balance of payments is to reduce tariffs (or import controls if they exist) or to appreciate. Where a country is fortunate enough to have a strong balance of payments its first measure to meet the problem should thus be to adopt one of these policies, and to offset the resulting downward effect on domestic activity by adopting a correspondingly more expansionary budgetary and monetary policy. But if the balance of payments is weak, and prices and incomes policies are found to be unacceptable or unworkable (at least in the short run), it is worth trying to vary the mix of budgetary and monetary policies in ways that will be most likely to give the desired stimulus to economic activity with a minimal upward effect upon the price level. Indeed, even if the balance of payments is strong enough for a tariff cut or an appreciation to be employed, it is important for a country that employs such measures not to rely on them alone, as they will have only a temporary effect; indeed, this can provide no more than a useful breathing space in which to evolve measures that can have a more lasting effect.

In choosing the appropriate combinations of monetary and budgetary measures to bring about a given effect on domestic activity, it may be possible to allow for the different effects upon the rate of inflation that may result from different policy measures. For example, particular taxes may be especially likely to raise the price level, or at least those indexes of consumer prices that are most commonly quoted as indicators of movements in the price level, and which are therefore often especially important in influencing people's expectations about inflation. These indexes probably also have considerable influence upon the wage and salary demands of employees and on the decisions of any arbitrators or conciliators that may make or influence the relevant decisions.

For example, increases in indirect tax rates, especially those that are levied upon important items of general consumption, are likely to increase the consumer price indexes especially sharply, as occurred in Australia in the latter part of 1970 and in South Africa in 1971. The very sharp rise in wage and salary increases that followed was due to many factors, but the rise in the consumer price index was presumably one of these; and, in any event, the sharp increases in it tended to raise people's expectations of a higher rate of inflation. These indirect-tax increases therefore seem in retrospect to have been misguided.

It is true that even increases in direct tax rates may eventually become built into the cost structure, though probably with a much longer time lag. Wage and salary earners may also take account of income-tax rates in formulating their wage and salary demands. But one could still argue that the immediate effect on prices and on wage and salary demands of a rise in indirect tax rates is more likely to be sharply upwards than that of a rise in income tax or company tax having the same effect on domestic demand. It is true that any tax reductions will, by stimulating demand, normally tend to have some upward effect on prices. But if the aim is to stimulate the economy with as little upward effect on prices as possible, reductions in indirect tax rates may well be less likely to stimulate a further rise in the price level than will cuts in income tax or company tax: indeed, it is possible that cuts in indirect tax rates might even reduce prices.

Such considerations as these should also affect the choice between measures of taxation and government spending. For if high tax rates are likely to become built into the cost structure and to stimulate higher wage and salary demands, there is an especially strong case for using tax reductions as a means of stimulating activity in a period of stagflation, rather than relying upon increases in government expenditure. For if the latter alternative is chosen tax rates will have to be higher than would otherwise have been appropriate; whereas if a rather less rapid rate of increase in government expenditure is chosen, it will be possible to achieve the same total level of demand by way of tax reductions that would not otherwise have been possible. Whatever the other arguments may be for a rapid growth of government expenditure, therefore, if there is a need to give a stimulus to activity in a period when prices are already rising uncomfortably rapidly, there may well be a case for giving rather more of the stimulus by tax reductions and rather less by way of increases in government spending than would be appropriate for an economy that was suffering from a less rapid rise in the price level.

The existence of a situation of stagflation may also have a bearing on the choice that should be made between budgetary and monetary measures of expansion. If interest rates are raised to check demand, voices from the business world are often heard urging that this is 'inflationary', by which they mean that the consequently higher costs are, in their view, likely to be passed on by way of higher prices. If this is so, it would constitute an argument for giving a high priority to reductions in interest rates as a measure to stimulate activity in periods when efforts are also being made to restrain price increases. But it is by no means certain that simply because certain costs have risen (in this case the cost of borrowing) businesses will in fact be able to pass the increases on by way of charging higher prices; indeed, the purpose of a tighter monetary policy is to restrain demand, which will to that extent make people less willing and able to pay higher prices. (Similar arguments can also be raised against the businessman's view that tax increases are 'inflationary' in the sense that if they affect the costs of businesses then they are likely to be passed on.) But, especially in a world where people have come to expect that full employment or something close to it will be maintained, it is possible that increases in interest rates (like those in certain tax rates) will give an additional upward twist to the general expectation of higher prices, and may to that extent be self-fulfilling.

But, on the other hand, there is a widely held view in the USA, (at least) that an expansionary monetary policy is especially likely to push up the price level. This is relevant because measures that allow the rate of interest to be kept down involve a faster expansion of the money supply than would otherwise be necessary, and in many countries there has been observed a close correlation between increases in the money supply and the rate of increase in the price level – however difficult it may be to say whether either of these causes the other. But if there is a widespread belief that there is such an association between prices and the money supply it may be that a faster expansion of the money supply (with the aim of keeping down interest rates) will tend to increase inflation through giving a further stimulus to expectations about inflation. Or it may be that if the alternative of tax reductions (and correspondingly higher interest rates) is preferred to an expansionary monetary policy, the tax reductions themselves will tend to check cost and income inflation.

There does not appear to be a widespread view in the four countries that an expansionary monetary policy is more likely to lead to a faster rate of inflation than is an otherwise equivalent reduction in tax rates or increase in government spending.[3] Nevertheless, expansionary monetary measures may well be more likely to raise the price level than are tax cuts (though not necessarily more so than higher government spending) if we accept the view argued in preceding paragraphs that high tax rates may tend to become built into the cost structure and to give rise to higher wage and salary demands. If this is so, a government may be able to minimize the stimulus that is given to inflation by its expansionary measures if it concentrates these measures upon tax cuts in periods of inflation, rather than on an expansionary monetary policy.

Seasonal fluctuations in the budget
Seasonal fluctuations in certain tax payments have presented something of a problem in Australia and New Zealand. Both countries have obviated most of the seasonal pattern of income-tax payments for employed persons by the use of Pay-As-You-Earn tax deductions; but the seasonal pattern of tax payments by companies has meant that there tends to be a severe strain on the liquidity of the banks and the public at certain times in the year.

---

[3] The Franzen Committee in South Africa, in its *Third Report (Fiscal and Monetary Policy in South Africa*, R.P. 87/70, Pretoria, 1970), para. 578, did, however, point out that 'During long periods of inflation an extension of bank credit may indeed encourage inflationary expectations so much that higher interest rates may result'.

This has meant in Australia that it has been especially easy to apply a credit squeeze at such times: that is, until 1971, when companies found that they could guard against such a seasonal stringency by borrowing overseas. By the same token, it had in earlier years been likely that measures of monetary control might in such periods have too great an effect (as they may have done in 1970), as the precise degree of the seasonal element in the fluctuations of liquidity is difficult to estimate and allow for. Similarly, in the part of the year when cash is relatively plentiful it becomes hard to apply a tight monetary policy. One solution – the preferable one – would be to move to a system of Pay-As-You-Earn for company-tax payments; and this has been done in New Zealand, though only for new companies. But so far as this is not possible, the issue of some sort of short-term government security that is attractive to companies with temporarily idle funds should be considered; even the existing treasury notes (in Australia) or treasury bills (in New Zealand) could serve this purpose if the rates at which they were sold to the public were attractive in relation to the prevailing level of market rates. Indeed, in the latter part of 1971, the rates on treasury notes in Australia had at last become attractive to companies with temporarily idle funds, and were purchased by them in considerable amounts.

INCOMES POLICIES

The main components of an incomes policy seem to be the setting of general targets for the appropriate development of major forms of incomes and prices; a finer breakdown of these overall targets to provide useful guidelines in individual wage and price decisions; and devices to induce adherence to these guidelines. On this definition, none of the four countries has (during the major part of the sixties) approached a fully fledged incomes policy, despite their concern about inflation. In Australia, the federal government has not been inclined to tamper with the existing system of award wage determinations under the Arbitration system and has not adopted a formal policy of restraint for over-award payments. In Canada, the opposition of trade unions and the highly decentralized wage-fixing structure have inhibited concerted efforts at formulating an incomes policy. In New Zealand (where, as in Australia, full employment had been achieved – until about 1970 – without intolerable inflation), the record of success generally imputed to the Arbitration Court in most of the post-war period was blotted by a 'zero wage' decision in 1968, and, after the unions had boycotted the Court a new Remuneration Authority (the influence of which cannot yet be adequately assessed) assumed some of the functions of the Arbitration Court, only the Remuneration Authority being henceforth empowered to approve any wage or salary increases of over 7 per cent. In South Africa, the complex dualistic labour market has been subjected to various interferences in the free flow of labour inter-regionally and vertically, but there has been no attempt at an incomes policy.

The reasons why these four countries have not opted for incomes policies along the lines defined above are obviously part of wide institutional and economic considerations from which no particular lessons of general application can be derived. But a study of comparative instruments of wage-fixing machinery may produce ideas about policies that may be useful elsewhere, if it could be shown that there is some causal connection between a particular form of wage machinery and the ability to contain wage inflation (assuming that to be the aim). For example, some commentators have admired those aspects of the Australian system of wage determination that are concerned with industrial relations and have felt that parts of its method could usefully be employed in their own countries.[4] This may be true, though the caveat of a British Royal Commission could be borne in mind that 'to transplant from one country to another legal institutions or principles which have stood the test of time . . . may be useless or even harmful if the social conditions of the country which seeks to adopt them differ from those which have given rise to their growth in their country of origin'.[5] There is, however, little ground for believing that the wage policies of any of the countries studied provide a ready-made model suitable for export to other countries that are intent on improving their own methods of attempting to control wage inflation. This view is reinforced by the recent decline, even in the Australian case mentioned, in the influence of the wage-fixing authorities (which control award rates only) over wages generally, and this has made it very doubtful whether their existing powers could be used to retard appreciably the rate of increase of average earnings or prices under current conditions.[6] Control over award wage rates is certainly not, therefore, an adequate substitute for an incomes policy; and the existence of

[4] See C. Grunfield, 'Australian Compulsory Arbitration—Appearance and Reality', *British Journal of Industrial Relations*, November 1971, p. 352.

[5] *Royal Commission on Trade Unions and Employers' Associations 1965–8: Report* (Cmnd. 3623, June 1968), para. 162.

[6] See J. P. Nieuwenhuysen and N. R. Norman, 'Australian Wages Policies: Issues and Tests', *British Journal of Industrial Relations*, November 1971.

such a system may well have inhibited the Australian government from adopting a more general incomes policy.

Furthermore, there is great doubt as to the usefulness of prescribing the forms of wages or incomes policy suitable for one country on the basis of experience elsewhere when the problem that the policies are aimed to meet (inflation) is an international one. Professor H. G. Johnson, for example, has attributed

'the world inflation . . . largely to a change towards inflationary behaviour on the part of the United States. The details of events in other countries can of course be used to tell a tale of domestic causation of inflation and in particular to blame inflation on the irresponsibility of the trade unions, but I would instead regard them merely as details in the process of transmission of world inflation, sparked by the United States, to the individual countries concerned.'[7]

The OECD has also outlined some of the major channels by which inflationary impulses may be transmitted from country to country. These include 'the impact on demand and incomes in other countries . . . cost and price effects; . . . the monetary impact of a balance of payments surplus on domestic liquidity creation . . . (and) finally, there are, no doubt, psychological effects'.[8] The problem of inflation and the role played by wage increases in causing it have produced a substantial literature analysing alternative means and experience of attempts at control.[9] Some elements of the institutional arrangements of the countries covered in this study may be transferable to other countries. But their general approaches to the macro-economic problems of price and income inflation do not seem to have provided useful and transferable examples for other countries to follow.

BALANCE OF PAYMENTS WEAPONS

It was stressed at the outset of this chapter that all measures of macro-economic policy affect both internal and external balance. But certain measures are often thought of as being generally directed at affecting the balance of payments, even though their internal effects are just as important. These include the use of the exchange

[7] The Inflation Crisis', *International Currency Review*, August 1971, p. 7. See also H. G. Johnson (ed.), *The Current Inflation*, Macmillan, 1971.

[8] OECD, *Present Policies Against Inflation*, June 1971, p. 31.

[9] See, for example, L. Ullmann and R. J. Flanagan, *Wage Restraint*, University of California Press, 1971.

rate, and of import controls and the general level of tariffs, including the temporary surcharge that has been imposed by certain countries to keep down imports. For want of a better generic term, these measures may be grouped under the heading of 'balance of payments' weapons, even though one must bear in mind their effects on the internal situation as much as their effects on the balance of payments.

The exchange rate
There is a clear contrast between Canada – which has (for a large part of the period we are considering) adopted a flexible exchange rate, with varying degrees of official intervention – and the other three countries. For Australia, New Zealand and South Africa have altered their exchange rates only rarely, and such changes as occurred were made at times when there were widespread changes in parities of the major countries of the world, so that they were by way of being a reaction to policies in the rest of the world rather than a conscious decision to make appropriate use of the exchange rate as one of the main measures of macro-economic policy.

The case for greater exchange-rate flexibility than that hitherto applied by Australia, New Zealand and South Africa rests on several grounds. In the first place, the variability of capital inflow and of export prospects for these countries means that the state of their external balance very is hard to predict for any prolonged period ahead, so that any exchange rate that might be adopted for a prolonged period is very unlikely to be that which will give the best results, taking good and bad years together. Some degree of readiness to alter the exchange rate, or to let market forces alter it within reasonably wide limits, would increase the likelihood of their being able to reconcile full employment with a strong (but not excessively strong) balance of payments: for it is especially important that the countries concerned should have another policy measure, in addition to budgetary policy, that can be fairly readily varied as conditions change, so that the dual objectives of internal and external balance can be successfully reconciled. It is true that something may be done by way of varying the mix of monetary and budgetary measures with an eye to maintaining internal and external balance; but the scope for doing this is in practice limited; and the relative efficacy of different budgetary measures on internal compared with their effects on external balance is not known with sufficient certainty for variations of the mix of different measures within the budget to be used to any great extent with this aim in mind.

The strongest internal argument for a more flexible exchange rate is that the efficacy of monetary measures for influencing internal balance is inevitably weak when exchange rates are fixed and when international flows of capital are as mobile as they have been in recent years (and as mobile as they are likely to continue to be into and out of the four countries so long as these countries obtain capital inflow on the sort of scale that they are likely to be able to use to good effect).

For so long as their exchange rates are not free to alter, any attempt by one of them to raise the level of its interest rates with a view to checking domestic inflation is not likely to have much success, as it will tend to bring about an offsetting inflow of capital. If, on the other hand, the exchange rate is free to vary, it will tend to appreciate if attempts to raise the level of interest rates attract more capital. The consequent appreciation will then help to keep down the increase in domestic expenditure and in domestic prices, thus making the monetary measures effective. This basic argument for exchange-rate flexibility is not yet widely appreciated in the four countries, but it is important that it should become widely understood and acted upon.

Both in South Africa and Australia there have apparently been doubts in some observers' minds about whether a greater degree of exchange-rate flexibility is feasible in these countries in the absence of a proper foreign exchange market. (In very recent years the first tentative steps have been taken in Australia towards encouraging the banks – which remain the sole dealers in foreign currency – to deal on their own account, and to compete with one another in foreign exchange dealings.) But in fact the greater flexibility of exchange rates that is required need not necessarily involve a fully fledged foreign exchange market. It is true that it would be helpful to build up the necessary expertise for such a market. But it does not seem to be essential that this should occur before the governments concerned would be able to make greater use of exchange-rate flexibility. For it would be possible for the authorities frequently to change the rate at which they will themselves buy and sell foreign exchange, in accordance with the country's changing internal and external balance; the central bank might thus be given a target level of reserves to maintain, and told to buy and sell at rates that would prevent the reserves rising or falling by more than a stated amount above or below that level. It should then have greater freedom to vary its monetary policy with an eye to internal balance.

A further reason why Australia, New Zealand and South Africa are likely to find it highly desirable to allow a greater freedom for their exchange rates to vary – either with market forces or by more frequent decisions of their governments – is that world exchange rates generally are likely to be more flexible than in the recent past, both through greater variation from day to day on either side of the official par value and also by more frequent changes in the official parities. This means that the major currencies are much less likely to remain in a fixed relationship to one another for prolonged periods than they have in the past. It would be difficult or impossible to decide with any confidence which currency should be the one on which Australia, New Zealand or South Africa should keep their parity fixed. For there is no reason whatever to expect that the fluctuations of sterling (for example) in terms of the currencies of the rest of the world would happen to coincide with what was an appropriate pattern of fluctuations for the Australian dollar (for instance).[10]

Other balance of payments measures
In two of the four countries – Canada and Australia – import controls were not used as a balance of payments weapon during the 1960s, although they were abandoned in Australia only in 1960. On the other hand, both New Zealand and South Africa employed import controls, and varied them to some extent in the light of both external balance and internal balance. New Zealand also applied tight controls over capital payments to other countries, as did also South Africa during some periods, whilst Australia limited the right of her residents to make capital payments overseas even when her reserves were high and her balance of payments strong, but did not

[10] It is true that it is necessary to quote the exchange rate for the currency of Australia, Canada, New Zealand or South Africa in terms of a particular major currency from day to day: but this matter of the daily quotation must be kept quite distinct (in minds of policy-makers and the public generally) from the very different matter of whether it is appropriate to keep the rate of exchange on that particular major currency unchanged for prolonged periods. For example, Australia chose at the end of 1971 to fix her exchange rate in future on the US dollar instead of on sterling; it would be thoroughly undesirable if this led to the adoption of inappropriate exchange rates for the Australian dollar in future merely as a result of the fluctuations that happened to occur in the US dollar as against the result of the world. It is also important to see that other irrelevant considerations, such as the exchange rate that a particular other country happens to adopt, should not be a dominant consideration in exchange rate decisions: quite irrationally, the New Zealand government elected late in 1971 (in advance of the Australian government taking its decision) to continue to keep its exchange rate at parity with the Australian dollar, when there was no presumption whatever that this rate (when chosen) would happen to coincide with New Zealand's interests.

in practice limit the rights of non-residents to withdraw their capital, and did not use variations in exchange controls over capital flows as a balance of payments' weapon over the period.

Of the two countries that did use import controls – New Zealand and South Africa – the latter used relaxations in these controls in a generally appropriate manner during the 1960s, with an eye to internal as well as external balance. Indeed, the fact that there was at that time scope for South Africa to relax import controls represented a useful safety-valve which could be used to prevent excess demand from leading to serious inflation at certain times during the mid-1960s. But by the early 1970s, with little scope remaining for using this safety-valve, and with the balance of payments under some pressure, it was no longer possible to use relaxations in import controls to restrain inflation, and, indeed, the devaluation of 1971 was necessary because the problem of external balance had by then become appreciable, even though import controls were reimposed in November 1971.

By contrast, New Zealand continued (for protectionist reasons) to apply a considerable range of import controls in 1971 – even when the state of the balance of payments did not seem to justify them, and when a general reduction in import controls would have been a useful way of overcoming what was then the principal problem of the rising level of domestic prices.[11]

There is a similar contrast between the generally appropriate policies pursued in the late 1960s and early 1970s towards tariff reductions and the use of the exchange rate by Canada, on the one hand, and the policies of Australia, on the other. In 1969 Canada brought forward some of the tariff reductions agreed upon in the Kennedy Round as a means of checking domestic inflation; in the same way, if reductions in tariffs had been made by Australia in the 1969–71 period, this could have made an appropriate contribution to overcoming the main problem of the time, which was domestic inflation, for there was at that time no serious external problem to inhibit the reduction of tariffs. In the same way, scope for the Canadian.dollar to appreciate in 1970 served to hold down the rise in prices in Canada, and an appreciation of the Australian dollar early in the 1970s could have had a similar effect, and need certainly not have been ruled out by the state of the balance of payments, which (as we have seen) was strong.

The balance of payments measures of temporary surcharges on

[11] These controls had, however, been very greatly relaxed between the early 1960s and the early 1970s.

imports was used by only Canada among the four countries, such a surcharge being imposed by that country on a wide range of imports temporarily in 1962, in order to strengthen the balance of payments. The use of a surcharge of this sort (preferably on all or most imports) seems less objectionable than use of import controls; it is therefore to be hoped that so far as these countries may be unwilling or unable to use the exchange rate they will consider such temporary surcharges on imports (or else prior cash deposits on imports) as a possible device rather than the introduction or further tightening of import controls.[12]

ISSUES FOR THE FUTURE

The four countries share many common problems of macro-economic policy, and many of these are also important in one form or another, to most other countries.

Early in the 1970s the principal problem seems to be that of preventing serious inflation without having to accept intolerably high levels of unemployment. It seems certain that if this is to be done successfully some form of prices and incomes policy will have to be devised, and it is likely to take different forms in different countries. For prices, some form of direct control over major price decisions should certainly not be ruled out, despite the well-known difficulties and disadvantages of price control. Perhaps some form of price tribunal, to which major price increases could be referred by the government and publicly discussed and justified, could be considered. If this was done, the political obstacles to submitting major wage and salary increases to some sort of arbitration authority should be less than if no direct attention were paid also to prices.

But, however much success one may optimistically assume for prices and incomes policies, it will still remain essential to devise appropriate combinations of macro-economic measures for maintaining a high level of activity and an adequately (but not excessively) strong balance of payments. Indeed, confidence in the will and the ability of the authorities to avoid appreciable unemployment may well be one necessary pre-condition for obtaining the full co-operation of trade unions in any sort of prices and incomes policy.

This will involve finding ways of making budgets sufficiently flexible to meet changing situations, as well as the adoption of

[12] The relative merits and defects of the principal balance of payments weapons are discussed in J. O. N. Perkins, *International Policy for the World Economy*, Allen & Unwin, 1969, chapter 2.

adequately flexible exchange rates. If we have to assume that a given country will be reluctant to use fairly frequent variations in its exchange rate as part of its normal policy, we shall probably have to assume that the efficacy of monetary measures for influencing internal balance in such a country will be greatly weakened, and budgetary measures will therefore have to be still more flexible and well chosen. If, however, a greater element of exchange-rate flexibility proves possible, this will facilitate the use of monetary policy for maintaining internal balance. and probably also enhance the efficacy of budgetary measures. It does not seem feasible or desirable for such countries as these to try to increase their freedom to have an independent interest-rate policy by cutting off their capital markets to some extent from those of other countries by means of detailed controls over external capital movements; to attempt to do this would inevitably cause distortions and inefficiencies, and it would be hard for them to enforce tight controls over many types of capital movements (and also over current account payments that may conceal capital movements). Moreover, all these countries are likely to continue to be able to use overseas capital to good effect for assisting with the development of their natural resources, and as a means of securing access to many forms of knowhow which their manufacturing industries (with their small scale of output by world standards) are not able to provide for themselves. Tight controls over capital movements would make it harder for them to obtain the capital they need. The appropriate conclusion would therefore seem to be that they should allow sufficient exchange rate flexibility to enable monetary policy to be used to good effect for playing its part in reconciling internal with external balance, whilst also looking for ways of making budgetary measures more flexible. In both these matters Canada has already given something of a lead to the other three.

Canada has also given a lead in the matter of keeping the internal capital market as free as possible from direct controls over particular interest rates and over the asset structure of banks and other intermediaries, as well as in pursuing a generally fairly liberal policy towards tariffs and controls over imports. It will be important for the other three to try to reduce or eliminate so far as possible the use of direct monetary measures over particular interest rates or asset structures, and also to reduce their tariffs and import controls, as a means of improving the allocation of their resources. They should certainly not attempt to use measures such as these for purposes of macro-economic policy; though reductions in tariffs and import controls can usually be made most readily when the balance of payments is strong. But if it remains weak, the alternative of devaluation should certainly generally be preferred to the continuance of tariffs or import controls that discriminate against particular imports; and where there are objections to using the exchange rate for this purpose, the alternative of a flat-rate tariff on imports (rather than import controls or a large number of different tariff rates), would be preferable, and variations in such a flat-rate tariff might also be used as a macro-economic weapon (though one that would be definitely second best to the use of the exchange rate).

RELEVANCE FOR OTHER COUNTRIES

Finally, it seems worth asking how far the conclusions outlined in this chapter are of relevance for countries other than those whose experience has been discussed in this book.

In the first place, virtually everything that has been said about budgetary and monetary measures and the relevance of exchange-rate flexibility to the internal efficacy of monetary and budgetary policy could have been said of virtually all developed countries (with the partial exception of the USA). For all of them have basically similar methods of using budgetary policy and central banking measures, and all of them are increasingly becoming integrated into the world capital market, so that flows of capital into and out of them are becoming very readily responsive to relative interest rates (as well, of course, as to other factors – including rates of return and expectations about exchange rates). It is true that the four countries under discussion are net capital importers, whereas most of the more developed countries of the rest of the world are either net capital exporters or have a capital outflow approximately balancing their capital inflow. But this difference does not appear to have any great bearing upon the responsiveness of net capital movements to interest-rate differentials, which depends primarily on the extent and efficiency of the links between a country's capital market and those of the rest of the world, and on whether investors have sufficient confidence in the political and economic stability of the country in question to move capital fairly readily into that country (and on whether they can move it out again if they wish). These characteristics of most developed and industrialized countries are now shared to a high degree with the four discussed in this book. Even in the matter of the degree of sophistication of their capital markets, the four countries are now broadly comparable to most of the other smaller or medium-sized developed countries, though the range of their financial institutions is not as great as in Britain or the USA.

The problems associated with 'stagflation', including those relating to prices and incomes policies, seem also to be shared with most other developed countries.

At the other extreme, the conclusions drawn in this chapter about the four countries have widely varying degrees of relevance for the less developed countries of the world, for the less developed (or 'developing') countries of the world are themselves very diverse in all the relevant respects. Some of them – India, for instance – have highly developed capital markets, and use budgetary and monetary measures in much the same way as do the four countries studied in this book. Most economies in the less developed parts of the world share in some measure with South Africa the problems of a dual economy, which make Keynesian macro-economic policies, as normally understood and applied, relevant to only a limited part of their problems of unemployment (or 'underemployment'); but so far as these measures can be applied to the problems of internal and external balance in any less developed country, the experience of the four countries certainly has some bearing on their problems. In particular, the internal and external macro-economic problems that result from fluctuations in export receipts from primary products are directly relevant to any less developed country. This means that what has been said in this chapter about the different balance of payments measures, and what is said in the New Zealand chapter about the role of stabilization funds, should be of interest to countries for which primary exports are of major importance.

On the other hand, the majority of less developed countries – though not some of the more prosperous among them – differ in certain relevant particulars from the group considered in this book. Their integration into the world capital market has not been carried so far as that of most developed countries, and therefore the difficulties for monetary policy resulting from the responsiveness of net capital movements (coupled with fixed exchange rates) is not so likely to be a problem for them as it has become for Canada and Australia, at any rate. New Zealand is probably still in a comparable position to many of the less developed countries in this respect, as fairly tight controls over capital movements have limited the extent of its integration into the world capital market.

The balance of payments of the four countries have in common with those of less developed countries a normal tendency to run current account deficits, financed by a varying and often highly unpredictable inflow of capital and/or transfers. For the four countries discussed in this book, this role is played by private capital; for most less developed countries it is played by foreign aid. But in both cases the variability of these flows presents problems of balance of payments adjustment from time to time, which are generally solved by either the use of import controls or the exchange rate. In these respects the four countries have a good deal in common with less developed countries generally. Moreover, as private capital inflow already plays an important role for certain less developed countries, and it is likely to play a more important role for many of them in the coming decades, those less developed economies will have more in common in this respect with the four countries to come.

The similarities are also likely to become greater as the range of financial institutions in more of the less developed countries becomes more diverse. As the scope for new financial institutions grows in these countries the techniques of monetary control available to their central banks are likely to become more nearly akin to those used in the four countries, and the lessons pointed by the experience of the four countries in the matter of direct monetary controls could therefore usefully be learned in advance in the developing countries, so that their central banks may encourage the development of security markets and market instruments of control, and refrain from keeping interest rates artificially low and from excessive emphasis on direct controls over bank lending and liquidity. Obviously, the institutional environment differs greatly from country to country. But the broad lessons of monetary, budgetary and exchange-rate policy discussed in this book are worth studying and applying in most countries of the less developed as well as the more developed parts of the world.

Index

Note: Where an entry in this index refers only to one country it is preceded by (A) for Australia, (C) for Canada, (N) for New Zealand and (S) for South Africa.